LESS SAFE, LESS FREE

LESS SAFE, LESS FREE

WHY AMERICA IS LOSING
THE WAR ON TERROR

DAVID COLE AND JULES LOBEL

THE NEW PRESS

NEW YORK
LONDON

Requests for permission to reproduce selections from this book should be mailed to:
Permissions Department, The New Press, 38 Greene Street, New York, NY 10013.

Published in the United States by The New Press, New York, 2007
Distributed by W. W. Norton & Company, Inc., New York

LIBRARY OF CONGRESS CATALOGING-IN-PUBLICATION DATA

Cole, David.
Less safe, less free : why America is losing the War on Terror /
David Cole and Jules Lobel.
p.   cm.
Includes bibliographical references and index.
ISBN 978-1-59558-133-4 (hc.)
1. Terrorism—Government policy—United States.   2. War on Terrorism, 2001–
I. Lobel, Jules.   II. Title.
HV6432.C62 2007
363.325'15610973—dc22   2007001657

The New Press was established in 1990 as a not-for-profit alternative to the large,
commercial publishing houses currently dominating the book publishing industry.
The New Press operates in the public interest rather than for private gain,
and is committed to publishing, in innovative ways, works of educational, cultural,
and community value that are often deemed insufficiently profitable.

www.thenewpress.com

Composition by dix!
This book was set in Minion

Printed in the United States of America

1   3   5   7   9   10   8   6   4   2

For Nina, Aidan, and Sarah

*　　*　　*

For Karen, Michael, Caroline, Sasha, and Myra

CONTENTS

ACKNOWLEDGMENTS

We have been talking about the ideas set forth in this book in one form or another since the terrorist attacks of September 11, and with more intensity since the launching of the Iraq War. We have benefited from presenting early versions of these ideas at a variety of symposia, fora, and workshops here and abroad, including at Columbia University's Mellon Seminar, NYU Law School's Center on Law and Security, Georgetown University Law Center, Northwestern University, the University of Chicago, Indiana University, Minnesota Law School, the University of Pittsburgh School of Law, Massachusetts Law School, the University of Texas Law School, Thomas Jefferson Law School, Clemson University, University College London's School of Public Policy, Fribourg Law School, USC Law School, Edinburgh University School of Law, Corpus Christi College at Oxford, King's College London, and the University of Fribourg and the University of Geneva in Switzerland.

We received invaluable comments on portions of the book and on its general argument from many friends and colleagues, including Nina Pillard, Karen Engro, Deborah Brake, Viet Dinh, Karen Engle, Noah Feldman, David Golove, Karen Greenberg, David Herring, Stephen Holmes, Anthony Infanti, Marty Lederman, David Luban, Staughton Lynd, George Loewenstein, Todd May, Jeff Rachlinski, Philippe Sands, Kim Scheppele, Steve Schnapp, Craig Rose, George Taylor, and Pete Wales.

We have also both been privileged to work firsthand on these issues with our colleagues and friends at the Center for Constitutional Rights, where we are both members of the board and cooperating attorneys. The Center's lawyers are a committed, talented, and spirited group, and their courage in standing up for principle and the rule of law, even when doing so is not the popular course, has inspired both of us in the writing of this book.

We could not have written this book without the support of our respective institutions, Georgetown University Law Center and the University of Pittsburgh Law School. We thank Dean Alex Aleinikoff at Georgetown and Deans David Herring and Mary Crossley at Pittsburgh for supporting this project generously throughout.

We also owe a deep debt of gratitude to those who have helped us research this book, including Georgetown students Brian Baak, Devon Chaffee, Marian Fowler, Irfan Murtuza, Rebecca Shaeffer, and Rachel Spitzer, and Pittsburgh students Sarah Vuong and Michael Lewis. They provided not only invaluable research but also thoughtful feedback on the ideas we were developing along the way. In addition, we'd like to thank the staff at the Georgetown University Law Library, the Pittsburgh Law Library, and the Document Technology Center at the University of Pittsburgh for their unstinting and always timely support.

Our editor, Diane Wachtell, provided careful and incisive editing, notwithstanding her many other duties at The New Press, and Sarah Fan provided unflappable support at the copy editing and galleys stage.

Finally, we thank our families, for putting up with the many late nights and weekends that we devoted to this project. They were supportive and understanding throughout and encouraged us every step of the way—even those too young to quite comprehend what their fathers were up to. In our view, a project like this must take the long view. Our greatest hope is that the arguments we put forth here might play some part in helping to make the United States a safer and freer society for our children as they grow up as part of the first post-9/11 generation.

INTRODUCTION

In order to fight and to defeat terrorism, the Department of Justice has added a new paradigm to that of prosecution—a paradigm of prevention.

U.S. Attorney General John Ashcroft,
Speech to the Council on Foreign
Relations, February 10, 2003

If we wait for threats to fully materialize, we will have waited too long.

President George W. Bush,
Commencement Speech at West Point,
June 1, 2002

In Steven Spielberg's *Minority Report,* set in the not-all-that-distant future, the Justice Department has hit upon a way—through the enslavement of psychic visionaries—to predict future crimes and thereby prevent virtually all wrongdoing. Would-be criminals are apprehended before they commit their heinous acts and punished under so-called pre-crime laws for their intent, which can be established, it is thought, with 100 percent certainty. But things go awry when it turns out that the psychics' visions can be manipulated, and an innocent man is wrongly implicated in a future murder that he does not intend to commit.[1]

President George W. Bush has no psychic visionaries, but in fighting what he has dubbed the war on terror, his administration has nonetheless adopted a sweeping new "preventive paradigm" that employs highly coercive tactics—from detention to coercive interrogation to war—not in response to concrete evidence of past or even ongoing wrongdoing, but preemptively, to thwart potential future threats. In isolation, neither the goal of preventing future attacks nor the tactic of using coercive measures is particularly novel or troubling. All law enforcement, after all, seeks to prevent crime, and coercion is a necessary element of state power. The force of law depends in part on the threat that violations will trigger a coercive response, such as arrest, prosecution, and imprisonment. When the end of prevention and the means of coercion are combined in the administration's "preventive paradigm," however, they produce a very troubling form of anticipatory state violence—undertaken before any wrongdoing has actually occurred and often without good evidence for believing that any wrongdoing will in fact occur. Such preventive coercion places tremendous stress on the rule of law.

In the name of preventing another terrorist attack, the Bush administration has treated the most fundamental commitments of the rule of law as if they were optional protocols to be jettisoned in the face of the threat of terrorism. The rule of law demands, at a minimum, equality, transparency, fair procedures, individual culpability, clear rules, checks and balances, and respect for basic human rights. Bush's preventive paradigm has violated each of these commitments, imposing double standards on the most vulnerable, operating in secret, denying fair trials, imposing guilt by association, intentionally obscuring clear rules, asserting unchecked unilateral power, and violating universal prohibitions on torture, disappearance, and the like. The greatest irony, however, is that while these compromises are defended as necessary to make us more secure, they have in fact made us more vulnerable to attack. They have wasted resources that could be more efficiently directed, cut off long-term options for illusory short-term gains, alienated our friends, and provided ideal recruitment fodder for our enemies. More effective strategies to prevent terrorism are available, but because the administration has favored dramatic and highly coercive actions, it has neglected the more important but less visible aspects of a successful counterterrorism strategy. Obsessed with playing offense, it has failed to put up a good defense.

In the name of preventing terrorism, the administration has locked up thousands of individuals without trial—within the United States and abroad—the vast majority of whom have never even been accused, much less convicted, of any terrorist act. President Bush invoked the "preventive" rationale to defend his secret order authorizing the National Security Agency to spy on Americans without probable cause that they had engaged in any wrongdoing, without a court order, and contrary to a criminal prohibition on warrantless wiretapping.

In the name of prevention, the president has claimed inherent and uncheckable authority to take whatever steps he deems necessary to "engage the enemy"—even where those steps have been prohibited by Congress. While many have criticized the Bush administration for its radical assertions of broad executive power, far too little attention has been paid to the close relationship between those assertions and the administration's preventive paradigm.

In the name of obtaining intelligence to prevent future attacks, the administration has employed a wide range of coercive interrogation tactics, including sleep deprivation; stress positions; extended exposure to extreme heat and cold; threatened attacks by dogs; injecting suspects with intravenous fluid and then barring them from using the bathroom so that they urinate on themselves; and waterboarding, in which the suspect is tied to a bench, immersed in water, and made to feel that he is drowning. Using the same preventive rationale, the administration has "disappeared" allegedly high-value al-Qaeda suspects into CIA "black sites"—a series of prisons in undisclosed locations where the government's conduct cannot be monitored and the suspect is completely cut off from the outside world. When our own secret detention centers and coercive methods are not enough, the administration has "rendered" suspects to be interrogated by foreign governments with even fewer scruples about their methods.

In these contexts, the preventive rationale has made thinkable tactics that have long been unthinkable in the United States. Not even the most ardent administration supporters defend coercive interrogation, disappearances, and renditions as permissible forms of investigation or punishment for past crime; they are invariably defended with some version of the familiar "ticking time bomb" hypothetical, in which extreme measures such as torture are said to be warranted to defuse a bomb and thereby save thousands of lives. What would be unacceptable as punishment suddenly becomes acceptable, at least to some, where information is urgently needed to forestall some future, hypothetical catastrophe.

The administration has even invoked the preventive paradigm to alter the grounds for starting a war. On September 17, 2002, the Pentagon issued a new National Security Strategy that justified what is, in effect, preventive war.[2] Established international law permits individual nations to go to war only in self-defense, meaning in response to an armed attack or an imminent armed attack. In its National Security Strategy, the administration pronounced this standard too constraining in an era of suicide terrorists and weapons of mass destruction, and maintained that we are justified in going to war even when we have not been attacked and face no threat of imminent attack. An "emerging" threat is enough, the document insists. The administration relied on this theory to justify the attack on Iraq in 2003, at a time when Iraq had neither attacked us nor posed any threat of imminent attack.

This strategy of employing force anticipatorily, before there is evidence of wrongdoing and before wrongdoing occurs, turns the law's traditional approach to state coercion on its head. With narrow exceptions, the rule of law generally reserves invasions of privacy, detention, punishment, and use of military force for those who have been shown—on the basis of sound evidence and fair procedures—to have committed some wrongful act in the past. The police can invade privacy by tapping phones or searching homes, but only where there is probable cause to believe that a crime has been committed and that the search is likely to find evidence of the crime. Arrest, too, requires probable cause of crime. People can be preventively detained pending trial, but only where there is both probable cause of past wrongdoing and concrete evidence that they pose a danger to the community or are likely to abscond if left at large. Individuals can be punished only upon proof of guilt beyond a reasonable doubt. And nations may use military force unilaterally only in response to an objectively verifiable attack or threat of imminent attack. Meanwhile, the rule of law absolutely prohibits other forms of state coercion—such as disappearances and torture—even where it can be shown without a doubt that an individual has broken the law.[3]

The preventive paradigm renders the rule of law virtually unrecognizable. The rule of law, after all, is designed to subject state power to careful checks, to scrupulously enforce the line between guilt and innocence, and to hold government officials accountable to clear rules. These ideals mix uneasily with the strategies of the preventive paradigm, which generally demand sweeping executive discretion, eschew questions of guilt or innocence (because no wrong has yet occurred), and substitute secrecy and speculation for accountability and verifiable fact. Where the rule of law insists on objective evidence of wrongdoing, the preventive paradigm relies on predictions about future behavior. Such predictions generally cannot be proved true or false; frequently rest on questionable assumptions, stereotypes, and preconceptions; and are especially vulnerable to pretextual manipulation. In times of crisis, moreover, the increased fear of a false negative—allowing a real terrorist to go free—becomes so great that high rates of false positives—detaining or punishing innocents, or attacking countries that do not intend to attack us—are deemed increasingly acceptable.

Where the rule of law demands fair and open procedures, the preventive paradigm employs truncated processes that are often conducted in secret, denying suspects a meaningful opportunity to respond to the charges against them. The need for preemptive action is said to justify the secrecy and the shortcuts, whatever the cost to targeted individuals. Where the rule of law demands that people be held accountable only for their own actions, not for their ethnic identity or religious or political views, the preventive paradigm paints in broad brushstrokes, frequently employing guilt by association and ethnic profiling to target suspected future wrongdoers. And where the rule of law absolutely prohibits torture and disappearances, the preventive paradigm maintains that these should be viewed as lesser evils to defuse the proverbial ticking time bomb. In short, the preventive paradigm treats the rule of law's most fundamental commitments as luxuries that we cannot afford in the face of a catastrophic threat.

The impetus toward prevention is understandable. All other things being equal, preventing a terrorist act is preferable to responding after the fact—all the more so when the threats include weapons of mass destruction and our adversaries are difficult to detect, willing to kill themselves, and seemingly unconstrained by any considerations of law, morality, or human dignity that we can recognize. There is nothing wrong with prevention itself as a motive or a strategy; think, for example, of preventive medicine. There are plenty of preventive counterterrorism measures that conform to the rule of law—such as increased protections at borders and around vulnerable targets; institutional reforms designed to encourage better analysis of data and information sharing among the many government agencies responsible for our safety; prosecutions for conspiracies to engage in terrorist acts; even military force and military detention when employed in self-defense. The real problems arise when the state seeks to inflict highly coercive measures— depriving individuals of their life, liberty, or property or going to war—on the basis of speculation about the future, without adhering to the processes long seen as critical to regulating and legitimating such force.

• • •

Abandoning the rule of law is not just wrong as a matter of principle. It is wrongheaded as a practical matter of security. The administration's turn to preventive coercion has actually made us more vulnerable to attack, not more secure. Even if one were to accept as a moral or ethical matter the "ends justify the means" rationales advanced for the preventive paradigm, the paradigm fails its own test: there is little or no evidence that the administration's coercive preemptive measures have made us more safe, and substantial evidence that they have in fact exacerbated the dangers we face.

Consider the most costly example of the administration's preventive paradigm: the war in Iraq. The preventive-war doctrine was critical to the administration's justification for starting a war in Iraq, as not even the administration could plausibly contend that Iraq was on the verge of attacking us. In fact, in the years before the United States initiated the war, Saddam Hussein seemed to have been successfully contained. But precisely because the preventive doctrine turns on speculation about non-imminent events, it permitted an administration—which for its own reasons had long sought to topple Saddam Hussein—to turn its focus from al-Qaeda, the organization that actually attacked us, to Iraq, a nation that did not. The preventive paradigm provided not only the theoretical justification for the Iraq War but also a critical piece of "evidence" for the war. To support the war, the administration repeatedly claimed a link between al-Qaeda and Saddam Hussein. One of the key pieces of intelligence offered to buttress that claim, it turns out, was itself obtained through a dubious preventive tactic—the rendition to Egypt and subsequent torture of Ibn al-Shaykh al-Libi. While tortured in Egypt, al-Libi falsely claimed that Iraq had trained al-Qaeda in the use of explosives and poison gas, a claim he subsequently (and more credibly) recanted.[4] As early as February 2002, the Defense Intelligence Agency (DIA) questioned the reliability of al-Libi's assertions, in part because of concerns that the information may have been obtained through torture. But long after the DIA raised these doubts, President Bush, Vice President Cheney, and Secretary of State Colin Powell all cited al-Libi's statements as evidence of an alleged link between Saddam Hussein and al-Qaeda—a link that has since been wholly discredited.

The Iraq War has by virtually all accounts made the United States, the Iraqi people, many of our allies, and for that matter much of the world, more vulnerable to terrorists. By targeting Iraq, the Bush administration not only siphoned off massive resources and expertise from the struggle against al-Qaeda but also played into al-Qaeda's hands by reinforcing its anti-American propaganda and by creating a golden opportunity to inspire, recruit, and train terrorists to attack U.S. and allied targets. In February 2005, CIA director Porter Goss told Congress that "Islamic extremists are exploiting the Iraqi conflict to recruit new anti-U.S. jihadists."[5]

Although Iraq had nothing to do with the so-called war on terror before we attacked it, our invasion and continued presence there have turned Iraq into the world's premier training ground for terrorists. As Goss admitted, "those who survive will leave Iraq experienced and focused on acts of urban terrorism. They represent a potential pool of contacts to build transnational terrorist cells, groups, and networks."[6] Military analyst Anthony Cordesman has identified thirty-two "adaptations" that the insurgents have developed since the war began, including "mixed attacks," in which one bomb follows another at some delay, in order to maximize injuries to first responders; improved infiltration of the Iraqi military and police forces; and increasingly deadly improvised explosive devices.[7] The insurgents have obtained access to large caches of Saddam Hussein's arms, most of which the U.S. military failed to secure. They have been able to demonstrate their "bravery" by repeatedly attacking the U.S. and Iraqi military and police forces. These attacks are videotaped and disseminated worldwide via the Internet to inspire those in the widely dispersed diaspora who might take the initiative to commit their own atrocities—as the world witnessed in the Madrid and London bombings of 2003 and 2005, respectively. And as of January 2007, over three thousand Americans and—depending on whose figures you use—tens of thousands to hundreds of thousands of Iraqi civilians have been killed in Iraq since the war began.[8] Virtually everyone agrees that the war in Iraq has made us less safe. What we seek to show is that one of the central reasons the war has been such a disaster is its origin as a preventive war.

The preventive paradigm in other aspects of the war on terror has been no more effective. According to U.S. figures, terrorist attacks worldwide increased by 300 percent between 2003 and 2004.[9] In 2005 alone, there were 360 suicide bombings, resulting in 3,000 deaths, compared to 472 such attacks spread over the five preceding years.[10] That hardly constitutes progress in the "global war on terror."

Still, administration supporters frequently note that other than the anthrax mailings in 2001, there has not been another terrorist attack in the United States in the more than five years since 9/11. The real question, though, is whether the administration's coercive preventive measures can be credited for that fact. There were eight years between the first and second attacks on the World Trade Center, after all. Stationing American troops in Baghdad where they can be blown up by suicide bombers may have *diverted* some terrorist attacks but can hardly be said to have *prevented* terrorism. In Chapter 4, we show in detail that the administration's claims of success in the war on terror are hollow. Here, a few highlights should suffice to make the point. A 2006 study of the Defense Department's own findings on the detainees held at Guantánamo, for example, revealed that only 8 percent of the detainees held at that time were even *alleged* to be fighters for al-Qaeda or the Taliban, and fewer than half the detainees were alleged to have engaged in any hostile act against the United States.[11]

As for terror cells, in February 2005, the FBI admitted in a secret internal memo that it had yet to identify a single al-Qaeda sleeper cell in the entire United States.[12] While the Justice Department claims to have charged more than four hundred persons in "terror-related" cases, the vast majority involved no charges of terrorism whatsoever, but only minor nonviolent offenses, such as immigration fraud, credit card fraud, or lying to an FBI agent.[13] Many of the administration's most highly touted "terrorism" cases have disintegrated under close scrutiny, most notably those against Captain James Yee, a Muslim chaplain at Guantánamo initially accused of being a spy; Sami Al-Arian, a computer science professor acquitted on charges of conspiracy to kill Americans; Sami al-Hussayen, a Saudi student acquitted on charges of aiding terrorists by posting links on a website; and Yaser Hamdi and José Padilla, the two U.S. citizens held for years as enemy combatants, but released from military custody when the government faced the prospect of losing in court. The government has convicted only five individuals for conspiring or attempting to engage in an actual terrorist attack since 9/11, and of those convictions, three cannot be attributed to the preventive paradigm and the other two involve highly dubious charges or evidence.[14]

In preventive-paradigm immigration initiatives, the administration called in 80,000 foreign nationals for fingerprinting, photographing, and "special registration," simply because they came from predominantly Arab or Muslim countries, sought out another 8,000 young men from the same countries for FBI interviews, and placed more than 5,000 foreign nationals here in preventive detention. Yet as of January 2007, *not one of these individuals stands convicted of a terrorist crime.* The government's record, in what is surely the largest campaign of ethnic profiling since the Japanese internment of World War II, is 0 for 93,000.[15]

One might object that this is the wrong way to measure success. If the administration's measures are preventing terrorism, there will not be terrorist convictions because the terrorism itself will never occur. It is possible that some of these preventive-paradigm measures deterred would-be terrorists from attacking us, or helped to uncover and foil actual terrorist plots before they could come to fruition. But if real plots had been foiled, and real terrorists identified, one would expect to see some criminal convictions. When FBI agents successfully foiled a plot by Sheikh Omar Abdel Rahman (popularly known as "the blind sheikh") and others to bomb bridges and tunnels around Manhattan in the 1990s, it not only foiled the plot but also ultimately convicted the plotters and sent them to prison for life.[16] The administration has boasted that it has foiled many terrorist plots since 9/11, but has not identified a single terrorist brought to justice for these purported plots.

The administration's claims of success are often questioned by people with inside knowledge. In October 2005, for example, President Bush claimed that the United States and its allies had foiled ten terrorist plots.[17] The *Washington Post*, the *Los Angeles Times*, and *USA Today* each reported that intelligence experts seriously questioned President Bush's claims.[18]

Consider just one of President Bush's ten success stories, the one about which he provided the most details: an alleged al-Qaeda plot to fly an airplane into the Library Tower, a skyscraper in Los Angeles. The perpetrators, described only as Southeast Asians, were said to have been captured in early 2002 in Asia. As far as we know, however, no one has ever been charged or tried for involvement in this alleged terror plot. Intelligence officials told the *Washington Post* that there was "deep disagreement within the intelligence community about . . . whether it was ever much more than talk."[19] A senior FBI official said, "to take that and make it into a disrupted plot is just ludicrous."[20] Bruce Hoffman, a terrorism expert at the RAND Corporation, said that Bush's account "doesn't really give us any more indication of whether this was a plot that was derailed or preempted, or a plot that was more in the realm of an idle daydream."[21] The *Los Angeles Times* reported that when the Library

Tower plot was first publicly disclosed, authorities "said that, at best, the alleged plot was something that had been discussed but never put into action."[22] Moreover, while U.S. officials claim to have learned about some of the plot's details by interrogating captured al-Qaeda leader Khalid Sheikh Mohammed, he was captured in 2003, long after the perpetrators had been arrested. As the *Los Angeles Times* put it, "By the time anybody knew about it, the threat—if there had been one—had passed, federal counter-terrorism officials said."[23] These facts—all omitted in President Bush's retelling—suggest that such claims of success need to be viewed skeptically.

One of the most oft-heard criticisms of the FBI in the wake of 9/11 was that it was too "backward-looking," overly concerned with amassing evidence in order to try alleged criminals for past crimes, and not sufficiently intelligence-focused, or "forward-looking." But this criticism ignores the fact that traditional measures of law enforcement investigation are, at their best, forward-looking and backward-looking at the same time, and that traditional tools are perfectly capable of disrupting plots and bringing would-be bombers to justice before bombs go off. Thus, it is traditional law enforcement methodology to conduct surveillance on a group of suspected criminals for an extended period of time before arresting them, in order to assess the scope of the threat the individuals pose, to identify others who may pose even greater threats, and to develop sufficient evidence so that once the individuals are apprehended, they can be successfully prosecuted and incapacitated. It appears that it was just such traditional police work, for example, that enabled British authorities in the summer of 2006 to avert an alleged plot to explode numerous aircraft flying from Great Britain to the United States.

As the Iraq War most vividly illustrates, it is not just that the preventive paradigm has not captured many terrorists. Wars against countries that do not threaten us and broad-brush measures that sweep up thousands of people who have nothing to do with terrorism consume scarce financial and human resources. Just as our military would have been put to better use had it concentrated on al-Qaeda, the agents and resources used to track down 93,000 Arabs and Muslims, none of whom were terrorists, would have been more effectively deployed had they targeted those whom we have some reason to believe actually pose some threat—beyond their mere ethnicity or religion. Registering 80,000 people whose only connection to terrorism is that they are Arab and Muslim immigrants is a colossal waste of resources. So, too, apparently, was the National Security Agency's domestic spying program, which, according to frustrated FBI agents, generated thousands of leads that were virtually all "dead ends or have led to innocent Americans."[24]

Because the administration has been so focused on swaggeringly aggressive coercive forms of prevention, it has devoted insufficient resources and attention to less glamorous but more effective preventive initiatives. We spend more in a day in Iraq than we do annually on some of the most important defensive initiatives here in the United States.[25] In December 2005, the bipartisan 9-11 Commission gave the administration failing or near-failing grades on many of the most basic homeland security measures, including assessing critical infrastructure vulnerabilities, securing weapons of mass destruction, screening airline passengers and cargo, sharing information between law enforcement and intelligence agencies, ensuring that first responders have adequate communications, and supporting secular education in Muslim countries. These measures are plainly not the Bush administration's priority.

The preventive paradigm has also had other collateral consequences. When the administration chooses to disappear al-Qaeda suspects into secret prisons and to use waterboarding to encourage them to talk, it may obtain intelligence that it might not otherwise have been able to gain, although one cannot ever actually know that. But such tactics foreclose any real possibility of bringing the suspects to justice for their alleged crimes, because evidence obtained in a "black site" would taint any attempt to prosecute. There is debate about whether torture ever results in reliable intelligence—but there can be no debate that it radically curtails the government's ability to bring a terrorist to justice. The lawless route the administration has chosen does not just harm its victims. It also does long-lasting damage to the government's own legitimacy. The goal of protecting innocent civilians from terrorist violence is indisputably legitimate. When laudable goals are pursued through dubious means, however, the legitimacy of the entire enterprise is compromised. That loss of legitimacy, in turn, makes potential allies less eager to work with us, creates new enemies, and inspires those already arrayed against us to adopt more radical tactics. Assuming that the principal terrorist threat at this juncture comes from al-Qaeda, or more broadly, a violence-prone fundamentalist strain of Islam, and that the "enemies" in this struggle are largely composed of Arab and Muslim men, it is all the more critical that we develop close positive ties with Arab and Muslim communities here and abroad. We need their eyes and ears if we are going to find the small number of persons actually planning to use violence against us. And we need their support if we are to succeed in isolating al-Qaeda from the wider circle of potential supporters. When we impose on these communities measures that we would not tolerate for ourselves, measures that fail to treat them with the respect and dignity owed all human beings, however, we sow distrust and enmity that impede the communication and cooperation we need and simultaneously fuel the anti-Americanism that we cannot afford.

Avishai Margalit, a philosophy professor at Hebrew University, has written that "terror as propaganda-by-action counts on one thing: the overreaction of its victims. Out of anger and frustration the victims will respond by punishing bystanders, who will react by becoming more radical in their feelings and more susceptible to recruitment."[26] Nothing could more perfectly meet the recruitment needs of al-Qaeda and its supporters than the abuse U.S. forces meted out to prisoners at Abu Ghraib, the legal black hole that is Guantánamo, the policy of rendering foreign nationals to third countries for torture, the practice of disappearing suspects into a network of secret CIA detention centers, or the war in Iraq. Defense Secretary Donald Rumsfeld identified the critical question in an October 2003 internal Pentagon memo: "Are we capturing, killing or deterring and dissuading more terrorists every day than the madrassas and the radical clerics are recruiting, training and deploying against us?"[27] While there is no certain metric for answering Rumsfeld's question, there can be little doubt that our preventive tactics have been a boon to terrorist recruitment throughout the world.

The extent of the damage to the United States' image was perhaps most dramatically revealed when, after the report of CIA black sites surfaced in November 2005, Russia, among several other countries, promptly issued a press release claiming that it had nothing to do with the sites.[28] When Russia feels the need to distance itself from the United States out of concern that its human rights image might be tarnished by association, we know that we have fallen far. The fact that European nations may have housed some of the black sites and cooperated in renditions has caused a firestorm of controversy in that region and will undoubtedly complicate future cooperation. Italy and Germany, for example, have indicted CIA agents for their part in the kidnapping and rendition of their residents.[29]

In short, we have gone from being the object of the world's sympathy immediately after 9/11 to being the country most likely to be hated the world over. The Bush administration squandered all the support we had in the wake of the attacks and its tactics have caused anti-Americanism to climb to all-time highs. In some countries, Osama bin Laden has a higher approval rating than the United States.[30] Once widely admired for our human rights record—with our experts consulting many of the world's governments about how to create a culture of democracy and respect for human dignity—we are now the object of sweeping condemnations by the United Nations Human Rights Committee, international nongovernmental organizations, and judges and political leaders across the globe. These developments are linked; much of the anti-Americanism is tied to the perception that the United States has pursued its war on terror in an arrogant, unilateral fashion, defying the very values that we had long championed.

Because the rule of law is a central element of popular conceptions of justice, those who adhere to it are likely to gain legitimacy and support in the all-important struggle for hearts and minds. Remarkably, however, that is not how the Bush administration sees it. In March 2005, the Pentagon warned in its National Defense Strategy that "our strength as a nation state will continue to be challenged by those who employ a strategy of the weak using international fora, judicial processes, and terrorism." [31] The proposition that judicial processes and international accountability—the very essence of the rule of law—are to be dismissed as a strategy of the weak, aligned with terrorism itself, makes clear that the administration has come to view the rule of law as an obstacle, not an asset, in its effort to protect us from the threat of terrorist attack. Such an attitude can only breed still more anti-Americanism, and still more terrorists willing to sacrifice their lives in striking a blow against us.

The administration's preventive paradigm has already embroiled us in a war universally recognized as a disaster, sacrificed thousands of lives, imposed untold hardships on millions of innocent civilians, undermined the system of international law that is so critical to world peace, and done grave and lasting damage to the reputation of the United States. Meanwhile, Osama bin Laden remains at large and terrorism worldwide is on the rise. The administration's claims that it is winning the war on terror are no more convincing than President Bush's "Mission Accomplished" claim of victory in the war in Iraq on the USS *Abraham Lincoln* on May 1, 2003.

Civil libertarians and government officials have long argued over the trade-off between liberty and security in times of war and national emergency. Civil liberties advocates often make the moral and ethical claim that liberty should not be sacrificed in the name of security. Security proponents respond that as a utilitarian matter we should be willing to sacrifice some liberty for more security when the stakes are especially high. While we agree that it is often wrong to sacrifice liberty, freedom, and rights in the search for security, we concede that trade-offs are inevitable and that in some circumstances sacrifices in liberty may be warranted if they can promise substantial improvements in security. The main point of this book, however, is that the choice is not simply between liberty and security, but between effective security measures and counterproductive ones. The administration's coercive preventive model not only sacrifices liberty but compromises our security.

This book has three goals: to illustrate the sacrifices in principle entailed by the preventive paradigm; to demonstrate that these sacrifices have made us less, not more, secure; and to propose an alternative counterterrorism strategy that treats the rule of law as an asset, not an obstacle, in the effort to win security for our nation. Part 1 describes the preventive paradigm in its law enforcement, intelligence, and military manifestations and shows that its adoption has resulted in deep, widespread, and morally dubious compromises in the fundamental commitments of the rule of law. Part 2 turns to results, and shows that there is very little evidence that these measures have in fact increased our security and substantial reason to believe that they have in fact rendered us more vulnerable to terrorist attacks. Finally, Part 3 offers an alternative to the preventive paradigm—one that seeks to prevent the next terrorist attack in ways that preserve rather than subvert the rule of law.

Our intention in writing this book is not so much to indict the Bush administration as to offer a case study in how not to fight terrorism. The preventive paradigm is not a Republican idea; if a Democratic president had been in office on September 11, 2001, many of the abuses we recount here would likely have happened anyway. The impulse to prevent another attack is a natural one, and with it often comes a rejection of rule-of-law values as luxuries we can no longer afford. Every prior national security crisis in the United States has triggered a preventive paradigm of one sort or another, as administrations of all political stripes have sought to use coercion to prevent a feared future attack. President John Adams enforced the Alien and Sedition Acts, President Lincoln suspended habeas corpus, President Woodrow Wilson prosecuted antiwar activists for their speech during World War I, Attorney General Palmer rounded up communists in the 1919 Palmer raids, President Franklin Delano Roosevelt interned Japanese Americans during World War II, and President Truman established loyalty review boards during the Cold War. In the wake of 9/11, two prominent liberal law professors, Bruce Ackerman of Yale Law School and Alan Dershowitz of Harvard Law School, have written books advocating the adoption of preventive coercive measures: detention and war, respectively.[32] And many Democrats joined their Republican counterparts in Congress to authorize preventive war in Iraq.

Our argument is that no matter who has employed it, anticipatory coercion has nearly always proved to be a grave mistake, not only as a matter of principle but also as a matter of effective security. Our long-term security turns not on locking up thousands of "suspected terrorists" who turn out to have no connection to terrorism; nor on forcing suspects to bark like dogs, urinate and defecate on themselves, and endure sexual humiliation; nor on attacking countries that have not threatened to attack us. Security rests not on exceptionalism and double standards but on a renewed commitment to fairness, justice, and the rule of law. Aharon Barak, president of Israel's Supreme Court, said it best in a case forbidding the use of "moderate physical pressure" in interrogating Palestinian terror suspects:

A democracy must sometimes fight terror with one hand tied behind its back. Even so, a democracy has the upper hand. The rule of law and the liberty of an individual constitute important components in its understanding of security. At the end of the day, they strengthen its spirit and this strength allows it to overcome its difficulties.[33]

The preventive paradigm, by jettisoning fundamental commitments to the rule of law, has compromised our spirit, strengthened our enemies, and left us simultaneously less free and less safe. If we are ready to learn from our mistakes, however, there is a way forward—through, rather than in spite of, a recommitment to the rule of law.

PART I

LESS FREE

1. PREVENTIVE LAW ENFORCEMENT AND INTELLIGENCE GATHERING

Maher Arar was introduced to the preventive paradigm on September 26, 2002. A thirty-five-year-old Canadian citizen, Arar had lived in Canada for nearly twenty years, but was born in Syria and held dual citizenship. He lived in Montreal with his wife and two children and worked as a wireless technology consultant. On September 26, he was changing planes at New York's JFK Airport on his way home to Montreal from Zurich. As he passed through immigration in order to catch his connecting flight to Montreal, U.S. officials pulled Arar aside. They ultimately incarcerated him for nearly two weeks at the Metropolitan Detention Center in Brooklyn, denied his requests for a lawyer, interrogated him at length, and ordered his removal on secret evidence alleging that he was a member of a terrorist organization. U.S. officials claimed that he had ties to al-Qaeda, a charge Arar denied.

Arar requested to be deported to Canada, his home, where he had been heading anyway, and for which he still held a connecting flight ticket. But federal authorities refused his request, and instead, after lying to the attorney his family had procured for him to prevent the attorney from gaining access to him, put Arar on a government-chartered jet to Jordan, where he was immediately transported to Syria. He spent the next year incarcerated in Syria without charges, most of it in solitary confinement in a three-by-six-foot cell that Arar describes as a "grave." During the initial weeks of detention, he was interrogated at length, placed in "the tire," which immobilizes prisoners for beatings, whipped with cables, and threatened with electric shocks. Syrian officials interrogated Arar with a dossier of questions that tracked those U.S. officials had asked him while he was detained in New York.

In the end, the Syrians released him, stating that they found no evidence that he had committed a crime, and he returned home to Canada (this time without changing planes at JFK). Canadian authorities never charged him with a crime either. In September 2006, an official Canadian inquiry concluded a multimillion-dollar investigation of the affair by fully exonerating Arar of any connection to terrorism, and in January 2007 the Canadian government agreed to pay Arar $11.5 million to compensate him for their part in his mistreatment.[1]

This is the preventive paradigm at work. U.S. officials suspected Arar of al-Qaeda ties, but evidently lacked solid evidence to back up the charges. If they had had such evidence, they would almost certainly have either charged him criminally in a U.S. court or designated him an enemy combatant and shipped him to Guantánamo Bay, where some 450 other enemy combatants are being held. Instead, under cover of secrecy, shielded from the inquiring eyes of Arar's attorney, and on the basis of secret evidence that he never had a chance to see or rebut, they shipped him to Syria. The only possible justification for sending him to Syria rather than to Canada is that Canada does not have a track record of arbitrary detention and torture; Syria does. At worst, from the United States' perspective, Arar would be incapacitated; at best, the Syrian security service might be able to extract valuable intelligence from Arar that could be useful in the war on terror.

Instead, Arar is today a free man, and the United States is accused of collaborating with Syria to torture an innocent man. The case has done tremendous damage to the United States' credibility with our neighbor to the north: in 2004, the Canadian edition of *Time* magazine named Arar "Person of the Year." (The American edition gave President Bush that honor.) And while Canada has officially exonerated Arar and admitted its part in the wrongdoing, the United States still has Arar on a watch list and has opposed any effort to hold American officials accountable in a court of law.

Arar is just one of approximately 160 persons whom the United States has reportedly "rendered" to third countries since September 11. Another is Khaled El-Masri, a German citizen who was arrested at the Macedonia border on December 21, 2003; held in a motel room for twenty-three days; and then shackled, blindfolded, and transferred by plane to Afghanistan. In Afghanistan, he says, he was beaten, interrogated, and photographed naked by persons El-Masri identified as Americans. According to El-Masri, one interrogator told him, "You are here in a country where no one knows about you, in a country where there is no law. If you die, we will bury you, and no one will know." In May 2004, more than five months after his initial detention, El-Masri was set free on an isolated country road in Albania. The U.S. ambassador admitted to the Germans that the CIA had wrongfully imprisoned El-Masri, but asked them to keep the matter secret. Like Arar, El-Masri has never been charged with a crime. The *Washington Post* has reported that he was initially picked up because his name was similar to an associate of a 9/11 hijacker, Khalid al-Masri. His release was apparently ordered by Secretary of State Condoleezza Rice upon realizing that his rendition was a case of mistaken identity.[2] On February 2, 2007, German prosecutors issued arrest warrants for thirteen CIA agents suspected of kidnapping El-Masri.

In Arar's case, federal officials were able to use (or more accurately, abuse) existing legal procedures—the immigration process—to effect Arar's transfer. Most renditions, by contrast, resemble El-Masri's: agents kidnap a suspect in one country, drug him, and covertly fly him to another country to be detained, using no legal process whatsoever. Before 9/11, rendition was employed as a last resort when extradition or deportation, the normal legal processes for removing a person from one country to another, were not available. The purpose of the enterprise was to bring individuals to justice where ordinary means for doing so were unavailable. These renditions often violated the law but at least were limited to persons who had already been investigated and indicted for past criminal conduct, but happened to be living beyond the reach of the law.

After 9/11, the Bush administration refashioned renditions in the preventive-paradigm mold. Where the original purpose of renditions was to bring individuals within the reach of the law to be held accountable for past wrongs, the new purpose appears to be to place suspects *beyond* the reach of any law that might protect them, in order to gather intelligence about potential future wrongdoing through coercive interrogation. Many of the countries to which the United States has rendered suspects are, like Syria, notorious for the use of torture as an interrogation tool. The Bush administration claims that it obtains "assurances" that the rendered suspects will not be tortured, but this defense seems implausible. If the individual is not being rendered to stand trial, what is he being rendered for, other than interrogation? And if interrogation is all we are interested in, why not conduct it in the country of residence? Why would we accept the assurances of a country like Syria on torture, when we do not appear to trust it on any other subject? And if we were not interested in obtaining information through tactics such as detention without charges and coercive interrogation, why was Arar not sent to Canada, which, unlike Syria, is our ally?

Renditions are defended as a way of preventing terrorist attacks by obtaining intelligence about and disrupting terrorist networks.[3] But like other aspects of the preventive paradigm, they entail substantial sacrifices in our commitment to the rule of law. Where the rule of law requires transparency, renditions are carried out in secret, undermining both the detainee's ability to defend himself and the public's ability to know what its government is doing in its name. Indeed, in El-Masri's case, the administration sought to keep its actions secret even after it had admitted, behind closed doors, that it had kidnapped and imprisoned an innocent man.

The rule of law requires fair procedures before a person's liberty is taken from him. Renditions for interrogation are designed precisely to avoid legal process. El-Masri, like most rendered suspects, was literally kidnapped. Because Arar was rendered through the immigration laws, he was afforded a hearing, but government officials did all they could to ensure that it was only pro forma. They held it on a Sunday evening and notified Arar's lawyer only by leaving a message that evening on her (closed) office voice mail. The government then flew Arar out of the country the next night, while prison and immigration officials misled Arar's lawyer during the intervening day about where he was to ensure that she could not seek judicial intervention. When, upon his return to Canada, Arar filed a lawsuit in the United States challenging the legality of his rendition to Syria, the government invoked a "state secrets" privilege and argued that Arar's claims must be dismissed because U.S. contacts with Syria and Canada could not be publicly disclosed.[4]

The rule of law requires a sound evidentiary basis before individuals are taken into custody. But because renditions involve no adversarial testing of the evidence, nor any kind of check by the other branches of government, they may be and reportedly have been carried out on very slim bases. One man was reportedly rendered solely because an al-Qaeda suspect offered up his name during a CIA interrogation; according to a CIA official, the man "turned out to be an innocent college professor who had given the al-Qaeda member a bad grade."[5] Arar and El-Masri similarly turned out to be entirely innocent.

Finally, the rule of law recognizes certain rights as fundamental to the individual, chief among them freedom from torture. The prohibition on torture is one of a handful of rules that international law recognizes as jus cogens norms, meaning that they are absolute, and their violation is *never* justified. The Convention Against Torture, which the United States has signed and ratified, unequivocally prohibits torture under all circumstances, specifically including wartime, and also prohibits a country from sending a person to any country where he faces a substantial risk of being tortured. Yet many of the Bush administration's renditions appear to be designed to send people not just to countries where they face a risk of being tortured, but *for that very purpose.*

In sum, renditions for interrogation, defended as necessary to prevent future terrorist attacks, violate several of the most fundamental cornerstones of the rule of law. These features, it turns out, are common to all the coercive measures that are employed as part of the Bush administration's preventive paradigm.

JUSTIFICATIONS FOR THE PREVENTIVE PARADIGM

Like renditions, virtually all of the Bush administration's most controversial initiatives in the war on terror have been defended in preventive terms. The use of coercive interrogation is perhaps the starkest example, because, as noted in the Introduction, no one suggests that such tactics are permissible to punish or investigate past crimes, but solely to prevent future wrongdoing. The *only* justification defenders of torture or cruel, inhuman, and degrading treatment offer is the need to prevent a greater future harm.

The Bush administration and its supporters have advanced preventive arguments to defend a wide variety of coercive interventions into the lives of individuals. The administration insists that indefinite detention of enemy combatants without trial or hearing is warranted, not as punishment for past wrongs, but to prevent dangerous individuals from doing harm in the future—for example, by rejoining enemy forces in a military conflict. As Secretary of Defense Donald Rumsfeld put it, the detainees at Guantánamo are not being held for stealing a car, but to stop them from returning to the battlefield and waging war against us in the future.

The natural inclination of most Americans, and indeed of people in many other countries, is to think in terms of criminal law and punishment rather than the law of war which has as its purpose first to keep the enemy off the battlefield so that they can't kill more innocent people. Another important objective is one I mentioned, intelligence gathering to save lives. And only last, is the issue of punishment an issue.

We need to keep in mind that the people in U.S. custody are not there because they stole a car or robbed a bank. That's not why they're there. They are not common criminals. They're enemy combatants and terrorists who are being detained for acts of war against our country and that is why different rules have to apply.[6]

In fact, by the government's own official assessment, less than half of those held at Guantánamo have engaged in any hostile acts against the United States, and as of late 2006, only ten individuals had actually been charged with committing war crimes.[7] Consistent with its preventive rationale, the army conducts annual reviews and releases those individuals who it concludes no longer pose a present or future threat to the United States. Thus far, over three hundred have been released. The predicate for Guantánamo detentions, then, is not past wrongdoing, but the likelihood of future hostile action.

The preventive paradigm also underlies the CIA's "black sites," a series of secret prisons holding allegedly high-value al-Qaeda suspects. In December 2005, Secretary of State Condoleezza Rice traveled to Europe, shortly after the *Washington Post* disclosed that several of the black sites had been located in eastern Europe.[8] Beset by questions about the prisons at every stop, Rice invoked the preventive paradigm to defend the administration's practices, claiming, "We have to remember that intelligence is key to this war on terrorism. If you cannot have good intelligence, you can't prevent an attack."[9] In September 2006, President Bush openly acknowledged the existence of the CIA program and sought to justify it by claiming that information obtained through the program had helped capture terrorists and prevent attacks.[10] He repeated this justification one month later as he signed the Military Commissions Act, which he lauded for permitting the CIA secret detention centers to go forward.

> This bill will allow the Central Intelligence Agency to continue its program for questioning key terrorist leaders and operatives like Khalid Sheikh Mohammed, the man believed to be the mastermind of the September the 11th, 2001 attacks on our country. This program has been one of the most successful intelligence efforts in American history. It has helped prevent attacks on our country.[11]

At home, the administration has also invoked the preventive paradigm as it has reshaped the nation's laws and adopted aggressive law enforcement and intelligence-gathering practices. One of the administration's priorities has been to cut off support to so-called terrorist groups, regardless of the nature of that support. Federal laws make it a crime to provide any sort of "material support" to an organization that has been labeled terrorist.[12] The administration defends these laws on explicitly preventive grounds. It does not maintain, for example, that the acts of donating a blanket or providing human rights training— both of which constitute prohibited material support—are themselves harmful. Instead, it argues that even bona fide humanitarian donations may "free up" other resources that can be used to conduct future terrorist activity.[13] Criminalizing such material support is preventive because it punishes people not for engaging in or planning harmful conduct but as a means to reduce the likelihood of future attacks.

The administration has advanced the same justification for pretextual immigration and criminal law enforcement targeted at Arabs and Muslims. Thousands of foreign nationals from predominantly Arab and Muslim countries have been singled out for detention, deportation, and prosecution since 9/11.[14] While many of those detained had committed immigration violations, and therefore had no right to remain in the United States, that fact did not distinguish them from millions of similarly situated foreign nationals from other nations living here. The justification for targeting Arabs and Muslims was that doing so might prevent future acts of terrorism: one of the deportees might have been a budding terrorist. In addition, Arab and Muslim terrorists abroad who see the United States cracking down on Arabs and Muslims here might think twice about attempting to enter to perpetrate terrorism. As Attorney General John Ashcroft said in a speech announcing the "paradigm of prevention" in October 2001, just one month after 9/11, "our single objective is to prevent terrorist attacks by taking suspected terrorists off the street."[15] As it turned out, according to an investigation by the Justice Department's own inspector general, few if any of these so-called suspected terrorists had any connection to terrorism, and the grounds for treating them as suspect was often little more than their ethnic and religious identity.[16]

The administration has similarly defended widespread and potentially sweeping infringements on privacy in preventive terms. The USA PATRIOT Act's very name invokes the preventive paradigm: Uniting and Strengthening America by Providing Appropriate Tools Required to *Intercept* and *Obstruct* Terrorism. That law expanded the government's ability to wiretap and search individuals without showing probable cause that they had engaged in or were engaging in any criminal activity;[17] again, the theory is that we need to keep track of what certain people are doing *before* there is any evidence that they may be involved in criminal activity so that we can prevent terrorist attacks. Similarly, the Patriot Act expanded the government's ability to demand records from libraries and other businesses without showing that the records pertained to a suspected terrorist.[18] That provision, too, was defended on the ground that preventing terrorists from acting may require investigating persons who have not (yet) committed any wrong.

The Pentagon's Total Information Awareness program, which was designed to gather and review massive amounts of computer data about individuals' everyday transactions, was similarly defended on the theory that through pattern recognition it might help us to identify potential terrorists before they act.[19] When the *New York Times* in December 2005 disclosed that President Bush had secretly authorized the National Security Agency to spy on Americans without court order and in violation of federal law, President Bush defended the program by claiming that it was a critical tool to prevent terrorist attacks, and Vice President Cheney boasted that the program had saved "thousands of lives."[20]

What unites all of these measures is not simply that they are justified on preventive grounds, but that they employ harshly coercive or highly invasive measures in anticipation of future wrongdoing, rather than in response to past acts. There are plenty of preventive tactics that do not involve the anticipatory application of substantial coercion. It is one thing to act defensively by hardening cockpit doors, sharing legitimately procured information between agencies to increase the likelihood of "connecting the dots," or screening airline passengers and luggage. It is another matter to lock up or disappear human beings; render them to countries known for torture; inflict cruel, inhuman, and degrading treatment or torture on them to compel them to talk; target ethnic and religious minorities for pretextual law enforcement and preventive detention; impose guilt by association; and intercept private telephone calls and emails without probable cause or a warrant. These methods—the heart of the Bush administration's preventive paradigm—employ coercion on the basis of speculation about the future, rather than in response to demonstrated wrongdoing in the past. Because of its anticipatory character, the preventive paradigm creates pressures to substitute suspicion for evidence as a basis for coercive action. Thus, instead of incarcerating people on the basis of proof beyond a reasonable doubt that they committed a past infraction, the preventive paradigm turns to detention as a preventive matter and employs it against individuals deemed suspect by virtue of their group identity or political affiliations.

This chapter will show that the preventive paradigm in law enforcement and intelligence gathering has resulted in serious departures from the core values we associate with the rule of law: namely, equality, transparency, individual culpability, fair processes, clear rules, checks and balances, and human rights. We do not intend to provide a comprehensive overview of the administration's counterterrorism measures, but rather to highlight certain troubling features of the preventive paradigm. At the chapter's close, we address and reject the claim that these preventive innovations are justified because we are fighting a war.

THE RULE OF LAW AND THE PREVENTIVE PARADIGM

The rule of law is an Enlightenment notion that state authority should be regulated and checked by rules that constrain the exercise of official power, subject state authority to democratic checks, and protect individual rights. It is the animating principle behind the Declaration of Independence and the Constitution. One of the rule of law's most important implications is that the state may generally employ harshly coercive measures, such as detention or punishment, only on the basis of past wrongdoing that has been established to a high degree of certainty by a fundamentally fair process. Thus, the state may use coercive force to stop, arrest, and punish, but only where it has evidence that an individual has committed or is in the course of committing a criminal infraction. The required degree of certainty increases as the level of coercive intrusion increases. A police officer may force a citizen to stop briefly for questioning if he has "reasonable suspicion" that crime is afoot, but needs "probable cause," a higher degree of suspicion, to subject the individual to formal arrest and custodial interrogation. The state needs proof of guilt beyond a reasonable doubt to secure a conviction and impose punishment of any kind. The critical threshold requirement for all of these intrusions is some evidence of *past* or *current* wrongdoing. While there are exceptions, the rule of law generally disapproves of imposing these types of coercion on the basis of speculation about future events. The state's monopoly on coercion creates the potential for grave abuse, and given the virtual impossibility of predicting the future, speculation about what someone might do in the future is generally an unsound basis for the exercise of such coercive force.

The preventive paradigm rejects the rule of law's presumption against employing coercive force on the basis of speculation about unpredictable future events. It features a variety of coercive interventions defended *expressly* on the need to prevent future harm, without any showing of past or current wrongdoing, even if the future harm necessarily cannot be predicted with the kind of accuracy possible when assessing responsibility for past actions. As President Bush put it, "If we wait for threats to fully materialize, we will have waited too long."[21] While the preventive impulse is salutary, the mobilization of coercive force in its name is dangerous. It not only risks inflicting grievous injuries in error but also corrodes the respect that the rule of law offers to regimes that play by the rules.

EQUALITY

In 1990, Congress ratified the Convention Against Torture and Other Cruel, Inhuman, and Degrading Treatment or Punishment (CAT), which categorically prohibits states from engaging in such conduct under any circumstance. When Congress was debating the treaty's ratification, some members raised concerns that the prohibition on "cruel, inhuman, and degrading treatment" might be too vague. Accordingly, Congress attached a "reservation" to the treaty providing that the United States understands those terms to be coextensive with the prohibitions in the Fifth and Eighth Amendments to the U.S. Constitution. The idea was that the substantive elaboration that these constitutional provisions had received would provide a concrete definition for the term "cruel, inhuman, and degrading treatment." Those constitutional provisions, in turn, had been interpreted to prohibit all use of physical coercion or threats thereof in criminal interrogations, all official conduct that "shocks the conscience," and punishment deemed cruel and unusual. On this understanding, the treaty prohibited U.S. officials from employing such tactics against anyone.

In 2005, however, as the Senate was considering whether to confirm Alberto Gonzales as attorney general, it learned that Bush administration officials had secretly drawn a different lesson from the reservation to the CAT. They interpreted it, Gonzales explained in response to a senator's question, to deny foreign nationals being held abroad any protection from "cruel, inhuman, and degrading treatment." [22] The administration's reasoning was that because the U.S. Constitution itself has not been generally interpreted to extend to foreign nationals outside our borders, and the prohibition on "cruel, inhuman, and degrading treatment" was coextensive with the constitutional provisions, that part of the CAT did not protect foreign nationals held abroad. As Abraham Sofaer, the former legal adviser to the State Department who presented the CAT to the Senate, argued, this reasoning is fundamentally inconsistent with the basic premise of the treaty, which is to protect the *human* right to be free from torture, not the *American* right to be free from torture, or the right to be free from torture *only in the United States*. [23] The administration's interpretation gave U.S. officials a green light to use any tactic short of outright torture, no matter how cruel, inhuman, or degrading, to interrogate foreign nationals detained outside U.S. borders. [24]

When Congress learned that the administration had concocted this loophole, Senator John McCain and others immediately vowed to close it. McCain proposed an amendment that prohibited the use of cruel, inhuman, and degrading treatment by U.S. agents wherever they acted and whatever the nationality of the person being interrogated.[25] President Bush initially threatened to veto the bill, but when McCain's amendment passed the Senate 90 to 9, the president realized that the veto option was foreclosed. He then dispatched Vice President Cheney to seek an explicit exemption from the prohibition for interrogations of foreign nationals abroad, or for CIA agents.

When McCain refused to budge and the House overwhelmingly approved the measure as well, President Bush signed the bill—but affixed a "signing statement" that essentially asserted that, as commander in chief, he could violate the prohibition whenever he deemed it appropriate to do so.[26] The signing statement announces that "the executive branch shall construe [the McCain amendment] in a manner consistent with the constitutional authority of the President to supervise the unitary executive branch and as Commander in Chief and consistent with the constitutional limitations on the judicial power." Journalist Andrew Sullivan translated this as code for: "If the President believes torture is warranted to protect the country, he'll violate the law and authorize torture. If the courts try to stop him, he'll ignore them, too."[27]

The controversy about cruel, inhuman, and degrading treatment is ultimately about the status of human beings. Senator McCain and Abraham Sofaer insist that what is cruel to do to an American in Louisiana is just as cruel to do to a foreign national in a secret CIA prison overseas. The whole idea of international human rights is that certain rights derive from human dignity, something we all hold by virtue of our common humanity. The right not to be treated in a cruel, inhuman, and degrading manner is a universalist claim and admits of no exceptions based on passport. On that understanding, it makes no sense to distinguish between the tactics that may be used to interrogate an American and the tactics used to question a citizen of Pakistan.

The administration's assertion that it was free to do to foreign nationals abroad what it could not do to Americans at home, however, was typical of many of the measures it has adopted in the war on terror. It has repeatedly sought to defend its most coercive preventive measures by invoking a double standard. It insists that the measures are reserved for foreign nationals, and are not being used against Americans. It may not be immediately obvious why the preventive paradigm would support such a distinction. As the Spanish and British learned in the Madrid and London bombings, terrorist attacks may be perpetrated by citizens as well as foreign visitors. But equality is the first principle to go in the preventive paradigm for a simple political reason: it is easier to defend preventive coercion as a political matter when the populace can be assured that the preventive measures will be applied only to "them," not "us." This argument serves an especially useful purpose in justifying preventive measures that would be unacceptable if employed more broadly.[28]

Precisely because it is so tempting for a collective to impose costs selectively on minorities, equality is the first principle of the rule of law. The motto etched in stone above the entrance to the U.S. Supreme Court reads, "Equal Justice Before the Law." The Constitution was initially adopted without a commitment to equality, an omission rectified only after the Civil War. Since then, the Fourteenth Amendment's equal protection clause has been the vehicle through which African Americans, other racial minorities, women, gays and lesbians, and others have advanced their claims to equal respect. International human rights treaties are also predicated on the notion that human beings are entitled to equal respect and dignity.[29] While the specific substantive commitments that equality entails are hotly disputed, there is general consensus that equal treatment is particularly essential where the state seeks to exercise coercive force over individuals.

The Bush administration's preventive paradigm has repeatedly transgressed the guarantee of equality. Immediately after the attacks of 9/11, it initiated a preventive-detention campaign

targeted at Arab and Muslim foreign nationals, ultimately subjecting over five thousand foreign nationals to preventive detention in the name of fighting terrorism.[30] Many were detained in
the initial weeks after the attacks on no charges at all. They were
picked up on the strength of such information as an anonymous
tip that there were "too many Middle Easterners" working in a
local convenience store.[31] They were held in secret. Many were
tried in immigration proceedings that were closed to the public,
the media, human rights observers, and even their family. When
some immigration judges ordered detainees released on bond,
the attorney general changed the rules to empower immigration
"prosecutors" to keep foreign nationals in custody even after an
immigration judge had ordered their release—simply by filing
an appeal, regardless of its chances of success.

When some detainees held on immigration charges agreed to
leave the country, thus obviating any legitimate need to detain
them, the administration responded by adopting a policy of
"hold until cleared." Under that policy, the detainees were not
permitted to leave, even after judges had ordered that they could
do so, until FBI investigators had satisfied themselves that the
individuals had no ties to terrorism. Virtually all were cleared.
Today, not one of the five thousand foreign nationals preventively detained in the name of fighting terrorism stands convicted of any terrorist crime.[32]

As a legal matter, this program of mass preventive detention
was possible only because the detainees were foreign nationals.
The administration was able to get away with locking up so
many persons without charges, holding and trying them in secret, and keeping them imprisoned even after judges ordered
their release, by exploiting the immigration laws for purposes
they were never designed to serve. As a political matter, it was
able to avoid public outcry because the detainees were foreign
nationals, not citizens.

Exploiting the same double standard, the United States called
in eighty thousand foreign nationals for registration, finger-

printing, and photographing, simply because they came from countries with predominantly Arab or Muslim populations; insisted that the hundreds of individuals incarcerated incommunicado at Guantánamo have no constitutional rights and no right of access to the courts; claimed the authority to use extrajudicial military tribunals to try and execute foreign nationals accused of terrorism, even though U.S. citizens accused of the same crimes may be tried only within the ordinary criminal justice system; and argued that Maher Arar's rendition to Syria violated no constitutional rights because, as a foreign national, he had no constitutional rights. To avoid constitutional scrutiny and deflect political accountability, the government in each instance pointed to the fact that the people targeted were foreign nationals.

Citizens and foreign nationals need not be treated identically in every respect. Foreign nationals must receive permission, for example, to enter the country; citizens are free to enter or leave at will. Foreign nationals among us may be expelled for violating reasonable conditions on their stay here; citizens may not be expelled, no matter how heinously they act. Citizens have a right to vote; foreign nationals do not. But when it comes to basic human rights, such as the right not to be locked up arbitrarily, not to be subjected to torture or cruel, inhuman, and degrading treatment, not to be disappeared, and not to be profiled on the basis of one's ethnic or religious identity, there is no rationale for treating those with British or Egyptian passports differently from those with U.S. passports. The threat to national security is the same whether a potential bomber is American or Saudi; the individual's interest in being treated in accord with basic human dignity also does not vary by nationality.

This issue arose shortly after 9/11 in Britain, where Parliament enacted a statute authorizing indefinite detention without charge of foreign nationals suspected of terrorist involvement who could not be deported. In a landmark ruling, the Law Lords, Britain's highest court, held that the law was incompatible with the European Convention on Human Rights because it impermissibly discriminated between foreign nationals and British nationals. British nationals and foreign nationals, the court reasoned, could both pose a threat of terrorism. Therefore, there was no justification for authorizing the detention of foreigners without also justifying the detention of nationals.[33] The rule of law insists that we not differentiate between Americans and citizens of other nations with respect to basic human rights. Yet the administration's preventive paradigm would be legally unthinkable and politically unacceptable without that double standard.

TRANSPARENCY

"Democracies die behind closed doors," wrote Judge Damon Keith in 2002, declaring unconstitutional Attorney General Ashcroft's blanket policy of closing to the public all immigration proceedings involving persons "of interest" to the 9/11 investigation.[34] Without knowing what elected representatives are doing, the people cannot exercise their right to self-government. Yet were it not for lawsuits seeking disclosure of confidential information or unauthorized leaks of classified material to the media, Americans would have little idea what the Bush administration has done in our name in the war on terror. We would not know about torture at Abu Ghraib, sexual abuse of prisoners at Guantánamo, or the rendering of suspects to third countries for torture. We would not know that the Justice Department drafted an opinion stating that the president can order torture even though Congress has criminally prohibited it; that the military detained boys as young as thirteen as enemy combatants at Guantánamo, or that the CIA disappeared al-Qaeda suspects into CIA black sites. We would be unaware that in the wake of the Patriot Act, the FBI issued tens of thousands of "national security letters," a form of administrative subpoena that requires banks, credit card companies, and phone and cable businesses to hand over information on customers secretly to the FBI without court order. And we would not know that President Bush ordered the NSA to conduct warrantless wiretapping of Americans in contravention of a criminal statute. The administration has sought to keep the American people in the dark regarding these and an untold number of other initiatives. Once they became public, many of these initiatives sparked widespread debate and controversy, inside and outside the United States, and the administration was compelled to retreat from some of its most extreme assertions of authority. Had it been left to the administration, those debates would never have occurred. The administration's reaction to disclosure of the NSA spying program was to threaten those who revealed the program with prosecution. As it stands, only the highest levels of the administration know how much more is still being done under cover of darkness.

"Preventive secrecy" has become the operative presumption. The administration claims that revealing information would help terrorists know what we are doing, learn what we know and do not know, identify our vulnerabilities, and prepare more effectively for future attacks. In the name of preventive secrecy, the administration in the first few months after 9/11 clandestinely arrested hundreds of foreign nationals and conducted hundreds of closed immigration trials. Prisoners detained abroad have been held even more secretly, under the theory that permitting outside scrutiny would obstruct the military's ability to gain information necessary to prevent future attacks. The detention facility at Guantánamo Bay has been shrouded in secrecy since its opening, and while the administration permitted the Red Cross highly restricted access to some detainees there, the highest-value suspects have been held away from the principal detention center, off-limits to any outside monitors. The administration conditioned the UN Human Rights Committee's access to Guantánamo on a ban on talking to any of the prisoners, a condition the committee rightly rejected. At Abu Ghraib, the army hid prisoners as "ghost detainees" off the books so that their treatment could not be monitored and evaluated. More secret still are the CIA black sites in undisclosed locations abroad, designed to avoid entirely the reach of legal oversight.[35]

The Patriot Act expanded authority for secret wiretaps and searches, regardless of whether investigations have anything to do with counterterrorism. (Wiretaps and searches can be kept permanently secret upon a showing that the target is an "agent of a foreign power," a term defined so broadly that it includes employees of foreign political parties and nonprofit groups, without regard to whether the parties or groups have ever engaged in violence.) The act also authorized the government to use secret evidence to freeze assets of charities suspected of ties to terrorist groups; that provision has been used to shut down more than half a dozen Muslim charities in the United States, without ever having to show in open court that the charities were engaged in any wrongdoing.[36]

Perhaps the most troubling invocation of secrecy has been the administration's invocation of the state secrets privilege to block judicial oversight of some of its most dubious practices. As noted above, it claimed that lawsuits challenging the rendition of Maher Arar and Khaled El-Masri for torture had to be dismissed because they involved secret information that could not be disclosed. The state secrets privilege is a judicially created doctrine designed to shield truly important secrets from disclosure through litigation. It is typically invoked in cases challenging the termination of CIA employees, where disclosure of the reasons behind the termination would reveal secret investigations or tactics. But unlike most privileges, which simply protect information from disclosure, the state secrets privilege can lead to wholesale dismissal of a lawsuit, where the government shows that it cannot defend itself without revealing national security secrets. In the rendition cases, the privilege threatens to foreclose any real accountability for a practice that is now a matter of public record. The district court and the court of appeals hearing El-Masri's challenge dismissed his suit on state secrets grounds.[37]

The administration resorted to the same defense in a series of lawsuits challenging the legality of the NSA spying program. The administration acknowledged that the NSA program existed, described its basic contours in public, and submitted to Congress a forty-two-page single-spaced memorandum defending the program's legality. That memo argued, among other things, that the president's power as commander in chief in the war on terror gives him exclusive, uncheckable authority to order warrantless wiretapping of Americans, regardless of what Congress has required. But when the administration's program was tested in the courts, its first response was to argue that, because the NSA program is a secret, its claim of uncheckable executive power could not be reviewed by the courts. The lower courts divided on whether the state secrets privilege demanded dismissal of the NSA cases, and in January 2007 the administration announced that it would terminate the program and thenceforth conduct wiretapping only pursuant to judicial oversight under FISA.[38] If the administration had succeeded on its privilege claim, however, it would have obtained through a claim of secrecy the very unchecked power it so controversially asserted.

Secrecy, of course, has its proper place. Confidential communications are essential to protect the frank discussions needed for a healthy deliberative process within the executive branch. Ongoing criminal and counterterrorism investigations legitimately rely on secrecy to avoid tipping off those under surveillance. The need to keep information close to the chest is at its height in wartime, when we need to keep the enemy guessing. At the same time, however, secrecy can be and historically has been used for illegitimate purposes—to conceal from the public misdeeds or mistakes and to evade accountability. As the Arar, El-Masri, and NSA cases illustrate, the administration has used secrecy to shield the preventive paradigm from meaningful oversight and constitutional challenge.

Just as with other values of the rule of law, transparency is perhaps most critical where the government seeks to employ highly coercive measures. It is not controversial, for example, to keep most internal White House policy deliberations confidential or to maintain secrecy while a wiretap is operational or an investigation is ongoing. But it is another matter to lock up a human being on the basis of secret evidence or closed hearings. If the state keeps the very fact of the detention secret, it has essentially engaged in the practice of disappearances, a tactic made famous by the military junta that ruled Argentina in the 1970s. This practice is condemned by international law because those held beyond public scrutiny are especially vulnerable to abuse. The United States severely criticized this practice when Argentina did it in the name of fighting terrorists in its dirty war, but the Bush administration has now adopted that tactic in its own war on terror.

Secrecy raises especially grave concerns when it denies an individual charged with wrongdoing a meaningful opportunity to defend himself. In immigration proceedings such as Maher Arar's, judicial hearings challenging the closure of Muslim charities, and the military detention tribunals being conducted at Guantánamo for enemy combatants, the administration has insisted on the prerogative of using secret evidence, not disclosed to the defendant, to justify the deprivation of life, liberty, or property. The most extreme example is the military tribunal, in which, under the administration's initial rules, defendants could be tried and executed on the basis of evidence that neither they nor their chosen civilian counsel had any opportunity to see or challenge, and in which the prosecution was not obligated to disclose exculpatory information—that is, evidence showing that the defendant is innocent—if it labeled the evidence confidential.[39]

There are undoubtedly legitimate reasons not to disclose to

enemy combatants all the evidence obtained against them, but those concerns must be weighed against the unfairness of trying a defendant on evidence that he cannot possibly rebut. Consider, for example, the following account of one of the hearings held at Guantánamo to determine whether a detainee had been properly categorized as an enemy combatant, from a district court decision declaring the hearing procedures unconstitutional:

> In reading a list of allegations forming the basis for the detention of Mustafa Ait Idr, . . . the Recorder of the CSRT [Combatant Status Review Tribunal] asserted, "While living in Bosnia, the Detainee associated with a known Al Qaida operative." In response, the following exchange occurred:
>
> DETAINEE: Give me his name.
> TRIBUNAL PRESIDENT: I do not know.
> DETAINEE: How can I respond to this?
> TRIBUNAL PRESIDENT: Did you know of anybody that was a member of Al Qaida?
> DETAINEE : No, no.
> TRIBUNAL PRESIDENT: I'm sorry, what was your response?
> DETAINEE : No.
> TRIBUNAL PRESIDENT: No?
> DETAINEE : No. This is something the interrogators told me a long while ago. I asked the interrogators to tell me who this person was. Then I could tell you if I might have known this person, but not if this person is a terrorist. Maybe I knew this person as a friend. Maybe it was a person that worked with me. Maybe it was a person that was on my team. But I do not know if this person is Bosnian, Indian or whatever. If you tell me the name, then I can respond and defend myself against this accusation.
> TRIBUNAL PRESIDENT: We are asking you the questions and we need you to respond to what is on the unclassified summary.
>
> Subsequently, after the Recorder read the allegation that the detainee was arrested because of his alleged involvement in a

plan to attack the U.S. Embassy in Sarajevo, the detainee expressly asked in the following colloquy to see the evidence upon
which the government's assertion relied:

DETAINEE: . . . The only thing I can tell you is I did not plan or
even think of [attacking the Embassy]. Did you find any explosives with me? Any weapons? Did you find me in front of
the embassy? Did you find me in contact with the Americans?
Did I threaten anyone? I am prepared now to tell you, if you
have anything or any evidence, even if it is just very little, that
proves I went to the embassy and looked like that [*Detainee
made a gesture with his head and neck as if he were looking into
a building or a window*] at the embassy, then I am ready to be
punished. I can just tell you that I did not plan anything.
Point by point, when we get to the point that I am associated
with Al Qaida, but we already did that one.

RECORDER: It was [the] statement that preceded the first point.

DETAINEE: If it is the same point, but I do not want to repeat my-
self. These accusations, my answer to all of them is I did not
do these things. But I do not have anything to prove this. The
only thing is the citizenship. I can tell you where I was and I
had the papers to prove so. But to tell me I planned to bomb, I
can only tell you that I did not plan.

TRIBUNAL PRESIDENT: Mustafa, does that conclude your
statement?

DETAINEE: That is it, but I was hoping you had evidence that you
can give me. If I was in your place—and I apologize in advance for these words—but if a supervisor came to me and
showed me accusations like these, I would take these accusations and I would hit him in the face with them. Sorry about
that. [*Everyone in the Tribunal room laughs.*]

TRIBUNAL PRESIDENT: We had to laugh, but it is okay.

DETAINEE: Why? Because these are accusations that I can't even
answer. I am not able to answer them. You tell me I am from
Al Qaida, but I am not an Al Qaida. I don't have any proof to
give you except to ask you to catch Bin Laden and ask him if I
am a part of Al Qaida. To tell me that I thought, I'll just tell
you that I did not. I don't have proof regarding this. What

should be done is you should give me evidence regarding these accusations because I am not able to give you any evidence. I can just tell you no and that is it.[40]

U.S. District Judge Joyce Hens Green concluded that at least in this setting, where life imprisonment was potentially being determined, secrecy could not be squared with due process and the rule of law. The government appealed, arguing that its hearings were fully adequate. In February 2007, a divided court of appeals ruled that the Military Commissions Act had eliminated the court's jurisdiction and reversed.[41]

Confidentiality can be used in two ways—as a shield and as a sword. When invoked to block the discovery of a secret program, its use is defensive. When used as a shield, the principal cost is to public accountability; if we cannot know what the government is doing in our name, how are we to subject it to democratic accountability? But secrecy can also be used offensively, as a sword, to justify the deprivation of an individual's life, liberty, or property, as in the military hearing transcribed above. The offensive use of classified information raises even greater concerns, because it allows the government to frustrate the adversarial process altogether. One simply cannot make a fair assessment of whether an individual is a terrorist without allowing the individual to respond to the evidence against him. At that point, secrecy is not just an obstacle to democracy but an aid to tyranny.

The full extent of the secrecy surrounding the government's initiatives in the war on terror is still unknown. It is possible that we have seen only the tip of the iceberg. But what we have seen already reflects a grave compromise of one of the core principles of the rule of law.

INDIVIDUAL CULPABILITY

The Supreme Court has proclaimed that, "in our jurisprudence, guilt is personal."[42] Guilt by association violates both basic tenets of fairness guaranteed by due process and the First Amendment right to associate freely. The constitutional requirement of individual culpability, however, poses a direct challenge to the preventive paradigm, which seeks to identify and incapacitate individuals based not on what they have actually done, but on what we fear they or others might do in the future. The preventive paradigm necessarily relies on predictions, which in turn often rest on characteristics other than an individual's own conduct.

As a result, times of crisis have often led to measures that deeply compromise the principle of individual culpability. In 1919, for example, after eight bombs exploded within the same hour in eight different cities, the federal government responded by rounding up several thousand foreign nationals in coordinated raids across the country. They were selected not for their involvement in the bombings but for their association with various communist organizations. None of the detainees were even charged with the bombings.[43] In World War II, after the surprise attack on Pearl Harbor, President Roosevelt authorized the internment of 110,000 Japanese Americans and Japanese immigrants, ostensibly out of concern that some among them might engage in espionage or sabotage, but solely on the basis of their Japanese ancestry. None were convicted of espionage or sabotage.[44]

In the Cold War, guilt by association reached new heights when the federal government imposed loyalty oaths, conducted congressional witch hunts, and prosecuted individuals for their association with the Communist Party.[45] So, too, in the preventive-detention campaign launched after the terrorist attacks of September 11, the FBI treated people as suspect based on their Arab or Muslim identity rather than their conduct. In each instance, the desire to preempt future harm led the government to sweep broadly and hold individuals responsible, not for their own actions, but for their association with groups considered suspect.

Perhaps the most systemic undermining of the principle of individual culpability is found in the federal laws prohibiting the provision of material support to groups labeled terrorist. These laws essentially resurrect the tactics of the McCarthy era; they hold individuals responsible not for their own involvement in or furtherance of any criminal activity, but for the groups they associate with. Someone who provides any sort of material support whatsoever to a blacklisted terrorist group is criminally liable, even if he can prove that his support had nothing to do with terrorism. These laws have proved to be the government's most frequently charged terrorism statutes in criminal cases, precisely because they do not require the prosecution to show any connection between the defendant's conduct and any actual terrorism. One of the material-support laws, an executive order issued by President Bush shortly after 9/11, goes even further and explicitly authorizes guilt by association in its pure form, empowering the secretary of the Treasury to freeze the assets of any individual or group found to be "otherwise associated" with anyone on a list of hundreds of "specially designated global terrorists," a term nowhere defined in the federal statutes.[46] In November 2006, a federal court declared the executive order unconstitutional because it imposed guilt by association.[47]

In the immigration context, Congress has gone still further, rendering foreign nationals deportable for mere membership in any group of two or more individuals that has ever used or threatened to use violence, regardless of whether the individual himself had any involvement or connection with violence. That law would make Nelson Mandela deportable for his association with the African National Congress. The Department of Homeland Security interprets the material-support ban in immigration law to apply even to those who are *coerced* into providing support to proscribed groups, thus barring asylum to persons forced at gunpoint to give Colombian guerrillas a plate of food or a glass of water.[48]

As noted above, the government defends its material-support

laws by arguing that support for a group's lawful activities frees up resources that the group can devote to terrorist ends. But if that "freeing up" theory were taken literally, it would eviscerate the concept of personal guilt. Any form of association beyond the most formalistic and symbolic involves some provision of support—whether through dues payments, contributions, or volunteering one's time or services. To say that one has a right of association, but no right to support the group with which one associates in any concrete way, is to render the prohibition on guilt by association a meaningless formality. In the name of preventing terrorism, the administration has done precisely that. Guilt by association, the Supreme Court declared, after witnessing the abuses of the McCarthy era, is "alien to the traditions of a free society and the First Amendment itself." [49] Yet it appears to be a central feature of the preventive paradigm.

FAIR PROCEDURES

Ordinarily, when the government arrests an individual, the law requires a prompt and fair court hearing to ascertain whether there is a sound basis for holding the detainee responsible for some past wrongdoing. When the government shifts to a preventive paradigm and sweeps up suspects based on fears about the future, however, a hearing may reveal only how little basis the government has for holding the detainee in the first place. Thus, there is a fundamental tension between the fair hearings envisioned by the rule of law and the desire to act preemptively. As noted above, the administration has detained thousands of persons, here and abroad, in the war on terror. It has used a variety of tactics to avoid providing fair hearings to those it detained. It exploited immigration powers to deprive immigrants here of the kind of hearing a criminal arrest would entail, and then concocted various strategies to deny the detainees even the minimal hearings usually required for immigration detainees. One of the reasons it did so, according to an internal investigation by the Justice Department's Office of Inspector General, was that it lacked the kind of evidence that would be required if a hearing were actually to take place. In many cases, all the government had were suspicions, predicated on little more than the fact that the detainee was Arab or Muslim.[50]

With enemy combatants, the administration went even further, denying that they were entitled to any hearings at all. In June 2004, the Supreme Court rejected that argument. In the case of Yaser Hamdi, a U.S. citizen held as an enemy combatant, the Court ruled that due process required that he be afforded a fair hearing before a neutral decision maker on whether in fact he was an enemy combatant.[51] Confronted with the obligation to hold a hearing, the government balked and released Hamdi, upon his (unenforceable) agreement to give up his American citizenship, go to Saudi Arabia, and remain there.[52] When it appeared that the Supreme Court would review the detention of José Padilla, the other U.S. citizen declared an enemy combatant, the administration abruptly changed course, releasing Padilla from military custody and charging him as a bit player in an ill-defined conspiracy to support terrorism abroad. By doing so, the government avoided ever having to establish in any hearing the truth of its press conference allegations that Padilla was a "dirty bomber."

The fact that the government released both Hamdi and Padilla from military custody in order to avoid hearings on its charges against them suggests that at least one of the government's objectives in taking them into military custody in the first place was precisely to avoid a hearing—perhaps because such a hearing might have revealed how weak the government's cases really were.

After the Supreme Court's June 2004 ruling that enemy combatants at Guantánamo could challenge the legality of their detentions in federal court, the administration belatedly provided the Guantánamo detainees with hearings before Combatant Status Review Tribunals (CSRTs), but as the transcript of one such tribunal, reproduced above, illustrates, the hearings themselves were often a charade. In addition to having to respond to secret evidence they could not see, the detainees had no right to the assistance of a lawyer and no right to compel witnesses to testify on their behalf. A study of the records of 102 hearing transcripts that the Department of Defense released to the public found that the government produced no witnesses in any of the hearings.[53] In only 4 percent of the hearings did the government disclose any documentary evidence to the detainee prior to the hearing. In more than half of the cases, the CSRTs relied exclusively on classified evidence. The tribunals denied every request by a detainee to inspect the classified evidence. In every case, the CSRT found the government's classified evidence reliable. In 48 percent of the cases, the government also relied on unclassified evidence, but this evidence was also almost always withheld from the detainee. In many cases the CSRTs relied on evidence allegedly obtained through coercive interrogation. While detainees were permitted a "personal representative"— not a lawyer—in more than a third of the cases the personal representative made no substantive argument whatsoever.

While hearings to determine the status of enemy combatants in wartime typically tend to be bare-bones affairs, that is because they are generally held near the battlefield, shortly after the detainees have been captured, and are principally designed to weed out civilians and unprivileged combatants from ordinary troops. Many Guantánamo detainees, by contrast, were apprehended far from any traditional battlefield, where the presumption ought to be that they are *not* combatants. They were held for years before they were granted any hearing at all, and the hearings took place thousands of miles away from the point of capture, sharply restricting the detainees' ability to put on any real defense. Even so, the CSRTs found that some thirty-nine persons had been wrongly deemed enemy combatants—and thus wrongly imprisoned for years. More than three hundred Guantánamo detainees have been released, suggesting that many would not have been detained in the first place had they been provided fair hearings.

If the administration has its way, a few detainees may have a more elaborate hearing—a trial for war crimes before a military commission. The administration initially created the rules for these tribunals out of whole cloth in a presidential order in November 2001. When the Supreme Court invalidated those procedures in June 2006, Congress resurrected the tribunals by enacting the Military Commissions Act. Even as reformed after the Supreme Court's ruling, however, the tribunal procedures allow the presentation of hearsay and scrubbed summaries of classified evidence, both of which are likely to deprive the defendant of an opportunity to cross-examine his accuser. The new rules exclude information obtained by torture, but permit testimony coerced by any means short of torture as long as the statement was extracted before enactment of the McCain amendment—and, as we have seen, the administration has employed a particularly expansive definition of "means short of torture."

Other initiatives in the war on terror similarly dispense with fair procedures. Consider, for example, the Kafkaesque process for designating groups as terrorist under the material-support laws. Two separate laws permit the government to blacklist groups and individuals as terrorist; it then becomes a crime to provide the designated entity with any "material support" or to have any financial transaction with it. Under one law, stemming from the 1996 Antiterrorism and Effective Death Penalty Act, and modified by the Patriot Act, the secretary of state may designate as a "foreign terrorist organization" any foreign group that has ever used or threatened to use a weapon against person or property.[54] In order to designate the group, the secretary must find that the group's activities undermine our "national defense, foreign relations, or economic interests."[55] Groups are designated in an internal executive process, generally without notice or any opportunity to participate. The law then affords the designated terrorist group thirty days from the publication of its designation in the *Federal Register* to file a challenge to the designation in federal court.

Even in the unlikely event that a foreign group happens to read the *Federal Register* in time, the challenge is essentially rigged. The court reviews only the evidence presented by the government; the designated group may not present evidence on its own behalf in court. The State Department may present its evidence to the court in confidence, so the group never sees it and cannot respond to it. Even if one could see the evidence, the legal standard gives the secretary of state virtually unfettered discretion. The courts have ruled that the key determination in the designation process—whether the group's activities undermine our "national defense, foreign relations, or economic interests"—cannot be second-guessed by courts.[56] As a result, the government effectively enjoys unreviewable authority to blacklist foreign groups and prosecute their domestic supporters.

A second terror-financing law creates even more sweeping executive power with even fewer procedural checks. Under an executive order issued shortly after 9/11 pursuant to the International Emergency Economic Powers Act (IEEPA), President Bush simply declared by fiat—without applying any evident criteria or offering any evidence or explanation—that twenty-seven groups and individuals were "specially designated global terrorists."[57] That listing resulted in an immediate freeze of any assets they had in the United States, and made it a crime for anyone to enter into any financial transaction with the group or individual.[58] The executive order also authorized the secretary of the Treasury to add others to the list based on findings that they provided services of any kind to, or were "otherwise associated" with, another blacklisted group or individual. Hundreds of individuals and groups have been so designated, some for mere association. Like the State Department process, the Treasury Department designation decision is made in secret, generally with no notice to the designated group until after the decision has been made. If a group or individual challenges the designation in court, the Patriot Act authorizes the government to defend its designation with secret evidence.[59] The IEEPA does not even define "specially designated global terrorist," so the executive branch is free to designate literally anyone it chooses, and it is not even clear what a court would review if a challenge were made. Not surprisingly, no entity has succeeded in challenging its designation under either material-support law.[60]

CLEAR RULES

While laws often take the form of general standards rather than precise rules, the goals of providing order, limiting official abuse of power, and settling disputes peacefully are all facilitated by clear rules.[61] Clarity is particularly important where the state seeks to exercise coercive power over individuals. Thus, the Supreme Court has long insisted that the constitutional prohibition on vague laws applies with special force to criminal laws, because transgressing such laws can result in a loss of liberty.[62]

The preventive paradigm, however, prefers open-ended standards to clear rules. When the state seeks to employ coercion based on fears about what individuals might do in the future, it prefers broad discretion, because determining what an individual will do in the future is simply not the kind of issue susceptible to clear rules. Accordingly, the Bush administration has sought to exploit ambiguity wherever possible, and to create ambiguity where it might be thought nonexistent—all in the name of expanding executive flexibility to act preventively.

Few rules are more clear than the prohibition on torture. International and domestic U.S. law erect an absolute ban, admitting of no exceptions. Yet in the wake of 9/11, this is just one of many clear rules that the Bush administration sought to make less clear in the interest of taking preventive action in the war on terror. Because the administration's initial response to the attacks of 9/11 was to round up as many suspects as possible, often on thin or negligible evidence, surveillance of suspects in the field to see who they were working with and what they were working on—ordinarily one of the most valuable sources of intelligence—was no longer an available option. This placed tremendous pressure on obtaining intelligence by interrogating suspects in custody. And that pressure led the administration to muddy the clear rules against torture and cruel, inhuman, and degrading treatment.

CIA agents tasked with extracting information from detainees worried that they might be vulnerable to prosecution under a federal criminal statute that forbids torture. So White House Counsel Alberto Gonzales turned to John Yoo, a young lawyer in the Justice Department's Office of Legal Counsel, to write an opinion allaying the CIA agents' fears. In the memo, issued in secret in August 2002, Yoo approached the torture prohibition as if he were a tax lawyer whose only job was to find loopholes in the code.[63] He argued that while it is torture to threaten a suspect with imminent death, threats of non-imminent death are not torture. He argued that torture was limited to the specifically intended infliction of severe physical pain, which he defined as limited to pain at the level associated with organ failure or death. Any physical pain short of that level, or any physical pain inflicted but not specifically intended to be at that level, was not torture. He argued further that the president has uncheckable constitutional authority as commander in chief to order outright torture, despite a federal criminal law and an international treaty signed and ratified by the United States categorically prohibiting torture under all circumstances, including wartime. (Yoo contended that those laws would be unconstitutional if they limited the president's options during wartime.) Finally, Yoo proposed unprecedented and expansive definitions of "self-defense" and "necessity" as defenses to liability were a CIA torturer to be brought to trial.

Armed with this opinion, the administration effectively jettisoned the absolute prohibition on torture and inhuman treatment contained in the CAT and the Geneva Conventions, and substituted an amorphous, ill-defined pledge to treat detainees humanely "to the extent appropriate and consistent with military necessity."[64] Administration officials assiduously avoided providing a clear definition for "inhumane treatment," and apparently maintained that such techniques as waterboarding, mock executions, physical beatings, and painful stress positions may be lawful depending "on the facts and circumstances of each particular case."[65] Captain Ian Fishback of the 82nd Airborne Infantry Division complained that, as a result, there were no clear rules for interrogations.[66] The results of this studied ambiguity can be seen in the abuse recorded at Guantánamo and Abu Ghraib, and unrecorded (as yet) in the CIA's black sites.

When Attorney General Ashcroft oversaw the roundup of more than a thousand foreign nationals in the first seven weeks after 9/11, he, too, substituted a vague standard for a clear rule. Had the detainees been arrested under criminal law, prosecutors would have been subject to a constitutional mandate to charge them immediately, and to justify their arrests within forty-eight hours before a federal judge by showing "probable cause" that they had committed a crime. Before 9/11, immigration regulations set out a similar bright-line rule, requiring that immigration charges be filed within twenty-four hours of any arrest. One of Ashcroft's first actions after 9/11 was to replace that twenty-four-hour rule with a new regulation providing that in times of emergency detainees need only be charged within a "reasonable" period of time.[67] What was "reasonable" turned out to be measured in weeks and months. The vagueness of the standard left the charging period largely to the discretion of executive officials.

At Guantánamo, the administration has also exploited ambiguity, asserting war powers as the justification for holding "the enemy," but refusing to be bound by the laws of war with respect to their treatment. The administration chose Guantánamo as the site for its detention facility precisely because it thought it could avoid any legal limits there. As one military intelligence officer reportedly told a detainee, "You are in a place where there is no law—we are the law." [68] When the administration applied any law at all, it proceeded under its own newly minted rules, including an open-ended definition of enemy combatants. Government lawyers have admitted that the Pentagon's definition of enemy combatant would encompass "a little old lady in Switzerland who writes checks to what she thinks is a charity that helps orphans in Afghanistan but really is a front to finance Al Qaeda activities"; a man who "teaches English to the son of a person the C.I.A. knows to be a member of Al Qaeda"; and "a *Wall Street Journal* reporter, working in Afghanistan, who knows the exact location of Osama bin Laden but does not reveal it to the United States government in order to protect her source." [69] By employing such a capacious standard, the administration gave itself what amounts to a blank check to detain an exceedingly broad category of individuals.

The same open-ended discretion can be seen in the material-support laws, which either offer no definition at all of "terrorism," or define it in terms that are not subject to judicial review, thereby granting the executive branch exceedingly broad leeway in the designation process. Similarly, when Attorney General Alberto Gonzales explained who is overheard by the NSA surveillance program, he described the category expansively to include not only members of al-Qaeda, but also a member of an organization affiliated with al-Qaeda, "working in support of al Qaeda," or "part of" an organization or group "that is supportive of al Qaeda." [70] Under this reasoning, a U.S. citizen living here who received a phone call from another U.S. citizen who attends a mosque that the administration believes is "supportive" of al-Qaeda could be wiretapped without a warrant.

Law does not of course always take the shape of clear rules. Many laws state general principles instead. They do so particularly where discretion is important, and where it is difficult to specify in advance all the contingencies that might arise. But as a

general matter, the more substantial the consequences for individual liberty, and the greater the potential for official abuse, the
more need there is for clear rules. What makes the preventive
paradigm particularly troubling is that it seeks to muddy the
waters precisely where clear rules are most important—where
the state seeks to take an individual's life or liberty or physically
coerce him into answering questions against his will.

CHECKS AND BALANCES

The rule of law would be little more than words on paper without a system of divided powers. It is the ability of separate
branches of government to check each other that gives force to
the rule of law, by ensuring that no one branch, and especially
no one person, is above the law. Thus, the most important structural feature of the Constitution is its division of authority into
three branches—legislative, executive, and judicial—each given
power to check the others. There is an inherent tension in simultaneously assigning the state a monopoly on coercive power and
subjecting the state to rules limiting that power: Who but the
state can enforce the rules against the state?[71] One of the central
purposes of a system of divided power is to ensure that different
institutions of government have incentives to keep the other institutions in line.

The preventive paradigm puts a premium, however, not on
checks and balances and accountability, but on flexibility, speed,
and initiative. Power almost inevitably shifts to the executive in
times of crisis, and for good reason. As a multimember deliberative body, Congress is not well suited to acting expeditiously.
The judiciary is by design reactive, not proactive, and its proceedings tend to move slowly. Moreover, in times of crisis, confidential decision making may be more essential, and the
executive branch is more likely to keep secrets than the legislature. At the same time, precisely because power shifts to the executive in times of crisis, it is especially important to maintain
the checking authority of the other branches. Even if the presi-

dent justifiably exercises the power of initiative, his actions should generally be subject to judicial and congressional oversight, and he must act within the bounds set down by the other branches, and by the Constitution.

The Bush administration has taken a different approach. In its view, the president as commander in chief cannot be restricted in how he conducts the war on terror. As commander in chief the president has uncheckable authority to select "the means and methods of engaging the enemy," and therefore neither Congress nor the courts can interfere in any way with his decisions regarding the detention of enemy combatants, the methods used to interrogate suspects, or the wiretapping of American citizens with the objective of tracking the enemy.

In the immediate aftermath of the 9/11 attacks, the administration's lawyers argued that statutes may not "place any limits on the President's determinations as to any terrorist threat, the amount of military force to be used in response, or the method, timing, and nature of the response."[72] In the August 2002 torture memo, the administration took the position that the commander in chief was not bound by international law or federal criminal prohibition on torture.[73] The administration invoked the same theory to defend President Bush's authorization to the NSA to conduct warrantless wiretapping on American citizens, in direct violation of another criminal prohibition. And even after suffering a lopsided defeat on the issue of clear, inhuman, and degrading treatment, President Bush appeared to assert that same power when, in the presidential signing statement attached to the McCain amendment, he stated that he would enforce the prohibition "consistent with my authority . . . as Commander in Chief."

These arguments have received a chilly reception in court. In *Rasul v. Bush*,[74] the case challenging the detention of enemy combatants at Guantánamo, the administration argued that permitting judicial review of the detention of enemy combatants "would raise grave constitutional problems" because it would "directly interfere with the Executive's conduct of the military campaign against al Qaeda and its supporters."[75] Not a single justice on the Court accepted the contention that the commander in chief could not be limited by congressional and judicial oversight. The six-justice majority ruled that courts could review the detainees' claims. Justice Scalia dissented, joined by Chief Justice Rehnquist and Justice Thomas, but they, too, agreed that Congress could have extended habeas jurisdiction to the Guantánamo detainees; they simply concluded that Congress had chosen not to do so.[76]

The administration similarly argued in *Hamdi v. Rumsfeld*, involving the detention of U.S. citizen Yaser Hamdi, that the Court could not review the factual basis for Hamdi's detention because that would impermissibly interfere with the president's power. The Court again rejected the assertion of unchecked executive power. As Justice O'Connor wrote for the plurality, "whatever power the United States Constitution envisions for the Executive in its exchanges with other nations or with enemy organizations in times of conflict, it most assuredly envisions a role for all three branches when individual liberties are at stake."[77]

In *Hamdan v. Rumsfeld*, the Court rebuffed this view of unilateral executive power for a third time. The administration argued that "the detention and trial of petitioners ordered by the President in the declared exercise of the President's powers as Commander in Chief of the Army in time of war and of grave public danger 'are not to be set aside by the courts without the clear conviction that they are in conflict with the Constitution or laws of Congress.'"[78] The Court nonetheless ruled that the president had violated both domestic military law—the Uniform Code of Military Justice (UCMJ)—and the Geneva Conventions, which govern the treatment of prisoners during wartime. Even assuming the president has "independent power, absent congressional authorization, to convene military commissions," the court explained, "he may not disregard limitations that Congress has, in proper exercise of its own war powers, placed on his powers."[79]

In August 2006, a federal judge rejected a similar defense of the NSA's warrantless wiretapping program. Judge Anna Diggs Taylor ruled that the president had violated the terms of the Foreign Intelligence Surveillance Act, which requires that national security and foreign intelligence surveillance be conducted pursuant to court orders. Like the Supreme Court, she, too, rejected the president's assertion of unilateral unchecked power, writing that "there are no hereditary Kings in America."[80]

The administration's view that the president is effectively above the law when acting as commander in chief is also contrary to earlier precedents; in fact, the Supreme Court has *never* found that Congress has improperly interfered with the president's powers as commander in chief. Until the recent trio of enemy combatant decisions, the best-known case concerned President Truman's seizure of steel mills during the Korean War. When a national strike threatened to close the country's steel mills, Truman ordered the secretary of commerce to seize them, contending that steel production was essential to the war effort and invoking his authority as commander in chief. The Supreme Court invalidated his order, noting that the president's power is to execute the laws, and no law made by Congress gave him authority to seize the steel mills.[81]

Justice Robert Jackson wrote a concurring opinion in the case that over time has come to be even more influential than the majority's. Jackson emphasized that the Constitution envisions overlapping powers, and that therefore assertions of executive power must be evaluated in the light of congressional action. Where the president acts pursuant to congressional authorization, his powers are at their zenith, and his actions must be upheld unless the political branches acting in concert lack all power to regulate the subject at hand. When, by contrast, the president acts in defiance of "the expressed or implied will of Congress," Jackson wrote, his power is "at its lowest ebb," and in this context "presidential power [is] most vulnerable to attack and in the least favorable of possible constitutional postures."[82]

Congress had previously considered—and rejected—granting the president authority to seize businesses during national emergencies, and so, Justice Jackson reasoned, President Truman was acting in contravention of Congress's implied will. Jackson dismissed President Truman's invention of executive war powers by noting that "the Constitution did not contemplate that the Commander in Chief of the Army and Navy will constitute him also Commander in Chief of the country, its industries, and its inhabitants."

Still earlier, in 1804, the Supreme Court held unlawful a seizure of a ship ordered by the president during a military conflict with France.[83] Congress had authorized the seizure of ships going *to* France, but the president had unilaterally authorized the seizure of ships coming *from* France as well. The Court reasoned that while the president might be able to act to seize such vessels had Congress been silent, Congress's decision to authorize seizures only of ships going to France implicitly negated authority to seize ships traveling the other way. As in the steel seizure case, the Court invalidated executive action taken during wartime that was said to be necessary to the war effort.

The only precedent that approaches the authority President Bush has asserted is President Nixon's infamous remark, made to David Frost while defending his own authorization of warrantless wiretapping during the Vietnam War, that "when the president does it, that means that it is not illegal."[84] Nixon learned the hard way that his theory of executive power was not acceptable; his authorization of the wiretapping program was listed in the articles of impeachment, and he was ultimately forced to resign. Yet President Bush has effectively revived the Nixon doctrine, with one modification—in his version, "when the commander in chief does it, it's not illegal."

HUMAN RIGHTS

Finally, the rule of law includes a commitment to fundamental human rights. Both our own two-hundred-year-old Bill of Rights and the international human rights movement of the last fifty years are predicated on the idea that a fair and just rule of law is not simply structural and procedural in nature, but must include substantive guarantees of certain rights inherent in human dignity. These include rights not to be subjected to torture and arbitrary detention, but also political rights of speech and association.

The administration's preventive paradigm has led to dramatic sacrifices in basic human rights. Rights of speech and association are threatened by the punishment of "material support" for blacklisted "terrorist organizations." Due process rights have been gravely undermined by reliance on secret evidence in enemy combatant hearings. The detention of suspects in the CIA's black sites violate the human rights not to be disappeared and arbitrarily detained.

Most dramatically, however, we have sacrificed our commitment to basic human rights in the context of coercive interrogations. The laws of war require at a minimum that all those captured in wartime be treated humanely, and international law prohibits both torture and cruel, inhuman, and degrading treatment. As we have seen, however, the administration sought to avoid these dictates through a series of strained legal interpretations in order to give its interrogators leeway to use coercion to obtain information from detainees. It claimed that the Geneva Conventions did not apply to the war with al-Qaeda, an interpretation firmly rejected by the Supreme Court, which ruled in *Hamdan v. Rumsfeld* that Common Article 3 of the Geneva Conventions applies to all conflicts between nation-states and nonstate actors.[85] It concluded that foreign nationals detained abroad could be subjected to cruel, inhuman, and degrading treatment. And it interpreted "torture" in Orwellian fashion, concluding that waterboarding, death threats, the use of dogs, and other extreme forms of coercion were available options for federal interrogators.

The results are reflected in the interrogation of Mohammed al-Khatani, allegedly the would-be twentieth hijacker in the 9/11 plot. (He was reportedly denied entry to the United States, and so could not take part.) Al-Khatani is being held at Guantánamo, where he has been subjected to extensive interrogation, all of it meticulously recorded in an army log book. That log, leaked to *Time* magazine and published in full, reveals that during his interrogation al-Khatani was held in total isolation—but for interactions with interrogators and guards—for 160 days straight. During one period, he was interrogated 48 out of 54 days, for 18 to 20 hours each day. He was threatened with dogs, put on a leash, and ordered to bark like a dog. He was stripped naked in front of female interrogators, and made to wear women's underwear and a picture of a naked woman around his neck. He was injected with intravenous fluids and denied access to a bathroom, so that he urinated on himself. The fact that the log book dutifully records each of these tactics suggests that the military interrogators believed that everything they were doing was acceptable. An internal military review of the al-Khatani interrogation concluded that he had been subjected to no inhuman treatment.[86]

There are few more powerful images of disrespect for human dignity than the images from Abu Ghraib. The administration sought to dismiss the abuse as isolated, but the greatest abuses at Abu Ghraib occurred shortly after the Pentagon sent the commander at Guantánamo to Abu Ghraib to assist them in making their interrogations more effective. There are as yet no pictures from the CIA's black sites, but inside accounts of the interrogations there make Abu Ghraib seem mild by comparison.[87] Yet as of February 2007, no high-level official had been held accountable for what went on at Abu Ghraib, the black sites, or Guantánamo. The only investigations that have taken place have been

conducted by the very agencies implicated in the wrongdoing—
the Pentagon, the CIA, and the Justice Department. And the
president publicly hailed Congress's enactment of the Military
Commissions Act for allowing him to resume operation of the
CIA black sites.

PREVENTION AND WAR

Does the war on terror justify these departures from the norm?
What is unacceptable during peacetime may be acceptable in
wartime. In peacetime, for example, the state generally may not
kill an individual without a trial and extensive appeals. Yet
killing without "due process" is the everyday stuff of war. In
peacetime, preventive detention is limited to persons who need
to be detained while they await trial for some specific past
wrongdoing, and to those who are so mentally disturbed that
they cannot conform to the law and pose a danger to others (a
showing that as a practical matter will always require some evidence of past wrongdoing). In wartime, by contrast, the state
may capture an enemy soldier simply because of his association
with the enemy, without regard to whether he has committed
any infraction.

But if war changes the calculus, one must be precise about
what war we are fighting. We do not reject the idea that we are involved in a military conflict with al-Qaeda—although we do reject the notion of a "war on terror." As many have pointed out,
one cannot fight a war against a tactic; the war on terror is a
rhetorical slogan, like the war on cancer or the war on drugs, not
a legitimate juridical concept. As an international legal matter,
however, al-Qaeda's attacks of 9/11 justified a military response
in self-defense, and as a domestic constitutional matter, Congress
authorized the use of military force against al-Qaeda. While some
argue that we would have done better to have pursued al-Qaeda
through domestic and international criminal justice mechanisms rather than by declaring that we were at war, the size and

nature of al-Qaeda's attacks, and the fact that al-Qaeda was so intertwined with the Taliban, made a military response a legally available option irrespective of the wisdom of that response.

In the wake of 9/11, the administration asked Congress to authorize the use of military force not merely against al-Qaeda, but against all those who would threaten us with terrorism in the future. Congress rejected that proposal. Instead it authorized the use of military force only against the perpetrators of 9/11 and those who harbor them, *not* against terrorism worldwide. Yet despite Congress's refusal to authorize an open-ended metaphorical war against an amorphous and ever-changing set of enemies, President Bush has acted as if he had been granted that power. In his first speech to Congress after 9/11, he described the conflict as a war on all terrorist organizations of global reach.[88] And the president's military order authorizing trial by military tribunal for terrorist offenses applied not only to al-Qaeda members but also to all foreign nationals alleged to have committed acts of international terrorism.[89]

The distinction between the metaphorical war on terror and the actual military conflict with al-Qaeda is critically important. It means, for example, that to the extent that wartime authorities are justified, they are justified *only* with respect to al-Qaeda and the Taliban, and not with respect to Hamas, Hezbollah, the Kurdistan Workers Party, or any of the hundreds of other organizations and individuals around the globe that the administration has labeled terrorists. It means that measures that might be acceptable against al-Qaeda, such as criminalizing all material support to it as the enemy in a military conflict, are not acceptable when extended to groups with which we are not engaged in military conflict. It means that one cannot defend the Patriot Act by invoking the war, as its powers are not limited to wartime or to a particular enemy. War powers are by definition temporary and limited exceptions to the norm. To treat the metaphorical war on terror as if it is a real war is to collapse the distinction between the exception and the norm.

Moreover, the existence of a military conflict does not mean that the rule of law is silent. There are rules for war—such as the rule that a nation may not attack another nation except in self-defense, that those detained as the enemy are entitled to a prompt hearing to ensure that their status has been properly determined, and that all detainees must be treated humanely. Disappearance, prolonged detention without hearings, and cruel, inhuman, and degrading treatment are not permissible even under the minimal rules that govern warfare. The Bush administration repeatedly invokes war as a justification for departures from peacetime norms, but at the same time is unwilling to be bound even by the laws that govern war. In the end, its preventive paradigm seeks to avoid the laws of peace or war.

Third, the administration often argues that it need not comply with the laws of war because we are engaged in a new kind of military conflict with an international terrorist group. But the novel nature of the conflict may well require *more* protections for detainees, not less. In a traditional war, it is relatively easy to identify who is fighting for the enemy, and therefore hearings to determine their status can be relatively minimal. In a war with a clandestine group that mixes in with the civilian population, by contrast, there is a greater danger of mistaken identity. Our troops likely had no idea who among the many they encountered in Afghanistan was an al-Qaeda member or fighter. They had to rely entirely on others' accounts. Moreover, a war with another sovereign nation may be more likely to be a limited affair, as the losing nation will eventually have an incentive to surrender in order to retain its sovereignty. A terrorist group like al-Qaeda, by contrast, has no incentive to surrender. Thus, when we detain a suspected al-Qaeda member, we may well have less certainty about who he is, and we may well be detaining him for much longer than we would an enemy combatant in a traditional conflict. These factors suggest that the hearings held to justify detention of al-Qaeda members should be more protective of the rights of detainees than the traditional status hearing required by the Geneva Conventions. In short, the invocation of war does not free the administration from the constraints of the rule of law, and the particular kind of conflict being fought against al-Qaeda may demand even greater restraint than a traditional war.

The preventive imperative has done systemic violence to the most fundamental elements of law. This should be reason enough, as a matter of principle, to look for another way to protect ourselves. As Senator McCain said in defending his amendment on cruel, inhuman, and degrading treatment, "this is not about who they are. It's about who we are." [90] As we will show in Part 2, however, there is also a very practical reason to resist the preventive paradigm; there is substantial reason to believe that it has actually increased our vulnerability to future terrorist attacks.

2. PREVENTIVE WAR

In September 2002, as the Bush administration was gearing up for a showdown with Iraq, the White House released its new National Security Strategy, a white paper announcing a radical shift in American military policy. The United States had previously adhered doctrinally, if not always in practice, to the rule that a nation may unilaterally launch a military attack against another nation only in strict self-defense, that is, in response to an armed attack or the threat of an imminent attack. Under established international law, any other use of military force requires approval of the UN Security Council, which must first find a "threat to the peace, breach of peace, or act of aggression," and then must authorize the use of force to remove that threat.

The 2002 National Security Strategy maintained that the threat of catastrophic attacks with weapons of mass destruction by rogue states and terrorists demanded a new approach. The new doctrine insisted that unilateral recourse to war is justified not only to preempt imminent attacks but also to forestall *nonimminent* threats where the threats are sufficiently serious:

> The greater the threat, the greater is the risk of inaction—and the more compelling the case for taking anticipatory action to defend ourselves, even if uncertainty remains as to the time and place of the enemy's attacks. . . . In an age where the enemies of civilization openly and actively seek the world's most destructive technologies, the United States cannot remain idle while dangers gather.[1]

This new strategy became a central tenet in the administration's foreign policy, and was reiterated, albeit in a somewhat subdued form, in its 2006 National Security Strategy.[2]

Like the preventive paradigm in law enforcement and intelligence, the doctrine of preventive war responds to a universal sentiment: we all want to avoid another terrorist attack. Moreover, the premise that terrorists today are less susceptible to deterrence or detection than the Soviet Union during the Cold War is not without basis. Yet the move to loosen the restraints on anticipatory state violence poses its own dangers—dangers that have been dramatically illustrated by the Iraq War itself, the first test of the administration's new policy. Like the preventive paradigm in law enforcement, the preventive-war doctrine leads to substantial sacrifices in fundamental commitments to the rule of law. Where the existing legal model for regulating war relies on clear rules, applied equally, requiring publicly disclosed, critically examined evidence and appropriate checks and balances, the preventive-war model permits ad hoc decision making fraught with double standards; based on suspicions, hunches, and secret intelligence; and unrestrained by institutional checks.

The question that has beguiled and perplexed politicians and commentators since the Iraq War began is how administration officials could have been at once so certain and so wrong in their claims that Iraq had weapons of mass destruction. Congressional committees and independent commissions have expended thousands of hours searching for an answer. For the most part, however, these analyses fail to identify the causal link between the administration's preventive-war paradigm and its massive intelligence failure.[3] The legal rules barring nations from resorting to war except in strict self-defense are designed to limit the use of state violence to situations in which objective evidence demonstrates a truly compelling need. By jettisoning these legal rules, the preventive-war doctrine paved the way for the administration's decision to launch a war based on astoundingly faulty intelligence.

SUBSTITUTING SUSPICION FOR EVIDENCE

Hans Blix's job was to keep Iraq in check without resort to war. UN Secretary General Kofi Annan and the UN Security Council coaxed Blix out of semiretirement in January 2000 to become director of the UN Inspection Committee (known by the unwieldy acronym UNMOVIC). A lawyer and longtime diplomat who had served fifteen years as the director of the International Atomic Energy Agency, Blix viewed his mandate as most lawyers would: to find solid, reliable evidence to determine whether Iraq had or was producing chemical or biological weapons of mass destruction. Like many, Blix had a "gut feeling" that Iraq was hiding such weapons. But as he wrote in his account of his experience as UN weapons inspector, he had not been "asked by the Security Council to submit suspicions or simply convey testimony from defectors." "Assessments and judgments in our reports," Blix felt, "had to be based on evidence that would remain convincing even under critical international examination."[4]

Blix's focus on hard evidence increasingly collided with the Bush administration's newly minted doctrine of preventive war. Because that doctrine justifies war as a way to preempt future, speculative threats, it substitutes suspicion, inferences, probabilities, circumstantial evidence, and hunches for the kind of solid evidence that Blix was seeking. As President Bush and national security adviser Condoleezza Rice argued, waiting for conclusive proof of Saddam Hussein's determination to obtain nuclear weapons was simply too risky, because "we don't want the smoking gun to become a mushroom cloud."[5] Paul Wolfowitz, deputy secretary of defense, similarly warned that after September 11, we could not afford to "wait until we have *certain* knowledge that attacks are imminent."[6] Just as the preventive paradigm permitted Maher Arar and others to be locked up or sent to other countries to be tortured based on flimsy intelligence and ungrounded suspicion, so, too, the preventive-war doctrine permits nations to be attacked based on inferences without conclusive proof.

The fundamental inference that American officials drew with respect to Iraq was not irrational: they reasoned that since the Iraqis would not produce clear evidence that all their weapons of mass destruction had been destroyed, they must still be hiding some. That suspicion, however, turned out to be wrong, and acting on it has now resulted in tens of thousands of Iraqis and Americans being killed and maimed over weapons that never existed.

Despite the theoretical justifications advanced by the 2002 National Security Strategy, the American public was unlikely to approve of a war based on overtly speculative inferences and suspicions unsupported by hard evidence. So before the war administration officials repeatedly asserted that they were not merely suspicious of Iraq, but actually "knew," were "absolutely certain," or had "no doubt" that Saddam Hussein had a reconstituted nuclear weapons program, had hundreds of tons of chemical and biological weapons, and was producing still more. On September 8, 2002, for example, Vice President Cheney stated on *Meet the Press* that we "know, with *absolute certainty* that he is using his procurement system to acquire the equipment he needs in order to enrich uranium to build nuclear weapons,"[7] while on *Fox News*, Secretary of State Colin Powell claimed that "there is *no doubt* that he has chemical weapon stocks."[8] The same day on CNN, Condoleezza Rice joined the administration's chorus of certainty, claiming that Iraq was importing aluminum tubes "that are *only* really suited for nuclear weapons programs."[9] A month later, in a speech in Cincinnati, President Bush again exuded certainty: "If we know Saddam Hussein has dangerous weapons today—*and we do*—does it make any sense for the world to wait to confront him as he grows even stronger and develops even more dangerous weapons?"[10]

The administration claimed to have very specific details of

Iraq's weapons of mass destruction. In his January 2003 State of the Union address, President Bush stated confidently that "the British government has learned that Saddam Hussein recently sought significant quantities of uranium from Africa," despite the views of the CIA, former U.S. ambassador Joseph Wilson, and a high-level State Department intelligence assessment in early 2002 that the allegation was unlikely to be true. At his presentation to the UN Security Council on February 5, 2003, Colin Powell dramatically held up a small vial of white powder and claimed that Iraq had declared past possession of 8,500 liters of anthrax, but that the UN Inspectors had estimated that Iraq could have produced almost 25,000 liters. Powell then proclaimed that "our conservative estimate is that Iraq today has a stockpile of between 100 and 500 tons of chemical weapons agent . . . enough agent to fill 16,000 battlefield rockets." He stated unequivocally that "*we know* that Iraq has embedded key portions of its illicit chemical weapons infrastructure within its legitimate civilian industry," despite a September 2002 Defense Intelligence Agency assessment that "there is no reliable information on whether Iraq is producing and stockpiling chemical weapons, or where Iraq has—or will—establish its chemical warfare agent production facilities."[11] On two big screens, Powell displayed satellite photographs of what he said were chemical and biological plants and drawings of what he claimed were mobile "biological weapon factories on wheels and rails," concluding with dramatic certitude that "we know that Iraq has at least seven of these mobile biological agents factories."[12]

As Powell was addressing the Security Council, Hans Blix and his inspection team were tracking down these claims on the ground in Baghdad. His inspectors searched almost seven hundred sites for potential evidence of prohibited chemical and biological weapons, including many sites identified by U.S. and foreign intelligence services. Blix reported that "at none of the many sites we actually inspected had we found any prohibited activity."[13] Blix wondered how there could be 100 percent certainty about the existence of weapons of mass destruction, but no knowledge about their location.

Blix's inspections undermined many of the administration's claims. While American officials asserted that they had identified Iraqi cleanup crews at a suspected chemical weapons site, Blix's inspectors found that there was no reason to believe the site was involved in any weapons activities. "It was a wild goose chase," one diplomat said.[14] Blix could not find any of the mobile bioweapon units Powell "knew" existed. After the war began, experts agreed that the function of the trucks pointed to by Powell was actually to produce hydrogen for weather balloons—as Iraqi officials had been saying all along.[15] The inspectors similarly tracked down decontamination trucks claimed by U.S. officials to be linked to the movement of chemical weapons, and found them to be innocent water trucks. Blix's team inspected most of the sites Powell described in his multimedia presentation, but found no "convincing evidence of any prohibited activity."

While Blix found no evidence to support the administration's claims regarding Iraq's possession of chemical and biological weapons, Mohamed ElBaradei, the director general of the International Atomic Energy Agency (IAEA), refuted the Bush administration's claims regarding Saddam Hussein's alleged nuclear weapons.[16] At a meeting of the Security Council on March 7, 2003—less than two weeks before the war began—ElBaradei reported that despite three months of inspections, including the inspections of all sites identified in satellite imaging as having suspicious activity, the IAEA had found no plausible indication of the revival of a nuclear weapons program. The IAEA concluded that the much-publicized aluminum tubes that Iraq had attempted to import were not likely to have been connected to the manufacture of centrifuges for the enrichment of uranium. And the IAEA and outside experts also determined that the reported uranium contracts between Iraq and Niger, cited by President Bush in his 2003 State of the Union address, were forgeries.[17]

The administration reacted to Blix and ElBaradei in much the same way that it later reacted to Ambassador Joseph Wilson's exposure of the phony Niger-Iraq uranium connection. Instead of carefully evaluating the inspectors' on-the-ground factual conclusions, administration officials attacked the messenger. On March 2, 2003, the *New York Times* reported that "a senior administration official" had charged that "the inspections have turned out to be a trap." Administration officials dismissed Blix as "more interested in pleasing all sides," afraid of being "the cause of war." [18] Donald Rumsfeld and Paul Wolfowitz sought to discredit Blix personally.[19]

In March 2003, Rumsfeld claimed that U.S. officials not only knew that Iraq had weapons of mass destruction but also knew their location. "We know where they are," he told *ABC News*.[20] Undeterred by the failure of Blix and ElBaradei to find any such evidence, President Bush launched war on March 19, announcing that "intelligence gathered by this and other governments *leaves no doubt* that the Iraq regime continues to possess and conceal some of the most lethal weapons ever devised." [21] In fact, every administration claim turned out to be wrong.

The assertion that Iraq had weapons of mass destruction, however, was only one piece of the equation for preventive war. Administration officials also cited the danger that Iraq would transfer such weapons to terrorist organizations, including al-Qaeda. Here, too, suspicions and surmise masqueraded as reliable fact. Even before the September 11 attacks, Wolfowitz suggested at internal meetings that there was an Iraqi connection to Osama bin Laden. After the attacks, Wolfowitz estimated that there was a 10 to 50 percent chance that Iraq was behind the attacks, an estimate based on no reliable intelligence data, and he and Rumsfeld pressed President Bush to confront Iraq immediately. President Bush had the same gut feeling, telling his advisers, "I believe Iraq was involved." [22] Powell, however, successfully argued against an immediate assault on Iraq, noting that there was no evidence of Iraqi complicity in the attacks.

Powell's argument was largely supported by the U.S. intelligence community, which generally concluded that Iraq and al-Qaeda had no collaborative relationship. Hussein and bin Laden were not natural allies; on the contrary, Hussein's secular regime was antagonistic to Islamic jihadists and radicals. Rumsfeld and Wolfowitz nonetheless pressured the intelligence community to find a connection, regularly asking senior intelligence officials if they had come up with "a smoking gun." A naval reserve officer assigned to assess the ties between Hussein and bin Laden was not asked to determine *whether* there was a connection, but was simply "told to show the connection." [23]

Eventually bits and pieces of evidence emerged. In October 2001, a Czech official claimed that an Iraqi intelligence officer had met in Prague with Mohamed Atta, the leader of the September 11 attacks, just five months before the hijackings. But by December, both Czech and American officials backed off, unable to establish that any significant meeting took place. In September 2002, Rumsfeld said that American intelligence had "bulletproof" evidence of links between al-Qaeda and Iraq. Rumsfeld refused to provide any details of this secret evidence, however, leading Senator Chuck Hagel, a Nebraska Republican, to respond, "To say, 'Yes I know there is evidence there, but I don't want to tell you more about it,' that does not encourage any of us." [24]

Nonetheless, by late September and October senior administration officials were repeatedly claiming that they had strong, albeit secret, evidence of a collaborative relationship between Iraq and al-Qaeda. President Bush claimed that Saddam Hussein was "dealing with al Qaeda," had "provided al Qaeda with chemical and biological weapons training," and that "you can't distinguish between al Qaeda and Saddam when you talk about the war on terrorism." Powell warned the Security Council of the "sinister nexus between Iraq and the al Qaeda terrorist network." [25] By the eve of the war, a majority of Americans thought that Saddam Hussein actually had something to do with the

September 11 attacks, even though the administration had carefully avoided directly making that claim. The administration's
claim was instead premised on its preventive paradigm: not that
Hussein had attacked us, or even that he would attack us, but
that he might provide dangerous weapons at some time in the
future to those who would.

But the Iraq–al-Qaeda link turned out to be just as fictitious
as the weapons of mass destruction. Rumsfeld's so-called bulletproof evidence was obtained by means of torture from Ibn
al-Shaykh al-Libi, who later recanted his claims.[26] Two high-
ranking leaders of al-Qaeda in American custody—Khalid
Sheikh Mohammed, al-Qaeda's chief of operations, and Abu
Zubaydah, an al-Qaeda planner—separately told their ques-
tioners that there were no substantive ties between al-Qaeda and
the Iraqi government.[27] The bipartisan 9-11 Commission's staff
concluded that there was no "collaborative relationship" between Saddam Hussein and al-Qaeda, a conclusion seconded by
the Senate Intelligence Committee.[28]

How did such weak evidence translate into such certainty on
the administration's part? The preventive-war doctrine provided the theoretical opening for the manipulation of evidence
that preceded the war with Iraq. The focus on inherently speculative future threats, coupled with the reasoning that the greater
the potential damage threatened, the less certain one need be
about its probability, justified reliance on suspicions, secret intelligence, and gut feelings, where the hard evidence was all to
the contrary.

Because it substitutes speculative prediction for solid factual
evidence, the preventive-war doctrine is particularly susceptible
to being invoked for pretextual reasons—and there is strong evidence that that is precisely what happened. Many suspect that
the administration's emphasis on illicit weapons and the Iraq–
al-Qaeda tie was a pretext to sell a war that the administration
actually launched for other reasons—oil, increased American
influence in the Middle East, spreading democracy, or simply

demonstrating U.S. resolve to our enemies. Indeed, after the war began, Wolfowitz admitted that the administration chose the weapons of mass destruction rationale for "bureaucratic reasons," as it was "the one reason everyone could agree on."[29]

Paul Pillar, the intelligence community's senior intelligence analyst for the Middle East from 2000 to 2005, concluded that the administration's invasion of Iraq was not in fact based on its concern about Iraqi weapons programs. In a 2006 article in *Foreign Affairs*, Pillar asserted that the administration's "decision to topple Saddam was driven by other factors—namely, the desire to shake up the sclerotic power structures of the Middle East and hasten the spread of more liberal politics and economics in the region."[30] For Pillar, what was most remarkable about prewar U.S. intelligence on Iraq was not how wrong it was, but that it played so small a role in the decision to go to war. Pillar, in charge of coordinating all of the intelligence community's assessments regarding Iraq, did not receive a single request from any administration policy maker for any such assessment prior to the war.[31]

Unlike Pillar, Blix does not claim that the administration acted for pretextual reasons. In his view, Americans allowed real fears to distort, shade, or color the actual evidence. In Blix's eyes, the administration in effect adopted a faith-based approach to war—it "knew" as if on faith that Hussein was evil, had dangerous weapons, and was associated with evildoers like bin Laden. Blix analogized the administration's approach to the Salem witch trials: "The witches exist; you are appointed to deal with these witches; testing whether there are witches is only a dilution of the witch hunt."[32] As in the Middle Ages, when people were convinced there were witches, "they certainly found them."[33]

Whether Pillar or Blix is correct, the preventive-war doctrine was the crux of the problem. The doctrine's focus on speculation about the future is dangerous not only because it makes it easier for unscrupulous politicians to manipulate suspicions and vague rules to achieve other, less noble aims but also because even when applied honestly, the doctrine is susceptible to costly and tragic miscalculations. Predicting future threats is not an exact science, and the judgments made are ordinarily not susceptible to proof. This is particularly true when the ultimate danger is deemed so great that the evidentiary standard regarding its probability is lowered. Thus, the administration relied on unverified claims from Iraqi defectors, which Vice President Cheney and others treated as more valid than the information gathered by the inspectors, even though the Defense Intelligence Agency concluded that most of the defectors' information was of little or no value, with much of it invented or exaggerated.[34] For example, the "central basis" for Powell's claim that Iraq had biological weapons turned out to be an Iraqi exile aptly nicknamed "Curveball," who German intelligence had determined was deranged and unreliable and turned out to be a fabricator.[35]

Powell later admitted that he had no "smoking gun, concrete evidence about the connection" between Iraq and al-Qaeda. "But," he continued, "I think *the possibilities* of such connections did exist."[36] General Richard B. Myers, chairman of the Joint Chiefs of Staff, similarly acknowledged the inherent limitations of intelligence. "Intelligence doesn't necessarily mean something is true," he said at a Pentagon news briefing after major combat ended in Iraq. "You know it's your best estimate of the situation. It doesn't mean it's a fact. I mean, that's not what intelligence is."[37] In the absence of hard evidence on Iraqi programs, officials developed a "mosaic," or a threat "picture," and "connected a lot of dots from multiple sources" to form a "judgment."[38] Or, as Donald Rumsfeld later conceded, we "did not act in Iraq because we had discovered dramatic new evidence of Iraq's pursuit of weapons of mass destruction. We acted because we saw the existing evidence in a new light through the prism of our experience on 9/11."[39]

The inflation of evidence to assert that dangerous threats exist is not unique to the Bush administration. When the Clinton administration in 1998 preemptively bombed what it claimed was a chemical weapons factory closely allied with al-Qaeda in the Sudan, officials claimed that they had conclusive, albeit secret, evidence to back up their claims. But much of the evidence turned out to be erroneous, and there was widespread skepticism, both at home and abroad, about the administration's claims.[40] The administration first asserted that the plant did not produce any medicine and was a heavily guarded chemical weapons facility, but later admitted that the factory was in fact the major pharmaceutical producer in Sudan, was unguarded, and had been visited routinely by foreign dignitaries, schoolchildren, and representatives of the World Health Organization.[41] Secretary of Defense William Cohen claimed that bin Laden had a clear financial interest in the plant, but in fact Salah Idris, a Sudanese businessman with no clear tie to bin Laden, had purchased the plant several months before the attack.[42] Here, too, the administration ignored or quashed dissenting voices in the intelligence community, including the State Department's Bureau of Intelligence, whose analysts concluded that the evidence tying the plant to bin Laden or to chemical weapons was weak and inadequate, as well as the head of the CIA Directorate of Operations and the chief of the CIA Counterterrorism Center, both of whom reportedly believed that the attack was not justified.[43]

Former Clinton administration officials continue to assert that the evidence was strong and the bombing justified.[44] We may never learn the truth because the administration rejected calls for an international inquiry from such diverse quarters as the Sudanese government, former president Jimmy Carter, and former Reagan administration adviser Abraham Sofaer.[45]

Psychologists and scientists have long recognized a deeply rooted tendency to interpret evidence in a manner that confirms one's preexisting beliefs.[46] As early as 1620, Sir Francis Bacon explained this phenomenon:

The human understanding when it has once adopted an opinion draws all things else to support and agree with it. And though there be a greater number and weight of instances to be found on the other side, yet these it either neglects and despises, or else by some distinction sets aside and rejects, in order that by this great and pernicious predetermination, the authority of its former conclusion may remain inviolate.[47]

This "confirmation bias" appears to have been at play in the run-up to the Iraq War, as U.S. officials cherry-picked the facts, exaggerating evidence supporting their position and disregarding contrary indications.[48] A high-level British assessment of the Bush administration's policy, written immediately after a secret conference in Washington in July 2002, reported that "military action against Iraq was now seen as inevitable," and "the intelligence and facts were being fixed around the policy."[49] As the Senate commission investigating the intelligence failure leading to the Iraq War observed, there was "a tendency of analysts to believe that which fits their theories," and they "simply *disregarded* evidence that did not support their position."[50] Indeed, the bias was so strong that even after the war, when David Kay, the CIA's chief hunter of weapons of mass destruction in Iraq, reported that there were no such weapons, CIA chief George Tenet responded, "I don't care what you say. You will never convince me they didn't have chemical weapons."[51]

Even without confirmation bias, intelligence analysts often exaggerate risks. Retired Israeli general Shlomo Brom has explained that intelligence estimates tend to be dire out of a desire to avoid being blamed for underestimating threats. "Intelligence analysts feel that by giving bleak assessments they decrease the threat to themselves," Brom says. The personal consequences of an assessment that misses what later turns out to be a serious threat are far greater than those that stem from an exaggerated assessment of a threat that does not come to pass.[52] If the analysts' dire threat assessment "ends up being correct, they will be heroes," but if it ends up being untrue, the error will frequently be ignored.

Paul Pillar suggests that assessments about ties between a government and a terrorist organization are particularly susceptible to abuse because "in the shadowy world of international terrorism, almost anyone can be 'linked' to almost anyone else if enough effort is made to find evidence of casual contacts, the mentioning of names in the same breath, or indications of common travels or experiences. Even the most minimal and circumstantial data can be adduced as evidence of a 'relationship.'" In addition, intelligence analysts—"for whom attention, especially favorable attention, from policymakers is a measure of success"—will feel a strong urge, "even if unconscious," to skew their analysis in the direction that they perceive policy makers desire.[53]

Law cannot rid us of these biases. But one of its functions is to create safeguards to counteract bias. One way of doing so is to require an independent assessment of the evidence. In theory, the UN Security Council serves that function with respect to any use of force beyond strict self-defense. In practice, it was doing just that, as it employed weapons inspectors, examined the evidence, and resisted the Bush administration's efforts to approve a war against Iraq. But when the Security Council resisted, the Bush administration simply bypassed that institutional check and unilaterally decided to strike.

Gideon Rose, managing editor of *Foreign Affairs* magazine, may have best captured the administration's case for going to war with Iraq. Rose likened the administration's insistence on a link between al-Qaeda and Iraq to the Dr. Seuss classic *McElligot's Pool*, in which a boy refuses to accept that his favorite fishing hole contains no fish. The boy imagines that the hole might be attached to a river, that fish might be swimming toward him, and

If such a thing *could* be
They *certainly would* be

"Encouraging toddlers to dream is fine," Rose maintains. "But shouldn't decisions about war and peace rest on a somewhat stronger foundation?"[54]

SUBSTITUTING OPEN-ENDED STANDARDS
FOR CLEAR RULES

The principle that nations may unilaterally use military force against other nations only in strict self-defense relies on a bright line to reduce resort to war. An armed attack is an objective fact. An imminent attack involves some amount of prediction, but is generally understood to require concrete evidence that the attack is indeed imminent, such as the massing of troops at the border. As Secretary of State Daniel Webster put it in 1842, self-defense is permitted only where the threat is "instant, overwhelming, leaving no choice of means and no moment of deliberation." Until recently, the United States accepted this imminence standard, at least in theory, even if it did not always honor it in fact. The Pentagon's definition of preemptive self-defense long echoed Webster's: "an attack initiated on the basis of incontrovertible evidence that an enemy attack is *imminent*."[55]

The preventive-war doctrine jettisons this bright-line rule for a more open-ended and less objectively verifiable standard. According to the Pentagon, preventive war is "a war initiated in the belief that military conflict, while not imminent, is inevitable, and that to delay would involve great risk."[56] No administration official argued that Iraq had plans to attack the United States or anybody else imminently. Rather, the administration's claims were based on a calculation of "inevitability" and "great risk." As President Bush put it, why would Saddam Hussein have gone to elaborate lengths to obtain weapons of mass destruction "except to intimidate or attack?"[57]

The decision to launch a preventive war invariably involves speculation about future events and intentions, judgments that defy clear rules. Thus, the National Security Strategy replaces the clear rule of self-defense with a vague balancing test in which the greater the threat, the less certainty there need be about its probability.[58] Former administration official John Yoo, an advocate of the preventive-war doctrine, recognizes that the doctrine substitutes a flexible cost-benefit standard for the UN Charter rule.[59]

The problem with this more open-ended standard was perhaps best described by Abram Chayes, the legal adviser to the State Department during the Cuban missile crisis, in explaining why the Kennedy administration refused to rely on preventive self-defense to justify its actions in that crisis. To permit preventive self-defense in the absence of an imminent attack, Chayes maintained, would mean that "there is simply no standard against which this decision could be judged. Whenever a nation believed that interests, which in the heat and pressure of a crisis it is prepared to characterize as vital, were threatened, its use of force in response would become permissible."[60] Because such a doctrine would eviscerate any clear limits on the use of force, Chayes argued that it would amount to a concession that "law simply does not deal with such questions of ultimate power."[61]

To be sure, the law frequently employs open-ended balancing tests. Determinations as to what constitutes negligence or how stringent environmental regulations should be frequently involve cost-benefit analyses. The Supreme Court has relied on balancing tests to determine such issues as the validity of state laws that impinge on interstate commerce. In general, however, the more significant the human interests at stake, the less appropriate are flexible, open-ended balancing tests. Under international law, for example, the prohibitions on torture, genocide, and summary executions are absolute and permit no balancing justifications whatsoever.[62]

The destructiveness of modern warfare similarly led the world's leaders to conclude that individual nations' resort to force should not be left to the discretion of national leaders. The UN Charter and customary international law reject Clausewitz's famous dictum that war is but the continuation of policy by other means. In order to restrain resort to war, the UN Charter adopted a clear rule. As Columbia law professor George Fletcher has explained, "Preemptive strikes are illegal . . . because they are not based on a visible manifestation of aggression; they are grounded in a prediction of how the feared enemy is likely to behave in the future."[63]

The Bush administration claims to have merely "adapt[ed] the concept of imminent threat" to a new strategic environment, in which terrorists and rogue states seek weapons of mass destruction and might attack a potentially infinite range of civilian targets. As Condoleezza Rice noted, "new technology requires new thinking about when a threat actually becomes imminent."[64] John Yoo argues that the post-9/11 world "renders the imminence standard virtually meaningless, because there is no ready means to detect whether a terrorist attack is about to occur."[65] Employing a sliding scale, Yoo argues that where the magnitude of the harm is great—as in a potential terrorist nuclear attack on the United States—a smaller degree of probability should suffice to warrant an attack.[66]

But substituting "probable" or even "inevitable" for "imminent" invites an inherently speculative enterprise. We simply cannot know whether the odds are 5 percent, 50 percent, or 90 percent that Saddam Hussein eventually would have obtained weapons of mass destruction and given them to terrorists to use against us. As Otto von Bismarck put it, rejecting similar arguments for preventive war, "one can never anticipate the ways of divine providence securely enough for that."[67]

But aren't there cases where it is virtually certain that another state will attack sometime in the future? As Donald Rumsfeld argued in defense of preventive military action against Iraq:

> think of all the countries that said, "Well we don't have enough evidence. . . . Maybe [Hitler] won't attack us. . . ." Well there are millions dead because of [those miscalculations]. . . . It wasn't

until each country got attacked that they said, "Maybe Winston Churchill was right." Maybe that lone voice expressing concern about what was happening was right.[68]

Hindsight, however, can be misleading. Until Hitler attacked Austria and threatened to attack Czechoslovakia in 1938, even Winston Churchill believed that Hitler might turn out to be one of those "great figures whose lives have enriched the story of mankind."[69] Churchill's "concern about what was happening" did not lead him to advocate preventive war in the 1930s, but rather a strong defensive alliance between Britain, France, and Russia to counter Nazi Germany's aggressive designs and actions.

In short, predicting the future is necessarily speculative, and therefore standards for waging war that are based on open-ended probabilities are extremely dangerous. International law reflects the considered judgment that it is better to avoid warfare unless a nation either has no choice but to defend itself from an attack or imminent attack or can convince the Security Council that a rogue state presents such a clear danger that an internationally authorized war should be fought on behalf of the community of nations.

DOUBLE STANDARDS

The preventive-war doctrine also depends on double standards. The doctrine would not be sustainable if applied across the board, and therefore rests on an assertion of American exceptionalism. Moreover, it is likely to be invoked only against our weakest foes, not against those who pose the most serious threats.

If every nation had the unilateral right to attack any other nation whenever it believed the danger of future attack was probable, the results would be calamitous. For this reason, former secretary of state Henry Kissinger, no dove, argued in 2002 that "it cannot be in either our national or the world's interest to develop principles that grant every nation an unfettered right of preemption against its own definition of threats to its security."[70] To do so in today's world would justify unilateral first strikes by both India and Pakistan, both Israel and Iran, both China and Taiwan, and both Ethiopia and Eritrea, to name but a few. After the Bush administration promulgated its preventive-war doctrine, Russia threatened a preemptive strike against Georgia, Australia threatened Indonesia and other Southeast Asian countries, and Japan threatened North Korea. During the Cold War, both the Soviet Union and China would have fit the West's definition of rogue states subject to a first strike, as would the United States itself from the vantage point of the Communist states.[71]

As these examples illustrate, the preventive-war doctrine would be untenable if it could be invoked by every nation. As such, it is necessarily, even if not explicitly, based on a double standard. Some openly acknowledge this. Robert Kagan, in his influential book *Power and Paradise*, argues candidly that the United States should "get used to the idea of double standards." In his view, the United States should use "force, preemptive attack, deception, whatever is necessary," even if others, in particular the Europeans, live in a "rule-based Kantian world."[72] Because of our military and political dominance, he suggests, we can do things that others cannot.[73] We can, and sometimes must, launch preventive strikes to remove dangerous threats; Russia, China, India, Pakistan, Israel, and Iran cannot. But such bravado is not a responsible or acceptable basis for international law or American foreign policy. If it is to have any legitimacy whatsoever, the "law of nations" must, as its name suggests, apply to *all* nations, not just some. A preventive-war doctrine for the United States alone cannot be squared with the rule of law's demand of equality, and therefore will not be accepted as legitimate by the international community.

The preventive-war strategy also violates the commitment to

equality in another respect. It permits and promotes selective targeting of the most vulnerable, not necessarily the most dangerous. Pakistan, North Korea, Russia, and Iran all posed much more serious dangers than Iraq in terms of weapons of mass destruction getting into the wrong hands; Iraq was attacked, Jonathan Schell has argued, "not because it [was] the worst proliferater but because it [was] the weakest." [74] By allowing nations to pick and choose which threats or bad rulers warrant a military response, the preventive-war doctrine substitutes expediency and exceptionalism for the principled decision making and uniformity required by the rule of law.

SHORT-CIRCUITING INSTITUTIONAL CHECKS

International law, like domestic law, depends on checks and balances for its enforcement. With respect to war, the checking function falls most notably to the UN Security Council. Absent a situation of strict self-defense, only it can authorize war. The preventive-war doctrine, however, effectively bypasses the Security Council by permitting unilateral use of force in situations that would ordinarily require the council's approval. By expanding the understanding of "imminent attack," the preventive-war doctrine thereby broadens the range of circumstances in which states may act without the Security Council's approval.

Consistent with this view, the Bush administration treated the Security Council as wholly optional as it prepared to launch its war against Iraq. It disregarded the ongoing work of arms inspectors appointed by the Security Council to determine the threat Iraq posed. And when a majority of the Security Council—including countries usually allied with the United States, such as Mexico, Chile, Germany, and France—refused to authorize war, the administration simply acted unilaterally. [75]

The UN structure for war authorization roughly parallels the structure of the U.S. Constitution on this subject. Under the Constitution, the president can act unilaterally in self-defense "to repel a sudden attack." In the absence of an actual attack or imminent threat, Congress must authorize warfare against another nation. The Constitution's framers felt that it would be far easier for one person to involve the nation in war than it would be to obtain the broad consensus necessary for legislative approval. As one framer put it, the Constitution was intended to "clog" rather than "facilitate" war.[76]

So, too, the UN Charter and international law require that the Security Council authorize war except where a nation must act to repel an armed attack or an imminent threat thereof. Here, too, the requirement that war be approved by a collective body representing several of the most powerful nations in the world was designed to limit recourse to violence, and to ensure that wars would be undertaken only where there was a broad consensus that they were necessary.

Some have defended the United States' ability to act unilaterally on the ground that the Security Council has proven to be a failure. In the face of that failure, the argument goes, the United States must act to protect both its own interests and those of the rest of the world. John Yoo has written that "the United Nations' rules on the use of force have become obsolete."[77] For Yoo, "by strictly confining the use of force to the point where states must ignore legitimate security threats, the leadership of the United Nations is condemning the Charter to obsolescence."[78] President Bush's challenge to the UN General Assembly either to take decisive action to disarm Iraq or become "irrelevant" suggested that the Security Council could "maintain relevance" only by supporting U.S. decisions.[79]

Critics of the UN process insist that the authority of the Security Council has been compromised by repeated violations of its prohibition on the use of force. During the thirty-five-year Cold War, the Security Council was paralyzed by the veto power wielded by the Soviet Union and the United States. The development of nuclear weapons and the rise of nonstate terrorism are said to have further undermined the viability of the UN Charter's rules. Cultural differences reflecting differing views on the use of force have destabilized the system. The rise of American hyperpower added still further strains. The divide over the Iraq War was simply, according to Tufts University professor Michael Glennon, the final nail in the Security Council's coffin.[80]

We discuss the broad challenges to the Security Council's role in Chapter 11. With respect to Iraq in particular, however, the Security Council performed its functions exactly as designed. It imposed a strict inspection process on Iraq. The inspectors were unable to find any weapons of mass destruction. The council accordingly determined that inspections should continue. The council's judgment that the dispute should be resolved peacefully accurately reflected the overwhelming international consensus. Had the council's wishes been adhered to, the United States would not be trapped in the quagmire that is Iraq. Thus, the Iraq War, rather than demonstrating the UN Charter's obsolescence, reaffirms the wisdom of its basic rules.

The preventive-war doctrine, like preventive law enforcement and intelligence gathering, has led the United States to make substantial sacrifices in its commitments to the rule of law. Where the rule of law demands hard evidence before one state may use violence against another, the preventive-war doctrine substitutes inescapably speculative predictions. Where the rule of law calls for clear rules, the preventive-war doctrine substitutes open-ended standards that magnify the chances of error. Where the rule of law insists on equal application to all, the preventive-war doctrine is tenable only as an instance of American exceptionalism. And where the rule of law requires institutional checks to counter aggression, self-interest, and bias, the preventive-war doctrine bypasses the principal institutional check on the use of force by radically expanding the situations in which states may unilaterally choose to attack other states. These sacrifices should be deeply troubling as a matter of principle to a nation that has prided itself on its commitment to the rule of law. And, as we will show in Part 2, these sacrifices in our principles have simultaneously compromised our security.

PART II

LESS SAFE

3. COLLATERAL CONSEQUENCES

When Attorney General Alberto Gonzales announced in late November 2005 that José Padilla had been indicted in a civilian criminal court, it came as some surprise that what he was charged with had nothing to do with what the United States had said about him for the more than three years that he was held in military custody as an enemy combatant. Padilla, a U.S. citizen born in Brooklyn, was arrested at O'Hare Airport in May 2002, held briefly as a material witness, and then designated an enemy combatant and transferred to a military brig in South Carolina. He was held there in military custody, for most of the time in solitary, incommunicado confinement, without access to a lawyer. In the government's first news conference about Padilla, which dramatically featured Attorney General John Ashcroft via satellite from Russia, government officials claimed that the United States had captured an al-Qaeda "dirty bomber." In subsequent press conferences, the government backed away from its dirty-bomb allegations, but claimed that Padilla was an al-Qaeda operative who had attended terrorist training camps, met with Khalid Sheikh Mohammed, the alleged mastermind of 9/11, and plotted to rent and blow up an apartment in the United States.

The criminal indictment of Padilla, however, made none of those claims. Instead, it charged Padilla only as a marginal figure in a vague conspiracy to provide financial support to unspecified terrorists abroad. No one in the indictment was alleged to have engaged in or plotted any violence whatsoever, here or overseas—much less detonating a dirty bomb—and the allegations specific to Padilla did not even claim that he provided financial support to terrorists.

The disconnect between the allegations aired in news conferences and the charges lodged in court was disturbing. If Padilla was in fact plotting with al-Qaeda leaders to unleash a dirty bomb in the United States, or even to blow up an apartment, shouldn't he be tried for those crimes and punished accordingly? Why did the government proceed instead on a paper-thin set of unrelated charges?

The answer is, in a word, torture. Administration sources explained to *New York Times* reporters that the reason they did not charge Padilla with more serious crimes was that the evidence allegedly supporting those charges was extracted from high-level al-Qaeda detainees—Khalid Sheikh Mohammed and Abu Zubaydah—through highly coercive tactics.[1]

Evidence obtained through torture would never be admissible in a court of law. The Supreme Court has long made clear that evidence obtained through any physical coercion, or even threats of physical coercion, is per se inadmissible. This rule is no mere technicality: such measures are said to produce inherently unreliable evidence and to "shock the conscience," and therefore cannot be condoned by admitting their fruits into a legal proceeding.[2]

The Padilla case illustrates one of the often overlooked costs of the Bush administration's preventive paradigm. Because evidence obtained through coercion is inadmissible in court, preventive coercive interrogation effectively immunizes the suspects and those they implicate from criminal prosecution. This problem infects not only the Padilla case but virtually everyone held at Guantánamo Bay, Cuba, Bagram Air Base in Afghanistan, and other detention centers in the war on terror. The United States is holding about 450 enemy combatants at Guantánamo, and another 500 at Bagram. Some of the detainees are alleged to be al-Qaeda fighters, some very high level leaders. Anyone who fights for al-Qaeda is guilty at a minimum of conspiracy to engage in terrorism, and may well be guilty of war crimes, as al-Qaeda has no right to engage in war and intentionally targets civilians. In theory, the United States should be able to try, convict, and imprison al-Qaeda fighters—in many instances, for the rest of their lives, but certainly until they no longer pose any real danger

Yet as of February 2007, not a single al-Qaeda fighter captured after 9/11 had been tried or convicted of any crime. Even before the Supreme Court in June 2006 ruled that the military tribunals created by the president were illegal, the administration had indicted only ten persons for war crimes trials.[3] One reason for the military's reluctance to hold war crimes trials was plainly the risk that any such proceeding would turn into a trial of the United States' own interrogation practices. It was not until March 2006, on the eve of the Supreme Court argument in the *Hamdan* military tribunal case, that the Pentagon barred the use of tortured testimony in its military tribunals, and it pointedly did not exclude testimony obtained through coercion that is deemed less than outright torture. In the wake of the *Hamdan* decision, Congress effectively sanctioned this practice, enacting the Military Commissions Act, which permits the admission of evidence obtained through coercion short of torture.[4] Defense lawyers are certain to make coercive interrogation a central issue in any proceeding. It is highly unlikely that the world will accept as legitimate any conviction obtained on the basis of coerced testimony. Congress's effort to jerry-rig the rules to ensure convictions will only reinforce the world's image of the United States as unwilling to adhere to fundamental precepts of the rule of law.

The administration's dilemma may be even deeper than this. There is substantial evidence that coerced testimony was relied upon by many of the Combatant Status Review Tribunals (CSRTs) set up in July 2004 to ascertain the status of Guantánamo detainees. The rules for the CSRTs do not preclude coerced evidence and require the tribunals to treat all government evidence as presumptively "genuine and accurate."[5] The Justice Department has argued in court that the CSRTs may rely on evidence "obtained through a non-traditional means, even torture."[6] And this is not an abstract issue. In many cases where transcripts of the tribunals have been made available, detainees told CSRT panels that their confessions had been coerced and were false, and that they could support that contention with medical evidence. In some cases, the CSRT panels deemed such claims sufficiently substantial to order that the torture allegations be investigated—but simultaneously classified the detainee as an enemy combatant, without even awaiting the results of the investigation.[7] If the federal courts ultimately rule that evidence obtained through torture or other coercive means cannot be used as the basis for CSRT decisions, the administration may be left with no legal basis to continue holding many of those now at Guantánamo.

In short, by electing early on to violate the universal prohibition against torture and cruel, inhuman, and degrading treatment in the name of "preventive" intelligence gathering, the Bush administration not only inflicted unconscionable harm on detainees from Abu Ghraib to Guantánamo but also painted itself into a corner. It is becoming increasingly unacceptable to hold so-called enemy combatants indefinitely without trial. But our interrogation tactics have shielded the vast majority of them from being held legally accountable in fair trials for the wrongs they may have committed. President Bush vowed shortly after 9/11 that he would capture the terrorists and "bring them to justice"; he repeated that vow in September 2006, when he announced that fourteen men who had been disappeared for years in secret CIA prisons were being transferred to Guantánamo.[8] But because of his authorization of coercive interrogation, the promise to bring terrorists to justice may well be impossible to fulfill.

Government interrogators were reportedly aware that their tactics would doom successful prosecutions. Officers from the Pentagon's Criminal Investigation Task Force, charged with developing criminal cases against the Guantánamo detainees, clashed with intelligence officers over the interrogation of Mohammed al-Khatani, the alleged twentieth hijacker. Military law enforcement officers argued that the best interrogation method was to develop rapport with the suspect, and that using coercive tactics would doom a prosecution. Intelligence agents refused that advice, explaining that their treatment of al-Khatani already prevented him from ever being put on trial, and then went ahead and used the cruel and inhuman tactics detailed above. Mark Fallon, special agent in charge of the Pentagon's task force, said, "We were told by the Office of Military Commissions, based on what was done to [al-Khatani], it made his case unprosecutable." As of February 2007, al-Khatani has not been charged with any crime.[9]

According to the pollsters, Americans reelected President Bush in 2004 in large measure because they trusted the Republicans more than the Democrats to keep them safe.[10] *New York Times* columnist David Brooks captured this sentiment while commenting on National Public Radio about the January 2006 Senate confirmation hearings for Justice Samuel Alito. Much of the hearing had focused on questions about Alito's views on executive power, sparked by revelations about the NSA warrantless wiretapping program. At the hearing, Republican senators generally defended the president, while Democrats raised questions about whether his actions were consistent with the Constitution's system of checks and balances. Brooks commented, "You saw people like Lindsay Graham, a Republican, saying 'I'm worried about terrorists.' You saw Democrats saying, 'I'm worried about the NSA.' That is a clear winner for the Republicans."[11]

But this should not be a partisan issue. Law and security need not be at loggerheads. The administration's repeated invocation of the preventive paradigm as a justification for treating law as a mere hindrance to be set aside in the quest for national security has in fact made us less safe. While the effects of counterterrorism policy are notoriously difficult to measure, there is little evidence that the administration's compromises with the rule of law have actually made us more secure, and substantial reason to

believe that they have made us more vulnerable to terrorist attacks over the long run. And as we will show in Part 3, the rule
of law does not leave a state helpless to protect itself against terrorists. For example, the administration had several lawfully
available options vis-à-vis Padilla. If government officials were
concerned that he was coming to the United States to commit a
terrorist act, but did not have evidence of any overt acts in furtherance of that act, they could have subjected him to close surveillance upon his arrival here and thereby uncovered evidence
that would have permitted a conspiracy prosecution. Alternatively, they might well have arrested him and charged him with
the very crimes with which he was eventually charged, as those
crimes date back many years, and presumably are based on evidence not tainted by the interrogation of Khalid Sheikh Mohammed and other black-site detainees. There is no evidence
that either of the coercive preventive measures employed with
respect to Padilla—his detention as an enemy combatant or the
use of coercion to develop (unusable) evidence against him—
contributed to making us safer.

In the following chapters, we will first show that the administration's claims of success regarding the preventive paradigm in
law enforcement and intelligence gathering are grossly exaggerated. In fact, there is little evidence that the preventive paradigm
has prevented terrorism, good reason to believe that it has made
matters worse, and every reason to believe that we could be
much safer if the administration had chosen a different course.
The administration's preventive coercive measures have limited
its long-term security options; tainted its efforts to identify, capture, and hold accountable al-Qaeda terrorists; and sown unnecessary division and distrust within the body politic.

We will also show that the preventive war in Iraq has similarly
undermined our security. It has diverted scarce resources from
the struggle with al-Qaeda and toward a country that posed no
threat of terrorism against us. It has sparked the recruitment of
more terrorists and offered them an invaluable training ground.

And it has emboldened rather than deterred so-called rogue states in their own race to develop weapons of mass destruction. Most troubling, the preventive paradigm—in Iraq, at home, and elsewhere around the globe—has exacted an astounding toll on the United States' image abroad and on the legitimacy of the struggle against terrorism. It bears the brunt of responsibility for the virulent anti-Americanism that now infects most of the world, from our bitterest enemies to our closest friends. That anti-Americanism, in turn, poses the greatest threat to our national security as we go forward.

The criticisms we offer regarding the ineffective and counterproductive character of the preventive paradigm are not limited to the particular initiatives of the Bush administration and the war in Iraq. Our concerns are not only with the incompetence of the Bush administration but also with the problems endemic to preventive coercion and violence. We conclude this section by pointing to deeper reasons for skepticism about adopting harsh coercive measures for preventive purposes. History demonstrates that executive officials of all partisan stripes tend to favor a preventive paradigm in times of national security crisis, and that such measures have rarely been necessary or even useful. And social psychology shows that there are deep-rooted reasons why government officials are unlikely to balance security and the rule of law fairly or accurately in times of crisis, and that therefore the preventive paradigm may be most ill-advised precisely when government officials are most likely to invoke it.

4. THE FAILURE OF PREVENTIVE LAW ENFORCEMENT

Has the preventive paradigm succeeded in its avowed purpose of making us safer from the threat of terrorism? The Bush administration's website, lifeandliberty.gov, claims that we are "winning the war on terrorism with unrelenting focus and unprecedented cooperation." It asserts that the U.S. government has captured or killed some three thousand al-Qaeda "operatives," including two-thirds of its leadership. It maintains that the government has disrupted 150 terrorist plots throughout the world (although President Bush in a speech in October 2005 claimed only 10). The website notes that the Justice Department has indicted more than four hundred people in what it calls "terrorism-related investigations" since September 11, and has obtained convictions in more than two hundred of these cases. It says the government has broken up terrorist cells in Buffalo, Detroit, Seattle, Portland, Oregon, and Virginia. And it boasts that it has deported more than five hundred foreign nationals linked to the investigation of September 11. Most important for Americans, other than the anthrax attacks in the fall of 2001, there has not been another terrorist attack on U.S. soil in the five years since September 11, 2001.

FALSE CLAIMS OF SUCCESS

But these claims of success do not withstand scrutiny. To the contrary, the evidence radically undermines the administration's case. Assessing the effectiveness of a preventive approach is admittedly difficult: how does one measure, much less assign causal responsibility for, what has *not* happened? But the existing evidence—from whom we are holding at Guantánamo to whom we have pursued and prosecuted at home—provides substantial reason to believe that we are not only less free, but less safe, as a result of the preventive paradigm.

GUANTÁNAMO: WORST OF THE WORST?

The best place to begin in assessing the preventive paradigm is the prison camp at Guantánamo Bay, Cuba. The camp was one of the administration's first steps in constructing the preventive paradigm: it was specifically designed to hold terrorism suspects in the name of preventing their participation in future attacks and obtaining intelligence from them. Since then, Guantánamo has become a symbol worldwide for the United States' approach to the war on terror, as its very creation and location reflect a decision to evade the rule of law. But has it worked? Are we holding hundreds of dangerous terrorists there, and thereby preventing them from launching the next attack? For a long time, the identity of those we had locked up at Guantánamo was shrouded in secrecy. But as more and more details emerge, it becomes increasingly evident how little this feature of the preventive paradigm has done to make us safer. With the exception of fourteen high-level detainees transferred from secret CIA prisons to Guantánamo in September 2006, there appear to be remarkably few actual terrorists held there—even according to the government's own assessment.

In January 2002, when the first detainees were airlifted to the American-leased Cuban outpost—bound, gagged, shackled, and blindfolded—General Richard Myers, chair of the Joint Chiefs of Staff, described them as the kind of prisoners who would chew through the cables on their transport plane to bring it down had they not been restrained.[1] Defense Secretary Rumsfeld labeled the men the "worst of the worst," and said they were "the most dangerous, best-trained, vicious killers on the face of the earth."[2] In June 2005, Rumsfeld insisted that all of the Guantánamo prisoners were "captured on the battlefield," and were "terrorists, trainers, bomb makers, recruiters, financiers, [Osama bin Laden's] bodyguards, would-be suicide bombers, [and] probably the twentieth 9/11 hijacker." [3]

In fact, the vast majority of those held at Guantánamo were not captured on the battlefield in Afghanistan, but in Pakistan, while others were picked up as far away from battle as Gambia and Bosnia. And the government's own accounts of who is detained there contradict Rumsfeld and Myers's hyperbolic claims. In a secret evaluation leaked to the *New York Times* in June 2004, the CIA reported that there were few high-value detainees at Guantánamo, and that interrogations there had yielded little actionable intelligence. [4] Michael Scheuer, who headed the CIA's al-Qaeda unit until 1999 and resigned from the agency in 2004, has said that fewer than 10 percent of the detainees at Guantánamo were high-value prisoners with information that might prove useful in the war on terror. The others, Scheuer said, were at best foot soldiers who knew "absolutely nothing about terrorism." [5]

The CIA's sober assessment was corroborated in early 2006 by the release of government records from the CSRTs, the tribunals belatedly charged with holding hearings to determine whether the detainees were in fact enemy combatants. A study by Seton Hall law professor Mark Denbeaux examined the written reports of the CSRTs on each of the 517 detainees held at Guantánamo in early 2006. [6] The CSRT reports—the government's best case for detention—divide the detainees into three categories based on their alleged relationship to al-Qaeda or the Taliban: "fighters," "members," or merely "associated with." Only 8 percent are said to be fighters. A further 30 percent are allegedly members of al-Qaeda or the Taliban, but not fighters. And a full 60 percent are said only to be "associated with" these groups, neither fighters nor members. Thus, the vast majority are held for associations that fall short of mere membership, and over 90 percent of these so-called enemy *combatants* are, by the government's own account, not fighters for the enemy.

Fewer than half of the Guantánamo detainees are alleged to

have undertaken any "hostile acts" against the United States, even though the military defines that term extraordinarily broadly. In one case, allegations that a detainee fled when U.S. forces bombed him, and that he was captured in Pakistan along with "other Uighur fighters," were sufficient to lead the CSRT to conclude that he had engaged in hostile acts against the United States.[7] In another case, the only evidence cited for hostile acts was that the detainee was a cook's assistant for Taliban forces, and had fled from a Northern Alliance attack.[8] Yet even treating cooking meals and fleeing from bombs as hostile acts, the CSRTs found that only 45 percent of the prisoners committed any such acts.

The Seton Hall study, moreover, significantly overstates the percentage of Guantánamo detainees alleged to be fighters or to have engaged in hostile acts. That is because it addresses only the 517 persons detained at Guantánamo in early 2006. By that time, over 250 detainees had already been released and were not part of the study. Assuming that the United States would not have released those it deemed to be fighters, this means that when the full Guantánamo population is considered, only about 5 to 6 percent of those held there were said to be fighters, and only about 30 percent were alleged to have engaged in hostilities.[9]

The high incidence of Guantánamo detainees *not* alleged to be fighters or to have committed any hostile acts is a function of the preventive paradigm. The administration swept broadly from the outset in part because it had little notion of who was and was not an al-Qaeda fighter. All but 5 percent of the detainees were captured by non-U.S. forces, often in exchange for generous bounties. U.S. and allied forces distributed flyers announcing rewards for bringing in al-Qaeda or Taliban members. One such flyer read as follows:

> Get wealth and power beyond your dreams. . . . You can receive millions of dollars helping the anti-Taliban forces catch al-Qaeda and Taliban murderers. This is enough money to take care of your family, your village, your tribe for the rest of your

life. Pay for livestock and doctors and school books and housing for all your people.[10]

In the poverty-stricken regions of Afghanistan and Pakistan, such offers appear to have prompted the capture of men who had little or no real connection to al-Qaeda or the Taliban. Members of the Uighur minority in China were reportedly turned in for $5,000 rewards, only to be determined years later to have had nothing to do with al-Qaeda or the Taliban.[11]

The preventive paradigm's harsh interrogation practices may also have contributed to the extended detention of innocents. Approximately thirty Guantánamo detainees were reportedly implicated by Mohammed al-Khatani, whom interrogators subjected to extended torture. In November 2002, three months into his brutal interrogation, an FBI agent reported that al-Khatani was "evidencing behavior consistent with extreme psychological trauma (talking to nonexistent people, reporting hearing voices, cowering in a corner of his cell covered with a sheet for hours on end.)"[12] Any information obtained under such circumstances is inherently suspect. Yet the CSRTs relied on his testimony to classify thirty others as enemy combatants.

The CSRTs relied on another detainee's testimony to implicate no fewer than sixty prisoners, or more than 10 percent of the entire prison population, even though this detainee's testimony was at times proved false. For example, this source claimed that Mohammed al-Tumani had attended a terrorist camp in Afghanistan at a specific time. Al-Tumani's CSRT representative proved that his client had not even entered Afghanistan until three months later, and that none of the other detainees whom the source placed at the Afghanistan camp at the time were in Afghanistan when the accuser said they were there. The tribunal nonetheless classified al-Tumani as an enemy combatant.[13]

In another instance, a prisoner had screamed at his interrogators after a long interrogation session, "Fine, you got me. I'm a terrorist." The CSRT treated this statement as a genuine admission, even though the interrogators themselves noted that it was obviously a sarcastic outburst, not intended as a statement of the truth.[14] Another man was treated as having admitted to knowing bin Laden when he admitted only to having seen him on television news.[15]

The bottom line is that the preventive paradigm as practiced at Guantánamo appears to have netted very few actual terrorists. And Guantánamo is an all-too-fitting symbol of the failure of the preventive paradigm.

IMMIGRATION ENFORCEMENT: 0 FOR 93,000

When Attorney General John Ashcroft first announced the "paradigm of prevention" in a speech in October 2001 in New York City, he vowed that the administration would use all laws within its power to round up suspected terrorists and prevent them from inflicting further damage upon us. He explicitly singled out immigration law, warning terrorists that if they "overstayed [their] visa by even one day," they would be locked up.[16] The administration subsequently adopted a zero-tolerance immigration policy toward immigrants and visitors from Arab and Muslim countries, on the theory that it would thereby root out the terrorists. But the nation's broadest campaign of ethnic profiling since World War II came up empty. The Special Registration program, which required 80,000 men from predominantly Arab and Muslim countries to register after September 11, resulted in not a single terrorist conviction. Of the 8,000 young men of Arab and Muslim descent sought out for FBI interviews, and the more than 5,000 foreign nationals placed in preventive detention in the first two years after 9/11, virtually all Arab and Muslim, not one stands convicted of a terrorist crime today. In these initiatives, the government's record is 0 for 93,000. Reviewing the results of the Special Registration program in particular, James Ziglar, commissioner of the Immigration and Naturalization Service on 9/11, stated that "what we did get was

a lot of bad publicity, litigation, and disruption in our relationships with immigrant communities and countries that we
needed help from in the war on terror." [17]

The bipartisan 9-11 Commission's staff concluded that all the
administration's immigration initiatives targeted at Arabs and
Muslims that it reviewed were a complete failure in identifying
terrorists. In addition to the programs identified above, it found
that a blanket twenty-day hold placed shortly after 9/11 on visas
issued to males aged sixteen to forty-five from twenty-six countries in the Middle East and North Africa, plus Bangladesh,
Malaysia, and Indonesia, "yielded no anti-terrorist information
and led to no visa denials." Similarly, it reported that the Visa
Condor program, which required additional screening of visa
applications from twenty-six predominantly Muslim countries,
had identified no terrorists, and that the CIA had withdrawn
from the program because it had uncovered no significant information. And it found that the Absconder Apprehension Initiative, a program that selectively targeted foreign nationals from
predominantly Muslim countries who had outstanding deportation orders, had identified no terrorists. [18]

In an attempt to obscure its failure to identify a single terrorist, the administration's website cites 515 deportations. But it
neglects to point out that most of these were carried out under
a "hold until cleared" policy that barred deportation—even
where immigrants agreed to leave the country—unless the FBI
had cleared the immigrant of any connection to terrorism. The
administration's reluctance to deport persons without clearing
them had a certain logic: after all, the last thing one would want
to do with a real terrorist would be to send him abroad, where,
beyond the reach of American surveillance, he could plan and
carry out further terrorist attacks against U.S. and allied targets.
But in light of that policy, these 515 deportations are misses, not
hits, in terms of identifying actual terrorists. How does deport-
ing hundreds of people the FBI has concluded are *not* connected
to terrorism make us any safer?

While the short-term result of the administration's ethnic-profiling campaign netted no terrorists, the long-term consequences may be to create terrorists. Many of those selectively targeted for deportation had U.S. citizen children, born and raised here but forced to leave in order to stay with their deported parents. If their families' treatment results in their alienation from the United States, they could become ideal recruits for terrorists fighting us. And as U.S. citizens, they will always have a right to return.

THE CRIMINAL RECORD

The Justice Department's record on criminal law enforcement ought to be an important bellwether of how the preventive paradigm is working. If the administration's preventive initiatives are successfully apprehending terrorists and disrupting terrorist plots, one would expect to see the results in criminal prosecutions. Conspiring to engage in a terrorist act is a serious crime. Omar Abdel Rahman, the blind sheikh, is serving multiple 240-year sentences for his part in planning to blow up bridges and tunnels around Manhattan long before 9/11. His conviction offers concrete evidence of a disrupted terrorist plot. Since 9/11, the Justice Department has used the criminal process "preventively" in a number of ways—bringing pretextual prosecutions against those it suspects but cannot prove are terrorists, pursuing material-support prosecutions that do not require proof of any actual terrorism, and detaining suspects as material witnesses to criminal investigations. But it has prosecuted a remarkably small number of individuals for actually planning, supporting, or engaging in terrorist acts.

The administration's claims of success in the criminal area are grossly inflated. In fact, the administration has a very low conviction rate in terrorism prosecutions, and has come up dramatically short in many high-profile cases. Its claims to have broken up five terror cells fall apart when one examines each purported "cell." It still has not identified a single al-Qaeda cell in the United States. And at the end of the day, it has obtained convictions in only five cases since 9/11 for attempting or conspiring to engage in terrorist acts. In three of those cases, the preventive paradigm cannot take credit for the prosecution, and the gravity of the threats posed by the other two is doubtful. In short, after five years, the government's preventive paradigm has little to show in terms of criminal convictions.

MISLEADING STATISTICS

The key to understanding the administration's claim that it has obtained more than four hundred criminal indictments and over two hundred convictions in "terrorism-related" cases is the word "related." These statistics are meant to be misleading, and they frequently succeed because listeners often drop the "related" and assume that the figures refer to *actual* terrorist cases. At a Senate Judiciary Committee hearing in May 2004, for example, after a Justice Department official cited the number of "terrorism-related" convictions, Senator Orrin Hatch, then chairman of the committee, interrupted and immediately mischaracterized them as convictions for "terrorist activities." The Justice Department official made no attempt to correct the senator, answering simply—and incorrectly—"Yes, sir."[19] In fact, few if any of the convictions were for terrorist activities of any kind.

In February 2007, the Justice Department's Inspector General released a comprehensive report on the department's terrorism statistics. It found that "the FBI significantly overstated the . . . number of terrorism-related convictions" it reported and that the U.S. Attorneys' offices did not accurately report any of the terrorism statistics the Inspector General reviewed.[20] Among other problems, it noted that cases were designated as terrorist without adequate support for that designation, and that both the FBI and the U.S. Attorneys' offices coded cases as terrorist-related at the outset of investigations and then failed to change the categorization when further investigation showed that the initial code was unfounded.[21]

In fact, the majority of the indictments and convictions the Justice Department labels "terrorism-related" are for minor, nonviolent offenses such as making false statements on a federal form, immigration infractions, or credit card fraud. In June 2005, the *Washington Post* examined these cases in detail, and found that only thirty-nine involved any convictions on charges related to terrorism.[22] The *New York Times* reached the same conclusion—also finding only thirty-nine convictions on terrorist charges—in a similar analysis conducted more than a year and a half later, in September 2006.[23] The *Post* noted that only one in fourteen of the more than two hundred convictions seemed to have any tie to al-Qaeda and that most involved no evidence of terrorism at all. Twenty of the convictions, for example, were of a group of men, mostly Iraqis, who had been involved in a truck-licensing scam, but who had been "publicly absolved of ties to terrorism in 2001."[24] New York University's Center on Law and Security similarly concluded, after reviewing the Justice Department's "terrorism-related" cases, that "the legal war on terror has yielded few visible results. There have been . . . almost no convictions on charges reflecting dangerous crimes."[25]

Nor are convictions on minor charges likely to be an effective preventive measure. In December 2003, a Syracuse University research institute found that the median sentence handed down in cases that the Justice Department had labeled "terrorism-related" in the first two years after September 11 was only fourteen days.[26] Such a sentence will do little to incapacitate or deter a would-be terrorist; it would merely give him two weeks in jail to plan his next attack.

FALLING SHORT

The government's website conspicuously omits reference to any of its failures in terrorist cases. In fact, however, the government has only a 29 percent conviction rate in prosecutions for federal crimes of terrorism since 9/11, as compared to a 92 percent conviction rate for felonies generally.[27] This is an astoundingly poor record, particularly given the climate of fear that ought to assist prosecutors in terrorism cases. Several of the government's most prominent cases have disintegrated when challenged.

For example, the Justice Department repeatedly touted the prosecution of Sami Al-Arian, a computer science professor at the University of South Florida, as a critical element of its war on terror, and as exhibit one in the case for why the Patriot Act was essential.[28] Al-Arian was indicted on some fifty counts, including conspiracy to maim and kill. Prosecutors called him the North American leader of the Palestinian Islamic Jihad. Yet after the prosecution presented eighty witnesses and hundreds of hours of taped surveillance over six months of trial, and Al-Arian's lawyers rested their case without calling a single witness, a Tampa jury found Al-Arian not guilty of the most serious charges against him, including conspiracy to murder and to aid a terrorist organization. The jury voted 10 to 2 in favor of acquittal on all other counts, including a charge of material support to a terrorist group and an immigration violation. A former FBI official told *Time* magazine that the FBI was pressured to make a case against Al-Arian despite weak evidence: " 'We were in shock, but those were our marching orders,' [said] the supervisor, who felt that the Justice Department was rushing to indict before it had really appraised the evidence." [29] In April 2006, the government dropped all remaining charges in exchange for Al-Arian's plea of guilty to one count of conspiracy to provide material support to a terrorist organization—by helping individuals with their visa applications—and his agreement to be deported. The agreement admits no involvement in or support of violence.[30]

In September 2003, the administration claimed to have uncovered an espionage ring at Guantánamo Bay, arresting a Muslim chaplain and three translators. Captain James Yee, the chaplain, was held for seventy-six days in solitary confinement; he was charged, not with espionage or sabotage, but with taking classified information off the base. Even that charge was subsequently dismissed when the government could not establish that any of the information was actually classified.[31] In an egregious act of vindictive prosecution, the United States then charged Yee with having pornography on his computer, and with having had an affair on Guantánamo—charges that plainly have nothing to do with national security, but were sure to end Yee's career as a chaplain, destroy his family, and forever tarnish his reputation. Those charges were eventually dropped as well, but not before the damage was done.

The government's cases against the Guantánamo translators also fizzled. The prosecutor initially filed thirty charges, some carrying the death penalty, against Ahmed Al Halabi, a twenty-four-year-old translator. After ten months, however, it dropped all the serious charges and accepted a guilty plea to four minor crimes, including taking pictures at Guantánamo without approval. Al Halabi was allowed to go free on the basis of the time he had already served awaiting trial.[32] A second translator, Ahmed Fathy Mehalba, also pleaded guilty to minor crimes, such as lying to investigators, and was set free a few months later.[33] The government dropped all charges against the third translator, Jackie Farr.[34]

The government suffered still another prominent defeat in its prosecution of Sami al-Hussayen, a Saudi student at the University of Idaho. Al-Hussayen was charged with providing material support to a terrorist group by including on his website links to other websites, some of which advocated jihad. It had no evidence that al-Hussayen himself ever advocated jihad, or that he even agreed with the content of the speeches on the linked websites. Under the expansive material-support statute used in al-Hussayen's trial, the government argued, that did not matter. But to an Idaho jury, it did. Showing more fidelity to the First Amendment than the prosecution had, the jury acquitted al-Hussayen on all terrorism charges.[35]

In May 2004, the government arrested Brandon Mayfield, a

Portland lawyer and Muslim convert, as a material witness, claiming that his fingerprints had been found on a suitcase near the Madrid train bombings. Spanish authorities objected that the fingerprints did not match Mayfield's, but the FBI disregarded those objections. Eighteen days later, the government dismissed its case against Mayfield, apologized, and admitted that, as the Spaniards had said all along, its fingerprint "match" had been a mistake.[36] The government ultimately paid two million dollars to settle a civil lawsuit Mayfield filed regarding his mistreatment.

In February 2007, a jury in Chicago acquitted two Palestinians of racketeering charges in another prominent "terrorism" trial. Muhammad Salah, a grocer from suburban Chicago, and Abdelhaleem Ashqar, a university professor, had been charged with distributing money to Hamas. The accusations related to support provided before Hamas was designated a "terrorist organization," and before Congress made material support of terrorist organizations a crime. Prosecutors argued that the support was nonetheless a crime because Hamas was a criminal enterprise, so any support to it violated anti-racketeering laws. In effect, the government sought to treat a political party with a concededly wide range of legal activities as if it were the Mafia. After a three-month trial, the jury acquitted the men of the racketeering charge and convicted them only on minor charges, including refusal to testify before a grand jury and obstruction of justice.[37]

Perhaps the administration's most prominent failures came in its cases against the two U.S. citizens held in military custody as enemy combatants. As already noted, the government was forced to back down in both José Padilla's and Yaser Hamdi's cases. It abandoned its efforts to hold Padilla as an enemy combatant when it faced a Supreme Court showdown on the legality of its actions, and it released Yaser Hamdi subject only to unenforceable conditions that he live in Saudi Arabia and surrender his U.S. citizenship, rather than provide him the hearing to which he was entitled.

EMPTY SUCCESSES

Even where the administration has managed to obtain a conviction on a terrorism charge, it is often not at all clear that it has actually identified a terrorist or made us safer. Virtually all of the convictions on terrorism charges the Justice Department has obtained since 9/11 involve no acts of terrorism per se, nor conspiracy to engage in terrorist acts, nor even the aiding and abetting of terrorist crimes, but only material support to a group the government has labeled terrorist. As explained in Chapter 1, the material-support laws broadly criminalize support to disfavored groups, regardless of the character of the support or its nexus to any actual terrorism.[38] Because they are so sweeping, a conviction under these laws does not mean that a terrorist has been convicted, or that any terrorism has been prevented.

Consider, for example, the prosecution of Lynne Stewart, a sixty-five-year-old criminal defense lawyer in New York City, and Mohammed Yousry, her translator.[39] In June 2000, while representing the imprisoned Omar Abdel Rahman, Stewart issued a statement from the sheikh to a Reuters reporter, and thereby violated an administrative agreement she had signed that barred her from helping Rahman to communicate with the outside world. After visiting Rahman in prison, Stewart told the reporter that he had withdrawn his personal support for a cease-fire then in place in Egypt. Two days later Stewart issued a clarification, explaining that the sheikh "did not cancel the cease-fire," but "left the matter to my brothers to examine it and study it because they are the ones who live there and they know the circumstances better than I." These statements prompted no response in Egypt. In the United States, the government appropriately revoked Stewart's visiting privileges and insisted that she sign a more restrictive agreement before visiting Rahman again. But that was before 9/11.

After 9/11, the government revived the matter and charged Stewart with providing material support for terrorism by issuing the statement. She and Yousry were convicted in February 2005 after a trial in which the government tried them alongside Ahmed Abdel Sattar, a far more culpable figure who had engaged in wholly distinct crimes. Among other things, without the involvement or knowledge of Stewart or Yousry, Sattar had issued a fake fatwa in 2000 urging followers to "kill [Jews] wherever they are." In his closing, the prosecutor repeated Sattar's "kill the Jews" fatwa more than seventy times. In addition, the prosecution introduced highly prejudicial evidence, including a tape of Osama bin Laden—played for the jury shortly before the anniversary of 9/11—and evidence of al-Qaeda's bombing of the USS *Cole*, even though there was no claim that Stewart, Yousry, or Sattar had anything to do with al-Qaeda or bin Laden.[40]

The case against Yousry was even weaker than the case against Stewart. As a mere translator, Yousry was not asked to sign the administrative agreement that Stewart signed and later violated. He played no role in Stewart's decision to issue the press statement. Nonetheless, for little more than the act of translation, the government charged and convicted Yousry of providing material support for terrorism.[41] The convictions of Stewart and Yousry provide two more cases in the Justice Department's "terrorism-related" conviction column, but it is difficult to see how they make Americans any safer.

WHAT TERROR CELLS?

All five of the "terror cells" that the administration claims to have disrupted in the United States were charged under the material-support laws, which make it possible to convict individuals without showing that they have actually undertaken, planned, supported, or even thought about furthering terrorist activity. None of the putative cell members was charged with, much less convicted of, attempting or conspiring to engage in any actual terrorist conduct. Indeed, there is little or no reason to believe that any of them were actual terrorists waiting to strike.

Even the "cell" that the CIA considered the most dangerous was never accused of engaging in or planning to engage in any terrorist activity. A group of seven young men in Lackawanna, New York, just outside Buffalo, were recruited by an al-Qaeda operative who lived in their community for some time and became a leader in the local mosque.[42] He convinced the seven to go to Afghanistan to attend an al-Qaeda training camp. They went in May 2001. Once there, they hardly acted as committed terrorists: one feigned injury and left after a week; three others also departed early; only three stuck around for the full six-week session. The FBI received a tip about the trip and closely monitored the young men upon their return to the United States. During a year and a half of intensive surveillance, the FBI found no evidence that any of the men were engaged in or plotting any criminal activity—not terrorism, not support of terrorism, not even a shoplifting spree. Nonetheless, shortly after the first anniversary of 9/11, federal officials arrested them. Deputy Attorney General Larry Thompson proclaimed that "United States law enforcement has identified, investigated, and disrupted an al Qaeda-trained terrorist cell on American soil."[43]

The men were charged with providing material support to a terrorist organization. The government's theory was that attending the training camp, without more, constituted the provision of support in the form of "personnel." But federal courts had already held unconstitutionally vague the statute's ban on the provision of "personnel" to terrorist organizations.[44] In addition, it was hardly clear that attendance at a camp even amounted to the provision of personnel as the statute uses that term. They may well have *received* support from al-Qaeda at the camp, in the form of lodging and training, but it was doubtful that attendance alone constituted the *provision* of support. The Lackawanna defendants had strong legal defenses on both statutory and constitutional grounds.

The men ultimately pleaded guilty, however, reportedly in part out of fear that the government might designate them as enemy combatants if they insisted on going to trial. That fear was not unfounded: Defense Secretary Rumsfeld and Vice President Cheney had both urged that the Lackawanna men be detained as enemy combatants from the outset, but the administration had chosen to pursue criminal charges initially. As Padilla's case showed, the government was perfectly capable of shifting individuals from criminal proceedings to military custody as enemy combatants. Whatever the men's reasons for pleading guilty, their convictions prove little about progress in identifying actual terrorists.

The Virginia "terror cell," which netted the government eleven "terrorism" convictions, involved a group of men in Virginia accused of playing paintball games, owning hunting rifles, and planning to fight for Muslim causes in Kashmir.[45] Four of the men are alleged to have attended a training camp run by Lashkar-i-Taiba, a militant group committed to driving India from Kashmir. One, Ali al-Timimi, was convicted of having urged some of the others, during a half-hour dinner conversation shortly after the 9/11 attacks, to fight with the Taliban in Afghanistan—*before* the United States attacked Afghanistan. As with the Lackawanna defendants, none of the men was ever charged with planning to undertake terrorist activity of any kind, here or abroad.

The three other "terror cells" are said to have been in Detroit, Seattle, and Portland, Oregon. Here, too, the evidence does not support the government's claims. The only "terror cell" prosecuted in Detroit was a group of men accused of having provided material support to terrorism in a case in which the government relied almost entirely on one informant's dubious testimony and never specified either a terrorist group or terrorist act that the individuals were alleged to have supported. Three of the men were nonetheless convicted in the first post-9/11 terrorism case to go to trial. But all of the convictions were subsequently overturned, and the men freed, when the government admitted that it had failed to disclose evidence that its principal witness, the informant, had lied on the stand.[46] The prosecutor was himself subsequently prosecuted for his misconduct in the case.[47] Nonetheless, these "convictions" are counted as successes on the government's website.

The Portland reference presumably refers to six men who pleaded guilty to attempting to travel to Afghanistan to fight alongside the Taliban. They never made it there. While the citizens among them could certainly have been tried for attempted treason, there was no allegation that any were involved in terrorism.[48] Finally, the Seattle case apparently refers to James Ujaama, a black civil rights activist who was detained as a material witness in July 2002 and originally charged with conspiring to open a terrorist training camp in the United States. The government ultimately dropped that charge and accepted a plea in which Ujaama admitted merely to having made a humanitarian donation to the Taliban—before 9/11. He was sentenced to little more than the time he had already served awaiting trial.[49] Thus, not one of the five "cells" that the government claims to have disrupted since 9/11 was convicted of conspiring to engage in any terrorist activity, here or elsewhere. In February 2005, the FBI admitted in a secret internal memo that it had discovered no actual al-Qaeda cells in the United States.[50] Nor has it identified any since.

THE BOTTOM LINE

Where, then, are the real terrorists? As of February 2007, more than five years after 9/11 and the launching of the preventive paradigm, the Justice Department had convicted only five individuals of attempting or conspiring to engage in a specific terrorist act. Of these, three were convicted without resort to the preventive paradigm at all. The convictions of the other two are attributable to the preventive paradigm, but two convictions is a distinctly unimpressive showing for a massive five-year law enforcement and intelligence campaign. And in both of the cases, there is reason to doubt that the defendants posed a true threat.

The only person convicted since 9/11 of actually attempting to carry out a terrorist act is the shoe bomber, Richard Reid. Reid's plot to ignite an explosive concealed in his shoe and bring down a transatlantic flight was undoubtedly a terrorist plot successfully averted. But the Justice Department's preventive paradigm can claim no credit. Reid was captured in the act not through any coercive preventive initiative, but simply because an alert flight attendant noticed a strange-looking man trying to set fire to his shoe.

Four others have been convicted of conspiring to engage in terrorist conduct. The most famous is Zacarias Moussaoui, who pleaded guilty in April 2005 to six counts of conspiracy to attack the United States and was sentenced to life imprisonment in May 2006. (The government went to great lengths and expense to see Moussaoui executed, perhaps because it had failed to bring anyone else to justice for involvement in 9/11. But it never showed that Moussaoui was in fact involved in 9/11, and the jury rejected the death penalty) Like Reid, Moussaoui's arrest cannot be attributed to the preventive paradigm, as he was arrested one month before 9/11, before the preventive paradigm had even been instituted.

Nor can the preventive paradigm take responsibility for the 2006 conviction of Shahawar Matin Siraj, a twenty-three-year-old Pakistani immigrant, for conspiracy to blow up a Manhattan subway station.[51] Siraj's conviction rested on taped statements to a paid government informant. Siraj objected that he was entrapped by the informant's impassioned entreaties. The government showed, however, that Siraj had made many statements approving suicide bombings long before he met the informant, thereby defeating the entrapment defense by convincing the jury that Siraj was "predisposed" to commit the crime. Siraj was never linked to any terrorist group, and it appears that the only person with whom he discussed his plans was the government informant. He may well have been a would-be terrorist, but he was identified and convicted not through the coercive initiatives of the preventive paradigm, but with one of the most traditional forms of investigation—an informant.

The preventive paradigm can claim credit for the conviction of Iyman Faris, an Ohio truck driver who pleaded guilty in May 2003 to providing material support to al-Qaeda in connection with a conspiracy to bring down the Brooklyn Bridge with an acetylene torch. Faris allegedly met with al-Qaeda's Khalid Sheikh Mohammed, and federal investigators reportedly learned of Faris's plot through the interrogation of Mohammed and through NSA wiretaps.[52] The only steps Faris took in furtherance of the plot, however, were to ask a friend where he could get welding tools and to research the Brooklyn Bridge on the Internet. He then concluded, not surprisingly, that the plot was unlikely to succeed, and abandoned it.[53]

The case of Ahmed Abu Ali may also be seen as part of the preventive paradigm. Abu Ali, a U.S. citizen and Virginia resident, was convicted in November 2005 of conspiring to kill President Bush. While attending university in Saudi Arabia, he was arrested by local authorities and imprisoned without charge for twenty months. There was evidence that the Saudis were detaining him at the behest of the United States. When a federal judge granted Abu Ali's family discovery into the relationship between the Saudis and the U.S. government in connection with his detention, he was released by the Saudis into U.S. custody and brought back to Virginia to stand trial.[54] The case fits the preventive paradigm, as the United States seemed to be willing to allow the Saudis to hold Abu Ali without charges until a federal court threatened to expose the arrangement. Abu Ali's conviction rested entirely on a confession he made while detained by the Saudi security services. He claimed that the confession was coerced through torture, a practice for which the Saudi security service is well known. But the federal trial judge dismissed that assertion and admitted the confession. His case is on appeal.[55]

In five years, then, the government has successfully prosecuted only five people for engaging in or conspiring to engage in actual terrorism. And as of January 2007, only two convictions—Faris and Abu Ali—can be attributed to the preventive paradigm—not a strong bottom line for "over 400 terror-related indictments."

WHAT TERROR PLOTS?

Some might argue that the real test of the preventive paradigm is not how many crimes have been prosecuted, but how many acts of terror have been prevented. It is certainly possible that some of the administration's preventive measures have disrupted terrorist plots. But there are three reasons to be skeptical of such claims. First, there is very little hard evidence that real plots have in fact been disrupted through the preventive paradigm. Where a real plot has been disrupted, one would expect at a minimum to see prosecutions for attempts or conspiracies to engage in terrorist activity. As the above review of criminal convictions reveals, there are virtually none. Second, even where there is reason to believe that an actual plot has been disrupted, it is often difficult to assign credit for the disruption: was it the preventive paradigm or some more traditional law enforcement or intelligence initiative? The chain of causation will often be unclear. Finally, even where a preventive-paradigm initiative seems to have foiled an actual plot, the question will always remain whether the plot could have been foiled without resort to the preventive paradigm.

In October 2005 President Bush sought to defend his administration's war on terror by claiming that the "United States and our allies" had disrupted a number of terror plots, both here and abroad. He vaguely cited "the intelligence community" as his source, but immediately many in the intelligence community questioned his assertions. The *Los Angeles Times, USA Today*, and the *Washington Post* all cited intelligence officials who said the White House "overstated the gravity of the plots by saying that they had been foiled, when most were far from ready to be executed."[56] One counterterrorism official said that "we don't know how they came to the conclusions they came to. It's safe to say that most of the [intelligence] community doesn't think it's worth very much."[57]

Only three of the ten plots named by the president involved alleged attempts to attack the United States, and there are reasons to be skeptical about the administration's claims in each case. The many grounds for doubting the reality of the first plot, an alleged plan to fly an airplane into the Library Tower in Los Angeles in 2002, are discussed in the Introduction. Most tellingly, despite the president's claims that the would-be perpetrators were captured years ago, no one has ever been charged with, much less convicted of, the crime.

The second alleged attempt on the United States was described only as a mid-2003 "plot to attack East Coast targets using hijacked planes."[58] The *Los Angeles Times* reported that the "White House refused to provide additional information" on this plot and that "counterterrorism officials said they were not certain what the White House referred to."[59] FBI deputy director John Pistole said that it "was more a threat than an advanced plot."[60] Again, no one has ever been charged for this "plot."

The only other "disrupted" plot on U.S. soil was José Padilla's alleged plan to blow up an apartment by setting it on fire with the gas left on—a charge that, as noted above, the administration is not willing to try to prove in court. Thus, there is little basis to conclude that any of the three allegedly disrupted terrorist plots targeted at the United States would have gone forward absent federal intervention.[61]

In the summer of 2006 the government announced that it had disrupted two more terror plots targeted at the United States. But once again, serious questions were raised about the reality of the threats. In June, the government arrested seven men in Florida and charged them with conspiracy to levy war against the United States by discussing and planning attacks on the Sears Tower in Chicago and the FBI building in Miami. But an FBI official admitted that the plot was "more aspirational than operational," as the men had neither weapons nor explosives, and the plots had not proceeded beyond the discussion stage in any meaningful sense.[62] One of the few concrete steps the group had allegedly taken was to purchase combat boots, hardly a critical element for blowing up a building in an urban setting. They also requested horses. Their only "connection" to al-Qaeda was with a government informant pretending to be an al-Qaeda member. According to the *New York Times,* an FBI official said that "the suspects apparently did not have written information on how to make explosives, details on the layout of the Sears Tower or any known link to a terrorist group."[63]

One month later, the government announced that officials in Lebanon had arrested three men accused of plotting to bomb train tunnels between Manhattan and New Jersey. Here, too, there were questions raised about whether the plot was a real threat or merely an aspiration. Government officials admitted that the evidence consisted only of discussions on an Internet chat room site, and one official stated that the men had never even met each other in person. New York police commissioner Raymond Kelly and federal officials admitted that the men had obtained no financing or explosives for the plot, and had never even been to New York. No criminal charges were filed in the United States, suggesting that criminal prosecution here may not have been possible, even though such a conspiracy would plainly be a crime under American law.

Proponents of the preventive paradigm might respond that it is better to be too early than too late in stopping terrorist plots, and that is certainly true, to a point. But if the government intervenes so early that one cannot tell whether the plot in fact had any real likelihood of coming to pass, the costs almost certainly outweigh the benefits. When the government intervenes too early, it loses the ability to gather intelligence about the involvement of others in the plot, or indeed about whether the plot was anything more than a pipe dream. An early intervention may ultimately lead to an acquittal or a conviction only on minor charges, neither of which are likely to forestall a real terrorist threat. Sheikh Omar Abdel Rahman could have been arrested early on as a material witness, but if he had been, he would likely be a free man today, rather than safely incarcerated for life.

TORTURED INTELLIGENCE

In September 2006, President Bush acknowledged for the first time that the CIA had disappeared suspects into secret prisons and subjected them to what he euphemistically called "alternative" interrogation tactics.[64] The president sought to defend the CIA's program of disappearance and coercive interrogation by claiming that the program had elicited valuable information that had "saved lives." He traced a fairly elaborate trail of leads assertedly developed by CIA interrogators using harsh tactics that he claimed led to the capture of several al-Qaeda leaders. Here, too, however, there is reason for skepticism.

In most instances, Bush provided insufficient details to test his claims. Bush essentially asked the world to trust him. But his track record provides little reason for trust. Whether it be the missing weapons of mass destruction in Iraq, the claim that Guantánamo held only the "worst of the worst," the denial that torture has been a central part of administration policy, or the assertion that Americans would be wiretapped pursuant only to court order, few of the administration's claims in the war on terror have withstood careful analysis.

Where details are capable of being checked, there is evidence that President Bush either exaggerated or lied with respect to the role of the tortured evidence. He claimed that harsh interrogation of one of the CIA's initial detainees, Abu Zubaydah, led to the identification and capture of Khalid Sheikh Mohammed, in part by revealing that Mohammed's nickname was Mukhtar. But according to intelligence officials, the government paid an informant $25 million for the tip that actually led to Mohammed's arrest, and the CIA knew Mohammed's nickname even before 9/11.[65] Bush also claimed that Zubaydah's interrogation led to the identification of Ramzi bin al-Shibh, but as *New Republic* writer Spencer Ackerman pointed out:

> A *Nexis* search for "Ramzi Binalshibh" between September 11, 2001 and March 1, 2002—the U.S. captured Abu Zubaydah in March 2002—turns up 26 hits for *The Washington Post* alone. Everyone involved in counterterrorism knew who bin Al Shibh was. Now-retired FBI Al Qaeda hunter Dennis Lormel told Congress who Ramzi bin Al Shibh was in February 2002.[66]

Moreover, an account of Zubaydah's interrogation, contained in Ronald Suskind's *The One Percent Doctrine,* paints a very different picture. Suskind's account, which like the president's is based on unidentified CIA and FBI sources, claims that Zubaydah's mental capacity and role in al-Qaeda were both highly questionable. He quotes an FBI official as saying that Zubaydah "is insane, certifiable, split personality. . . . He knew very little about real operations, or strategy. He was expendable, you know, the greeter . . . Joe Louis in the lobby of Caesar's Palace, shaking hands." When the CIA informed the president of its doubts about Zubaydah, the president's response to Director George Tenet was, "I said he was important. You're not going to let me lose face on this, are you?"[67]

Suskind's sources confirm that Zubaydah was tortured but also suggest that he provided useful information only when the torture *stopped.*

> According to CIA sources, [Zubaydah] was water-boarded. . . .
> He was beaten, though not in a way to worsen his injuries. He was repeatedly threatened, and made certain of his impending

death. His medication was withheld. He was bombarded with deafening, continuous noise and harsh lights. He was, as a man already diminished by serious injuries, more fully at the mercy of interrogators than an ordinary prisoner. Under this duress, Zubaydah told them that shopping malls were targeted by al Qaeda. That information traveled the globe in an instant. Agents from the FBI, Secret Service, Customs, and various related agencies joined local police to surround malls. Zubaydah said banks—yes, banks—were a priority. FBI agents led officers in a race to surround and secure banks. And also supermarkets—al Qaeda was planning to blow up crowded supermarkets, several at one time. . . . And the water systems—a target, too. Nuclear plants, naturally. And apartment buildings. Thousands of uniformed men and women raced in a panic to each flavor of target. . . .

Then there was a small break. A CIA interrogator, according to sources who monitored the program, was skilled in the nuances of the Koran, and slipped under Zubaydah's skin. The al Qaeda operative believed in certain ideas of predestination— that things happen for reasons preordained. The interrogator worked this, pulling freely from the Koran. Zubaydah believed he had survived the attacks in Faisalabad, when several of his colleagues were killed, for a purpose. He was convinced that that purpose, in the fullness of time, was to offer some cooperation to his captors, something a dead man couldn't do. And he did cooperate. He gave up one body: José Padilla. . . . After a bit, Zubaydah said that Mukhtar's real name was Khalid Sheikh Mohammed.[68]

If Suskind's portrayal is correct, it appears that Zubaydah provided the details that Bush cited not in response to torture or coercion, but in response to clever, noncoercive interrogation, the kind that police routinely use—and are permitted to use— in traditional criminal investigations.

In short, the preventive paradigm in the war on terror has resulted in the detention and ethnic profiling of literally thousands of persons with no connection to terrorism, but has identified few actual terrorists. Immigration measures have come up short. Virtually all of the criminal cases in which the government has actually brought terrorism charges involve claims of material support to terrorist groups, not any actual terrorist conduct or even conspiracy to engage in terrorist conduct. Many of the government's cases have fallen apart, as, in its zeal to notch up "victories" in the war on terror, it has overcharged individuals, relied on questionable witnesses, and engaged in unethical and illegal conduct. It has yet to identify a single al-Qaeda cell within the United States. While its campaign has undoubtedly unearthed criminal conduct, immigration violations, and a handful of suspicious characters, in the end the administration has little if any basis to claim that its preventive law enforcement and intelligence-gathering measures have much, if anything, to do with the fact that there has not been another terrorist attack within the United States since the anthrax mailings shortly after 9/11.

5. THE COSTS OF OVERREACHING

Thus far, we have shown that the administration's claims of success for the preventive paradigm are hollow. But the complete picture is worse than that. It is not just that the preventive paradigm has come up with so little. There is substantial reason to believe that it has actually made us—and the world—less safe, increasing the risks of terrorism for us, our allies, and others worldwide. We are not only no better off as a result of the preventive paradigm—we are worse off.

President Bush has long boasted that the United States is waging a "global war on terror." But if that's the relevant battlefield, the numbers are especially discouraging. In April 2004, the State Department reported that terrorist incidents throughout the world had dropped in the previous year, a fact Deputy Secretary of State Richard L. Armitage promptly cited as "clear evidence that we are prevailing in the fight" against terrorism.[1] Two months later, a chagrined Secretary of State Colin Powell acknowledged that the department had miscounted, and that in fact terrorism worldwide had *increased*. For example, where the initial report stated that the number of injuries resulting from international terrorist incidents had fallen by almost one-quarter, from 2,013 in 2002 to 1,593 in 2003, the corrected report stated that in fact terrorist-related injuries had nearly doubled, to 3,646.[2]

There is no sign that matters are improving. In 2005, the State Department eliminated numbers from its annual terrorism report altogether, saying they were too difficult to track accurately. Soon thereafter, however, a leak suggested another reason for the omission: government analysts had found that international terrorist incidents worldwide had jumped threefold from 2003 levels, with 651 attacks in 2004 resulting in 1,907 deaths.[3] The National Counterterrorism Center (NCTC), using a broader definition, identified 3,192 international terrorist attacks in 2004, resulting in the "deaths, injury, or kidnapping of almost 28,500 people."[4] In 2006, the government attributed 3,000 deaths to 360 suicide bombings in 2005, a dramatic increase over historical levels. By contrast, in the five years from 2000 to 2004, there were an average of 94 suicide attacks per year.[5]

In 2006, *Foreign Policy* surveyed more than one hundred top foreign policy experts, principally former executive branch and military officials. The group was evenly divided between those who identified themselves as conservative (30), moderate (39), and liberal (30). Fully 84 percent of all experts agreed that we are not winning the war on terror, including 71 percent of those who described themselves as conservative, and 90 percent of those who described themselves as moderate; 86 percent of the experts felt that the world today is a more dangerous place for the United States and Americans than it was on 9/11.[6] Two years earlier, James Fallows reached the same conclusion, writing that "among national-security professionals there is surprisingly little controversy. Except for those in government and in the opinion industries whose job it is to defend the Administration's record, they tend to see America's response to 9/11 as a catastrophe."[7] So much for progress in the global war on terror.

The preventive paradigm has undermined our security in three fundamental ways. First, it has led to the misguided expenditure of resources on initiatives that do not protect us, diverting scarce resources from measures that would likely be more effective. Second, it has closed off long-term options for security as a consequence of poor short-term choices. Third, and most importantly, by adopting dubious means to pursue its end, it has undermined the legitimacy of the struggle against terrorism, which has in turn increased division at home, reduced the likelihood that we will find willing allies abroad, and provided ideal recruiting fodder to our adversaries, who by most accounts are stronger and more numerous than ever.

WASTED RESOURCES

The rule of law is not designed primarily for efficiency. It serves higher values, such as dignity, equality, and fundamental fairness. Nonetheless, one of its by-products is often to focus government resources on those who pose concrete threats to society. By restricting the occasions on which the state may use coercive force, and especially by requiring evidence of individualized suspicion before the state can invade privacy or deprive people of their liberty, the law helps to keep government resources trained on those who objectively pose the greatest threat. Once government abandons the objective standards of individualized suspicion and probable cause, it is free to sweep broadly—and in times of crisis, it inevitably will. That path often leads to the detention and targeting of innocent people who pose no threat at all.

History shows that the broad preventive-detention roundups that occur in times of crisis are likely to substitute the impermissible criteria of race, ethnicity, religion, political opinion, and affiliation for objective individualized suspicion of criminal activity. In 1919, the United States responded to a series of terrorist bombings by rounding up not bombers, but communists. In World War II, we responded to the fear of espionage and sabotage by sweeping up more than 110,000 Japanese Americans, most of them U.S. citizens, who were deemed suspect for nothing more than their ethnic identity. None was ultimately found to have been a spy or saboteur. In the Cold War, we turned our focus back toward communists, purportedly in the name of forestalling a Soviet-backed overthrow of the U.S. government, and extended it to "fellow travelers" who associated with suspected communists, regardless of any evidence linking them to any criminal, much less security-threatening, conduct. No more than a handful of the millions of Americans targeted by anti-communist initiatives turned out to be actual spies; none posed a real threat of violent overthrow of the government. In the Vietnam and civil rights era, the search for communists expanded to justify government infiltration and disruption of antiwar, black power, and civil rights groups. Once again, while the government swept broadly—Martin Luther King Jr. was among its prime suspects—few if any of these political activists were shown to pose any real threat to the nation.[8]

The British had similar experiences with mass preventive detention directed at suspected terrorists in Northern Ireland.[9] Following the Easter Uprising of 1916 in Dublin, the British government interned over 2,500 suspected rebels. Treatment of the internees caused public protests in Britain and the United States, and in December 1916 the government declared an amnesty. While interned, some of the rebels, including Michael Collins, used the opportunity to recruit adherents to their cause from the internees. In 1971, the British again rounded up 342 suspected terrorists, some of whom turned out to be in their eighties. Apparently most of the IRA leaders had been tipped off and were not captured. Large numbers of the detained were released after being questioned. As one historian of the period concluded, "internment barely damaged the IRA's command structure, and led to a flood of recruits, money and weapons. It was a farce."[10]

Each of these eras is remembered for widespread violations of basic civil rights and liberties. What is often overlooked, however, is the more practical consideration that vast resources were wasted by directing government coercion not at those whose conduct posed a genuine threat, but at those deemed guilty or suspicious on the basis of group identity or political ideology.

The aftermath of 9/11 was no different. As noted above, the administration launched a nationwide ethnic-profiling campaign that targeted approximately 90,000 Arab and Muslim men, netted not a single individual convicted of a terrorist offense, and no doubt cost millions of dollars. Had the government responded in a more targeted fashion, it would not have

wasted so many resources on the innocent, and could have re-
directed its resources toward more long-lasting and concrete
investments in security, by, for example, protecting vulnerable
targets or shoring up the capabilities of first responders.

Similarly, FBI agents have protested that President Bush's
NSA warrantless-wiretapping program generated hundreds of
bad leads, forcing them to devote scarce resources to tracking
down information that led to dead ends.[11] Sweeping surveillance
programs will inevitably gather vast amounts of useless information, and the resources required to sort through the chaff to
find the wheat might be better spent focusing on those whom
the government actually has an evidentiary basis for suspecting.

One effect of the Foreign Intelligence Surveillance Act (FISA)
is to focus surveillance before vast amounts of useless information are gathered, and before individual privacy is invaded. FISA
permits wiretapping for foreign intelligence or national security
purposes. It does not require evidence of wrongdoing, but it
does require some showing that the targeted individual is an
"agent of a foreign power," which includes members of international terrorist organizations. That showing must generally be
reviewed by a federal judge before approval to wiretap is
granted. In addition to protecting the privacy of innocent persons, these statutory requirements focus the energy and resources of intelligence agencies on those who are most likely to
be foreign agents. Where these requirements are bypassed, as
under the administration's NSA program, the number of false
leads will inevitably rise, and as the FBI complaints illustrate,
that increase imposes further costs down the line, not only on
the privacy of those unnecessarily intruded upon, but on the resources of the intelligence and law enforcement agencies.

FORECLOSING OPTIONS

In addition to wasting scarce resources on individuals who pose
no threat, the preventive paradigm may undermine or foreclose

altogether certain long-term security options. In dealing with al-Qaeda, it is especially important to think long-term, as the organization—or more accurately now, the movement—has already demonstrated a tenacious ability to survive and adapt. The same is true for the more generalized threat of catastrophic terrorism. That threat stems more from the increased availability of the technology for weapons of mass destruction than from any particular group. Even if al-Qaeda disappeared, that technological reality would remain. Protecting against terrorism is a decidedly long-term challenge. Yet the Bush administration's preventive paradigm, despite its avowedly forward-looking orientation, has repeatedly made poor short-term decisions that have sacrificed our long-term security interests.

As the discussion of José Padilla's case in Chapter 3 illustrates, the decision to use inhumane and degrading interrogation methods has already forced the administration to forego the prosecution of serious crimes because it obtained evidence by tainted interrogation methods. Some might argue that this cost would be worth bearing if interrogators were able to identify and defuse a ticking time bomb. But the information the United States has sought is generally not of an emergency nature—after all, how could a detainee who has been held incommunicado for months or years at Guantánamo or in a CIA black site have information about a *ticking* time bomb? Instead, the information sought is more systemic in nature: who plays what role in the organization, where are its safe houses, how does it operate in the field, what codes and methods does it use for communications, what are its sources and avenues for financing, where is it focusing its recruitment efforts, and the like.

That information is undeniably valuable, but if one long-term goal is, as President Bush has repeatedly said, to bring the terrorists to justice, then using coercive methods of interrogation is virtually certain to backfire because the information obtained will be unusable. The bind in which the administration finds itself is illustrated by the fact that despite its claims to have captured two-thirds to three-quarters of al-Qaeda's leadership since 9/11, not a single al-Qaeda leader has been held accountable for any wrongdoing.

Administration supporters will argue that focusing on bringing al-Qaeda leaders to justice reflects an outmoded, pre-9/11 mindset. But short of summary executions, there is no realistic alternative. As the world's reaction to Guantánamo has made clear, we cannot hold detainees forever without some sort of trial. Under the laws of war, a nation can hold enemy combatants for as long as the conflict continues. But in that scenario, the individuals can look forward to being repatriated at war's end. If we defeated al-Qaeda by capturing or killing all of its leaders and fighters, we would then be required to release all our al-Qaeda suspects—thereby likely restarting the conflict. If the fighting against al-Qaeda continues indefinitely, neither the international community—nor, for that matter, U.S. courts—are likely to tolerate indefinite, lifetime detention of alleged terrorists without trial. Thus, the only acceptable long-term solution is to hold al-Qaeda operatives responsible in fair trials for the crimes that they have committed—and that is likely to be impossible if so much of our information about al-Qaeda stems from coerced interrogations.

Similarly, President Bush's decision to bypass FISA—and Congress—in secretly authorizing the NSA to conduct warrantless wiretapping on Americans has long-term security costs. Consider, for example, the reaction of the judges who head the secret court known as the Foreign Intelligence Surveillance Court, which reviews requests for all national security and foreign intelligence searches and wiretaps under FISA. When the chief FISA judges learned of the NSA program, they instructed the administration not to submit *any* applications for court-approved surveillance based on information derived from the NSA program.[12] Thus, if the NSA developed evidence through its program that an individual was a member of a terrorist organization, it could not use that information to authorize further surveillance under FISA.

The NSA's extralegal character is also likely to have had costly consequences in terms of intelligence analysis and coordination. One of the most frequent criticisms of the pre-9/11 relationship between law enforcement and intelligence agencies was that they failed to share information. And one of the most commonly cited causes for this failure was "the wall," an administrative practice in which, out of (often unfounded) concern about violating FISA, law enforcement and intelligence agencies acted as if there were a wall between them, literally barring them from sharing information. In fact, there were many other causes for the failure to share information, chief among them a general distrust between the agencies and an understandable concern for protecting sources. But "the wall" was nonetheless often cited by Bush administration officials as a real impediment to "connecting the dots."

Ironically, by secretly authorizing the NSA program, President Bush effectively erected a new wall. Since the administration was not allowed to use any information obtained from the NSA program in any way to develop an application for a FISA wiretap or search, law enforcement and intelligence agents must have had to create a new wall between the NSA and intelligence and law enforcement agents using FISA to investigate terrorism. Similar concerns would likely have mandated a wall between federal prosecutors and the NSA, because if information obtained through an NSA warrantless wiretap led to information introduced against a defendant in a criminal case, it would jeopardize both the admissibility of the evidence and the secrecy of the NSA program.

The decision to authorize the NSA program in violation of FISA has also had other significant costs. The administration has expressed concern that the extensive public discussion of the NSA program has compromised its utility by tipping off al-

Qaeda. But if that is the concern, the administration has only itself to blame. The program has garnered so much public attention because of the way the administration implemented it—bypassing the courts and Congress and unilaterally ordering conduct that violates federal law. Had the administration proposed amendments to FISA as one more section of the wide-ranging Patriot Act in 2001, there would have been some public debate about the program, but if the program was as limited as the administration has described it, it would not have been controversial. Moreover, had the administration sought judicial approval for its wiretaps from the FISA courts initially, instead of waiting to do so until the program had been publicly disclosed, there might well have been no public exposure at all. In short, it was the lawless way that the administration proceeded that is responsible for the public attention the NSA program has received.

Preventive detention and preemptive prosecutions also often close off more long-term security options. When government officials are investigating an ongoing criminal conspiracy, the last thing they generally want to do is lock up the individuals under investigation. As long as the suspects remain free, they offer the potential for further intelligence gathering. A wiretap on a suspect's phone will disclose his contacts, and may provide reliable, firsthand intelligence as to the scope of the operation, the identity of other participants, and the group's future plans. If one of the participants can be encouraged to turn state's evidence, or if an undercover agent or informant can infiltrate the conspirators' group, he or she may be able to develop still more intelligence.

By contrast, when a suspect is arrested and detained "preventively," the threat he poses may be neutralized in the short term, but any further intelligence about his compatriots is likely to be much more difficult to obtain. Those working with him are put on notice that the government is aware of the plot. Tapping the suspect's phone or following him as he visits co-conspirators is no longer an option. It was for this reason that eight former high-level FBI officials criticized the Bush administration's roundups after 9/11. William Webster, former director of both the FBI and the CIA, explained that an effective counterterrorism investigation often involves lengthy surveillance, "so when you roll up the cell, you know you've got the whole group." When, by contrast, arrests are made prematurely, "you may interrupt something, but you may not be able to bring it down. You may not be able to stop what is going on." [13]

The general point should be clear. Acting preventively in disregard of the rule of law tends to cut off subsequent options and trigger legal sanctions that limit the utility of information or evidence obtained through the initial preventive measure. The Bush administration, eager to incapacitate potential terrorists and gather "actionable intelligence" to prevent future attacks, locked up thousands of individuals who posed no risk of terrorism whatsoever, and then gathered intelligence in ways that rendered much of the information unusable for perhaps the most important long-range goal of the conflict with al-Qaeda— bringing its leaders to justice and holding them accountable for the atrocities that they have committed.

SACRIFICING LEGITIMACY, GENERATING RESENTMENT

- Shortly before the first anniversary of the London subway and bus bombings of July 7, 2005, al-Qaeda released a recruitment video. It featured a young American convert to Islam, Adam Gadahn. Instead of ranting against the West, Gadahn argued calmly that people should join al-Qaeda's struggle because of the way the United States has treated Muslims. He criticized the United States for attacking and killing civilians in Iraq, for capturing Muslims and relegating them to Guantánamo, and for handing them over "to the American and British-backed despotic regimes of the Islamic world to be brutally interrogated." In short, he invoked our own tactics—indiscriminate attacks, indefinite detention, inhumane treatment, and renditions—as reasons to rally against us, and in support of al-Qaeda.[14]

- "You should have seen his cell phone." A young Muslim man we met in Florida was describing his encounter with a young boy in a pharmacy in a rural town in Saudi Arabia in 2005. The boy did not speak English, but he was evidently very eager to show our American friend his cell phone. On the screen were brutal torture images from Abu Ghraib. "When young boys have images of Abu Ghraib on their cell phones, you know we are in trouble," said our friend.

- The day after the *Washington Post* broke the story about the CIA's secret detention centers, Russia issued a press release claiming that it had nothing to do with the secret prisons.[15] (The previous day's news had reported that some of the detention centers were based in eastern Europe, although it did not identify specific countries.)

- In June 2005, an Italian judge signed warrants for the arrest of thirteen officers and operatives of the Central Intelligence Agency, accusing them of abducting an Egyptian cleric from a city street in Milan two years earlier, and rendering him to Egypt for questioning. The Italians had been investigating the cleric with the help of U.S. intelligence officials. As one senior Italian investigator said, "we do feel quite betrayed that this operation was carried out in our city, . . . undermining an entire operation."[16]

- In early 2007, a German court issued arrest warrants for thirteen CIA agents for their part in the rendition of German citizen Khaled al-Masri.[17]

The deepest and most long-lasting consequence of the sacrifices we have made in the name of the preventive paradigm is to the legitimacy of the struggle against terrorism itself. Once a leading exponent of the rule of law, the United States is now widely viewed as a systematic and arrogant violator of the most basic norms of human rights law—including the prohibitions against torture, disappearances, and arbitrary detention. That loss of legitimacy in turn makes us more vulnerable to terrorist attacks, as it makes cooperation with others in our defense more difficult and fuels the animus and resentment that inspire the attacks against us in the first place. As the bipartisan 9-11 Commission recognized, the fight against terrorism is fundamentally a struggle for hearts and minds. There is no alternative, because there is no way to build a fortress that will repel all terrorist attacks. By throwing aside fundamental precepts of the rule of law, the preventive paradigm makes it that much more difficult for the United States to appeal to the hearts and minds of those who might turn against us.

As the world's strongest superpower, it is particularly important that the United States be seen to act legitimately and fairly. Our disproportionate share of power is itself likely to make other nations and their citizens wary. If we are seen as using that authority responsibly, in accordance with international law, to shore up rather than to break down the rule of law, in ways that respect the concerns of other nations and of human dignity, we are more likely to be seen as legitimate. As any leader instinctively knows, it is far better to have people follow your lead because they view you as legitimate than to have to try to compel others by force to adhere to your will.

The goal of defending ourselves against terrorist attacks is unquestionably legitimate. No one disputes the right of a nation to protect itself against attacks on its soil, much less against attacks on its innocent civilians. The world recognized that the United States suffered a grievous armed attack on 9/11, and widely supported our military response in Afghanistan. But when one pursues a legitimate end through illegitimate means, one sacrifices the legitimacy of the enterprise. No matter how just it is to seek to protect civilians from terrorist attacks, the effort will not be viewed as legitimate if it relies on torture, coercive interrogation, waging war against those who have not attacked or threatened to attack us, renditions, and indefinite detention without hearings.

The cost of sacrificing legitimacy begins at home. When

the administration advances aggressive assertions of executive power, it unnecessarily sows division. For example, had President Bush sought congressional or judicial approval for his NSA spying program at the outset, instead of bypassing Congress and the courts, the program would likely have garnered widespread support. A strong leader seeks to unite the nation when it faces serious threats—actions like the NSA spying program have unnecessarily divided us. That division in itself is costly, for a nation deeply divided is likely to be less effective in marshaling its resources against a common enemy.

More generally, because it so radically challenges basic commitments to the rule of law, the preventive paradigm is likely to erode trust in government at the very moment when trust is most needed. Trust is particularly essential during a military conflict or other national security crisis. In such periods, the government by necessity cannot share all the information it has about the threat that it faces, but at the same time needs the support of the population in mobilizing an effective response. The only way to obtain that support without being able to show in detail the nature of the threat is by building trust. But when the administration is shown time and time again to have pursued initiatives of questionable legitimacy, and to have broadly invoked secrecy to evade accountability, trust will inevitably erode.

Nowhere is the maintenance of trust more important than in Arab and Muslim communities within the United States. Given al-Qaeda's ideological commitments and ethnic makeup, al-Qaeda operatives are likely to seek support from these communities, as did the al-Qaeda leader who convinced the young men from Lackawanna, New York, to attend an al-Qaeda training camp. Our law enforcement agents need to work closely with Arab and Muslim communities if they are to develop the intelligence necessary to identify, monitor, and counteract potential threats therein. But if members of these communities feel that they have been unfairly targeted in a broad-brush way for little more than their ethnic and religious identities, cooperation will be difficult. As Sadullah Khan, director of the Islamic Center of Irvine, California, told the *Washington Post* in 2007, "How much cooperation can we give . . . at the same time we ourselves are part of the problem in [their] eyes?" [18]

The sweeping roundups and widespread profiling conducted in the first two years after 9/11, coupled with the continuing perception that authorities have selectively directed a zero-tolerance policy at their communities ever since, have made Arabs and Muslims understandably nervous about coming forward. As Britain has learned, the cost of distrust is not merely in foregone intelligence; the British were shocked to learn that the July 7, 2005, suicide bombers were young men born and raised in Great Britain itself. The Arab and Muslim population in the United States is as a general matter more integrated and less alienated than their counterparts in Europe, but that fact only underscores the opportunities federal officials have squandered by treating these communities as suspect.

The negative consequences of illegitimate initiatives are not limited to a divided domestic polity. There can be little doubt that the administration's "war on terror" has radically undermined the United States' standing throughout the world. Even before the administration launched its preventive war against Iraq, much of the world had come to view the United States' actions in the war on terror with deep skepticism and antagonism. A Pew Research poll conducted in 2002 found that 80 percent of French citizens, 85 percent of Germans, 68 percent of Italians, and 73 percent of the British felt that the United States was acting mainly in its own interest in the war on terror, while only small minorities thought the United States was taking into account the views of its allies. [19] Another 2002 study found that favorable attitudes toward the United States had fallen in nineteen of twenty-seven countries polled. [20] More than half of the people in all of the following countries felt that U.S. foreign policy did not consider the interests of others: Canada, Great Britain, Italy, France, Poland, Ukraine, Czech Republic,

Slovak Republic, Russia, Bulgaria, Jordan, Lebanon, Egypt, Turkey, Mexico, Brazil, Argentina, Japan, South Korea, and Senegal. Majorities in Jordan, Lebanon, Egypt, Turkey, Indonesia, South Korea, and Senegal opposed the U.S.-led war on terror.[21]

The cause of these reactions—even before the Iraq War—is no mystery. Foreign press and foreign governments alike have been highly critical of many of the administration's coercive preventive measures, most of which have, after all, been selectively targeted at foreign nationals and expressly defended on that ground. It would be difficult to name a single country, friend or foe, that has *not* criticized the mistreatment of detainees at Guantánamo and in Iraq. Similarly, the administration's post-9/11 campaign of ethnic and religious profiling sparked widespread resentment, especially in the countries whose nationals were targeted by the program—the very countries we need to work most closely with.[22]

To fight an international foe like al-Qaeda, we need international cooperation. We do not have the resources, contacts, or cultural expertise to identify and assess risks that might arise in any of literally dozens of nations around the world. Yet because an attack could be planned and launched from almost anywhere, we need to develop wide-ranging intelligence. The only way to do that is to work with the citizenry and intelligence agencies of other nations. For this reason, both Stansfield Turner, former director of Central Intelligence, and Paul Pillar, former deputy chief of the CIA's Counterterrorism Center, have argued that success in countering terrorism critically depends on fostering strong relationships with foreign governments and their intelligence agencies.[23] Strong relationships—with governments, intelligence agents, or ordinary citizens—depend on trust. And trust is precisely what is lost when the United States is viewed as acting illegitimately, in particular toward Arabs and Muslims.

Disregarding basic principles of the rule of law also provides cover for other nations that may be only too happy to follow suit, and that in turn can raise security costs for the United States. As Human Rights Watch has reported in its annual World Reports, since 9/11 many repressive regimes around the world have used the United States' shortcuts in the war on terror as license to adopt their own harshly coercive measures, often directed not at terrorists but at dissidents or opposition parties.[24] Such repression invariably breeds resentment among those targeted or those associated with the targeted groups, and increases the likelihood that the opposition will turn to violent means. Moreover, to the extent that a nation's repressive measures are seen as linked to the United States, it plays into the hands of the propaganda of al-Qaeda and other violent extremists who seek to portray the United States as responsible for repression far beyond its borders.

Perhaps most fundamentally, when we sacrifice legitimacy, we drive bystanders into the terrorists' camp. Terrorists cannot hope to win a straight-out military struggle, so they instead fight an ideological battle. Their attacks are designed to trigger overreaction from the nation under attack, and they then use that overreaction to garner support for their cause. The al-Qaeda videotape described above chillingly illustrates the phenomenon, as the speaker calmly cites our own tactics as justification for supporting al-Qaeda. That young children are now carrying images of Abu Ghraib around on their cell phones points to the fallacy of the preventive paradigm; when we sweep away the rules in the name of preventing the next attack, we foster the conditions that make the next attack that much more likely.

The very terminology of the "global war on terrorism" further fuels this problem. The term "war on terror" suggests that there is a legitimate military conflict going on, in which both sides have a right to fight. As a matter of law, that is not the case—al-Qaeda has no "right" to fight. By treating them as enemies in war rather than as international criminals, we have inadvertently raised their status. By contrast, the British steadfastly

refused to accept the Irish Republican Army's efforts to characterize their struggle as a war, because the British understood
that such a label would legitimize IRA violence.

At the same time, the administration's "global" rhetoric of
good and evil reinforces al-Qaeda's message that this is a conflict
between Islam and the West, and gives credence to the view that
a suicide bomber in Cairo, Chechnya, or Jerusalem is striking a
blow in a "global jihad" against the United States and the West.
The administration's insistence that the "war" is not simply
against al-Qaeda, but against all terrorist organizations of potentially global reach, gives other terrorist organizations an incentive to band together and treat us as the enemy.[25] As former
NSC counterterrorism experts Daniel Benjamin and Steven
Simon have noted, jihadist ideology is now spread through
thousands of Internet websites, which reproduce images of terrorist attacks around the world in an attempt to gain support for
the terrorists' causes.[26] By casting al-Qaeda as the center of a
worldwide movement in which all terrorism is somehow connected, we play into its own grandiose self-perceptions and reinforce al-Qaeda's mystique for potential sympathizers around the
world. By responding to al-Qaeda's attack by declaring "war on
terror," we have unwittingly helped to transform al-Qaeda from
a relatively discrete organization headquartered in Afghanistan
and Pakistan into a decentralized, widely dispersed global political movement, in many ways more difficult to monitor, confront, and neutralize. As the bombings in Madrid and London
illustrate, the next attack is as likely, if not more likely, to come
from individuals inspired by al-Qaeda's propaganda—with limited or no actual connection to al-Qaeda itself.

In sum, there is little evidence that the preventive paradigm has
made us safer and considerable grounds for concluding that we
are in fact worse off. What progress has been made in the war on
terror is likely attributable to traditional law enforcement and
military tactics, most significantly the military mission against

al-Qaeda in Afghanistan. The administration's coercive preventive measures, by contrast, have largely come up short. We have not brought a single al-Qaeda leader to justice and have subjected many al-Qaeda suspects and innocent people to abuse that may well make it impossible ever to do so.

There is admittedly an inescapable degree of uncertainty here. One cannot know whether any of the "plots" President Bush claims were "disrupted" would ever have come to fruition in any event. "Better safe than sorry" is the administration's mantra, and it makes sense where there is solid evidence of concrete plans. But when that impulse leads to the arrests, renditions, military detentions, and pretextual prosecutions of thousands who pose no actual concrete threat, and about whom officials merely have vague, factually unsupported suspicions, it is far from clear that we are better off. Resources spent targeting people who do not pose a threat could be better spent on initiatives that might actually make us safer. Breaking the rules now makes holding others accountable for breaking the rules later difficult if not impossible. And when "preventive" actions appear to be selectively targeted at particular segments of the population—in this case, Arabs and Muslims—they generate resentment toward authorities in those communities. The preventive paradigm has generated substantial negative costs, created corrosive distrust toward American law enforcement within Arab and Muslim communities within the United States, and sparked intense and unprecedented anti-Americanism abroad. In short, we are not only less free, but less safe, as a result of the preventive paradigm.

6. THE FAILURE OF PREVENTIVE WAR

On May 1, 2004, President Bush, dressed in a flight suit, landed aboard the aircraft carrier USS *Abraham Lincoln* to declare Saddam Hussein's ouster a "victory in the war on terror."[1] Later that month, he told a Polish broadcast interviewer that "we found the weapons of mass destruction."[2] Since then, over three thousand Americans and at least ten to twenty times as many Iraqis have died in Iraq, and we still haven't found any weapons of mass destruction.[3] Undertaken in the name of keeping Americans safe, the Iraq War is widely seen as a security disaster: it has diverted billions of dollars and massive resources from pursuing al-Qaeda and other threats, inspired many to become terrorists, provided an invaluable training ground for those who do become terrorists, bogged down the U.S. military, and dramatically increased anti-American sentiment around the world. Meanwhile, the war has motivated Iran and North Korea to accelerate their development of weapons of mass destruction in order to deter another "preventive" attack by the United States, while at the same time assuring these countries that, given the resources tied up in Iraq, there is no way the United States could respond militarily in the short term to such efforts. As an initial test of the preventive-war doctrine, the Iraq War has been a spectacular failure. That failure cannot be dismissed as the product of a few unfortunate missteps, but reflects deeper, intrinsic problems with the preventive-war doctrine itself.

"FIGHTING THEM OVER THERE": THE IRAQ WAR AND U.S. SECURITY

There is little disagreement among security experts that the war in Iraq has undermined the struggle against terrorism. As James

Fallows reports, "it is hard to find a counterterrorism specialist who thinks that the Iraq war has reduced rather than increased the threat to the United States."[4] A 2006 bipartisan survey of more than one hundred top U.S. foreign policy experts found that 87 percent agreed that the war in Iraq has made the American people more vulnerable to global terrorist networks.[5] In April 2006, a classified National Intelligence Estimate, representing the consensus views of all sixteen federal spy agencies, concluded that the "the Iraq conflict has become the 'cause célèbre' for jihadists, breeding a deep resentment of US involvement in the Muslim world and cultivating supporters for the global jihadist movement."[6] Harvard University terrorism expert Jessica Stern put it most succinctly when she concluded that the United States "has taken a country that was not a terrorist threat and turned it into one."[7]

The damage to our security done by the war in Iraq takes many forms. The invasion of a predominantly Muslim Middle Eastern nation that had neither attacked us nor threatened an imminent attack has inspired a powerful and resilient insurgency within Iraq. The scale and tenacity of the insurgency has made a mockery of U.S. prewar plans, which predicted that we would have as few as 35,000 troops in Iraq by the fall of 2003. Instead, as of early 2007, we still had over 140,000 troops in Iraq, the president's "surge" had added 20,000 more, and the army had to extend enlistments involuntarily and drop its standards for recruitment in order to meet its personnel needs.[8] Even so, there are serious questions about the adequacy of our troop levels, but the war is so unpopular that seriously increasing our military presence there or instituting a draft here are politically out of the question.

Administration officials predicted that American troops would be welcomed in Baghdad as liberators. Instead, overwhelming majorities in the Sunni community, and even a significant percentage of Shiites, view the United States as an occupier, not a liberator.[9] For many Iraqis, President Bush's declaration at the war's outset that the "day of your liberation is near" had an all too familiar ring, echoing British Major General Stanley Maude's line upon entering Baghdad in 1917 that "our armies do not come into your cities and lands as conquerors or enemies but as liberators." [10] In both cases, Western invasion and occupation inspired a bitterly tenacious insurgency. As Pulitzer Prize–winning journalist Anthony Shadid reports, most of the Iraqi insurgents share a "religious ideology that, in message and appeal, was a direct consequence of [the U.S.] occupation." [11]

The reservoir of insurgents in Iraq appears to be almost limitless. The Brookings Institution estimates that as of January 2004 there were 3,000 to 5,000 insurgents. By January 2005, the insurgency's estimated strength had grown to 18,000, despite the fact that an estimated 25,000 insurgents were killed or detained in 2004. By that count, the insurgency found 43,000 new adherents in 2004 alone. The trend has continued. In 2005, another 25,000 insurgents were estimated to have been killed or captured, yet by January 2006 insurgent strength was effectively unchanged, at 15,000 to 20,000. The average number of daily insurgent attacks, meanwhile, grew from 61 per day in January 2005 to 180 per day in October 2006.[12] While these Brookings estimates are necessarily rough, they suggest that killing or capturing a large number of insurgents will not end the insurgency.

In addition to the growing and increasingly violent opposition among Iraqis, the war has also attracted many foreign fighters. The majority of these fighters appear to be not hardened terrorist veterans but new recruits to global jihad drawn to the struggle by the Iraq War.[13] The Israeli scholar Rueben Paz analyzed the biographies of 154 foreigners killed in Iraq and found that "the vast majority of [non-Iraqi] Arabs killed in Iraq have never taken part in any terrorist activity prior to their arrival in Iraq." [14] Similarly, a Saudi study of some three hundred Saudis captured in Iraq and three dozen killed in suicide attacks found that most were moved to embrace radical jihad by the conflict in Iraq.[15] Our invasion of Iraq has created a new generation of terrorists. And as CIA director Porter Goss warned in 2005, many of these new terrorists will eventually take the training they gain in Iraq and put it to use elsewhere by targeting American and Western targets—much as the Afghanistan mujahedin, the guerrillas whom we trained and supported in fighting the Soviet Union, eventually turned and attacked us, in Nairobi, Kenya, Yemen, and New York City.[16]

The war against al-Qaeda and the Taliban in Afghanistan closed down al-Qaeda's training camps, but by invading Iraq we opened a much more effective, realistic, and deadly training camp there (while simultaneously allowing al-Qaeda to regroup in the hills of Pakistan). Iraq has provided terrorists with real-time experience in urban guerrilla warfare, and, as noted in the Introduction, has helped Iraqi insurgents to hone their terrorist skills—recruiting and deploying suicide bombers, building more powerful bombs, improving their intelligence and infiltration tactics, and developing more sophisticated plans of attack.[17]

The insurgents have benefited from access to large caches of Saddam Hussein's arms, most of which the U.S. military failed to secure. While Iraq had no weapons of mass destruction, the size of its conventional weapons arsenal astounded even military experts. There were approximately 130 known Iraqi ammunition storage points, some of which were bigger than towns and held an estimated six hundred thousand tons of artillery shells, rockets, aviation bombs, and other ordnance. As of early 2006 most were still unsecured.[18] In October 2004, the *New York Times* reported that 380 tons of high explosives HMX and RDX had disappeared from an Iraqi weapons site called al-Qaqaa. RDX, or Royal Demolition Explosive, was the type of explosive used in the USS *Cole* bombing. Two experts have calculated that the "amount lifted from al-Qaqaa would be enough to sink the entire U.S. Navy twice over."[19] HMX, or High Melting Explosive, is a perfect detonator for a nuclear device, or for attacks on large buildings, because it is twice as powerful as an ordinary explosive and not easily set off by accident.[20] U.S. troops also left un-

guarded another major Iraqi nuclear facility called Tuwaitha despite the pleas of IAEA chief Mohamed ElBaradei to secure nuclear material stored there.[21]

The war in Iraq has also led to increased terrorist acts beyond
Iraq. A report by Britain's top intelligence and law enforcement
officials concluded that "events in Iraq are continuing to act as
motivation and a focus of a range of terrorist related activity in
the U.K."[22] That analysis was seconded by the Royal Institute of
International Affairs, an influential private research organization in Britain, which concluded that Britain's participation in
the war in Iraq had made it more vulnerable to terrorist attack. A
videotaped statement by one of the four British Muslims involved in the July 7, 2005, suicide-bomb attacks on London's
transportation system said the attacks were motivated by images
of Muslims being killed in Iraq.[23] Similarly, a perpetrator in a
failed London bombing told his Italian captors that the bombers
prepared for the attacks by watching "films on the war in Iraq."[24]
So too, the March 11, 2004, Madrid train bombings, which
killed 191 people and injured over a thousand, were carried out
by a terrorist cell whose members had virtually no prior terrorist experience or training, but who were enraged by the war in
Iraq. Reportedly, the "decisive bit of inspiration" for the Madrid
bombings were two bin Laden tapes urging attacks against "the
countries that participate in this unjust war," and specifically
mentioning Spain.[25]

The Iraq War has widely reinforced the Islamic jihadists' contention that the United States is an overly aggressive and anti-
Islamic power. Counterterrorism experts Daniel Benjamin and
Steven Simon argue that the "foremost effect of the invasion was
inadvertently to affirm the jihadist argument."[26] As the former
U.S. diplomat John Brady Kiesling has written, "the more ag-
gressively we use our power to intimidate our foes, the more foes
we create and the more we validate terrorism as the only effective weapon of the powerless against the powerful."[27]

The popularity of *Metal Storm*, one of the best-selling books in Turkish history, vividly illustrates the anti-Americanism that the invasion has promoted in the Islamic world. The book's plot features a U.S. surprise attack on Turkey in 2007, which Turkey repulses by enlisting help from the European Union and its old enemy, Russia. The book, reports the *Christian Science Monitor,* "is clearly sold as fiction, but its premise has entered Turkey's discourse in a way that sometimes seems to blur the line between fantasy and reality." [28] The Turkish political elite keenly read the book, leading an American diplomat to admit that "we're really pulling our hair out trying to figure how to deal with this." [29]

Metal Storm's success reflects the fact that Turkish citizens, like those of many other Muslim nations, view the United States as an aggressor nation. Majorities in each of four predominantly Muslim countries surveyed by the Pew Global Attitudes Project in 2005 expressed concern that U.S. military power may be turned against them, including 67 percent of Jordanians, 65 percent of Turks, 80 percent of Indonesians, and most disturbingly, given its nuclear capabilities, powerful radical opposition, and precarious government, 71 percent of Pakistanis. [30] The enmity is so deep that one year after the invasion of Iraq, a majority of Jordanians and Moroccans, and a substantial minority in Turkey and Pakistan, thought that suicide bombings against Americans and other Westerners in Iraq were justifiable. [31] Majorities in all four of these nations doubted the sincerity of the war on terrorism and believed that it was an effort to control Mideast oil and dominate the world. [32]

While Americans might dismiss such views as misguided or misinformed, they nonetheless have real consequences for our security. The fact that so many people in the Islamic world feel that suicide bombings against Americans are justified makes them more likely to support terrorist operations and less likely to cooperate with American efforts to bring would-be terrorists to justice. As Benjamin and Simon have argued, one needs to view the terrorist threat as concentric circles. The inner circle, relatively small, consists of those already committed to engaging in terrorist attacks. Outside that circle is a much larger ring, composed of people who share many of the inner circle's ideological commitments and deep-rooted frustrations, and who are therefore at risk of moving into the inner core.[33] Given this reality, an effective response to terrorism needs to focus not only on capturing or killing the inner circle of terrorists but also, at least as importantly, on limiting migration from the outer to the inner circle. The Iraq War has done virtually nothing to further the goal of capturing or killing the inner circle, since before we attacked their country Iraqis posed no real threat of terrorism to us. On the contrary, by all accounts al-Qaeda has exploited the Iraq War to transform outer-circle fundamentalists into inner-circle militants.[34] "A price that's being paid for this intervention," claims one former Bush administration senior official, is that "Iraq has become a magnet for anti-Western, anti-American beliefs."[35]

President Bush's principal response is that "we are fighting them over there so that we don't have to fight them here at home."[36] But that slogan ignores the obvious fact that if we were not occupying Iraq, the Iraqi insurgents and many of the foreign militants would not be fighting us at all, here or there. The more appropriate strategic question is whether our actions are helping al-Qaeda and other anti-American terrorist groups recruit more terrorists than we are killing or capturing. With respect to the invasion of Iraq, the answer to that question is almost certainly yes.

These unfortunate consequences were entirely foreseeable. Our own intelligence community predicted that war and occupation would increase sympathy for the terrorists' objectives and make Iraq a magnet for extremists throughout the Middle East.[37] Paul Pillar, the CIA's top analyst for the Middle East during the run-up to the war, explains that

> the assessment was that the terrorists would get a boost, though not just in recruitment. The war would expand popular support

for some terrorist objectives, probably expand financial contributions, and be portrayed as validating some of the terrorists' propaganda. Al Qaeda would endeavor to capitalize on the situation by accelerating or expanding operations.[38]

Before the war began, a senior American intelligence officer observed that the looming American invasion was already being used as "a recruitment tool by al Qaeda and other groups. . . . And it is a very effective tool."[39] British intelligence agents concurred, advising Prime Minister Blair before the war that "al-Qaida and associated groups continue to represent by far the greatest threat to western interests, and that threat would be heightened by military action against Iraq."[40] As one U.S. expert on bin Laden, Peter Bergen, points out, the U.S. attack on Iraq was a propaganda gift that "bin Laden could not have imagined in his wildest dreams." Bergen explains: "The United States invaded an oil-rich Muslim nation in the heart of the Middle East, the very type of imperial adventure that bin Laden has long predicted is the 'Crusaders' long-term goal in the region."[41]

At the same time that our undertaking in Iraq has contributed to a dramatic growth in terrorism there and around the world, it has reduced our ability to respond effectively to the increased threat. Army morale has clearly suffered; a poll of U.S. troops in Iraq conducted in January and February 2006 found that over 70 percent of the service members believed that the United States should withdraw completely from Iraq within a year and only 23 percent felt we should "stay as long as needed."[42] Since the invasion, increasing numbers of young army officers are leaving the service as soon as their initial commitment is fulfilled.[43] The army fell more than 6,600 recruits short of its goal of enlisting 80,000 troops in 2005, the first time it missed its annual target since 1999 and the largest shortfall in twenty-six years.[44] A 2006 report commissioned by the Pentagon warned that the U.S. army was being stretched by its deployment in Iraq and Afghanistan into a "thin green line" that could easily break.[45]

Preparation for the war diverted much of the intelligence community's attention from al-Qaeda to Iraq. As Paul Pillar has pointed out, feeding the administration's "voracious appetite" for information on Iraqi weapons of mass destruction and on the presumed Iraq–al-Qaeda link consumed an enormous amount of the intelligence community's time and attention. To Pillar, "it is fair to ask how much other counterterrorism work was left undone as a result."[46]

The cost of the Iraq War has been enormous, in lives lost, soldiers and civilians wounded, and economic resources wasted. As noted above, by February 2007, over three thousand Americans and at least ten to twenty times that number of Iraqis had died in the war, while tens of thousands more had been wounded.[47] Official figures put the direct cost of the war through December 2006 at approximately $400 billion, and climbing by approximately $8 billion each month.[48] In 2005, the Congressional Budget Office estimated the war's eventual total cost as between $400 billion and $600 billion.[49] Independent experts put the cost even higher. Nobel Prize–winning economist Joseph Stiglitz estimates that the total economic cost could actually run to $2 trillion.[50] Stiglitz's study includes direct and indirect costs not included in the official budgetary estimates, such as long-term costs for lifetime disability and health care for over 16,000 injured soldiers, one-fifth of whom have serious brain or spinal injuries, and the cost of repairs on and replacement of military equipment.[51]

Resources and energy siphoned off to the Iraq War could have been better spent hunting al-Qaeda, reinforcing protections at U.S. borders, ports, and potential targets, protecting nuclear weapons sites in the former Soviet Union, and rebuilding and developing Afghanistan to decrease the likelihood that terrorists will find fertile ground there. For example, while Hong Kong uses American technology to scan all containers that pass through two of its ports' terminals, as of early 2007 most cargo containers still went through American ports unscanned because of a lack of scanners, a shortage Robert Bonner, the commissioner of Customs and Border Protection, conceded was due to "budgetary constraints."[52] Stephen Flynn, a terrorism expert at the Council on Foreign Relations, estimates it would cost $1.5 billion to install the Hong Kong systems at every major container port worldwide, less than 1 percent of the cost of the Iraq War to date.[53] FBI monitoring of terrorist funds has fallen dramatically since 2002, but when the bureau requested eighty more accountants and analysts to track terrorist funding, it was turned down.[54] Yet at the same time federal contracts with Halliburton in Iraq were valued at more than the FBI's entire $5 billion budget.[55] And although $6.8 billion is needed to outfit emergency personnel with proper radios to prevent the tragedy that occurred when firefighters and police at the World Trade Center could not warn one another of the buildings' impending collapse, first-responder programs fell victim to budget cuts in 2005.

Meanwhile, as we shifted our attention to Iraq, we have seen a troubling resurgence of Taliban and al-Qaeda activity in Afghanistan. The Center for Defense Information reports that 2005 was the deadliest year in Afghanistan since the start of U.S. operations there in late 2001.[56] U.S. troop deaths almost doubled from the previous year, and 2006 was even bloodier, with a resurgent Taliban surprising the Americans with the ferocity of its offensive.[57] British intelligence reported in October 2006 that al-Qaeda had fully reconstituted itself in the hills of Afghanistan and Pakistan and poses as great a threat as ever.[58] Meanwhile, there has been a precipitous increase in the number of suicide bombings and IED—improvised explosive device—attacks, leading many analysts to conclude that an "Iraqization" of Afghanistan has begun. There is growing evidence of an Iraqi connection to the upsurge of insurgent activity in Afghanistan, as foreign fighters are returning to Afghanistan from Iraq, bringing increasingly sophisticated bombs and techniques.[59]

The war has also caused serious tensions and strains with our NATO allies, including such strong friends as Canada and Germany, both of which opposed the war. Election campaigns in both countries after the war were dominated by politicians playing to the anti-American mood, and in Canada prominent columnists now question whether the government should cooperate with the United States on future terrorism cases.[60]

Anti-American attitudes, which as we have seen were already on the rise before the Iraq War as a result of the way we pursued the war on terror, grew to unprecedented levels in the wake of the invasion. Majorities in most countries believe that President Bush deliberately lied about Iraq and that the war on terrorism is not a sincere attempt to reduce international terrorism. Tying the Iraq War so tightly to the war against terror might have been a useful political tactic for convincing Americans to support the war initially, but it has hurt international support for the effort against terrorists. In many countries, support for the U.S.-led war on terror slipped dramatically after the invasion of Iraq. Sixty-three percent of Spaniards, for example, supported the war on terror in 2003, before the Iraq War, but by 2006 only 19 percent did so. Similarly, in Japan, support for the war on terror plummeted from 61 percent in 2002 to 26 percent in 2006. In Canada, historically a strong ally, only 45 percent support the war on terror. Similarly, in France, Britain, and Germany, popular support for our antiterrorism efforts substantially declined between 2002 and 2006, dropping below 50 percent. In Jordan, support for the U.S. war on terror dropped to 2 percent immediately after the start of the Iraq War, before rising slightly to 16 percent in 2006.[61]

Most remarkably, in Britain, France, Spain, and Russia, more people cite the U.S. presence in Iraq as a danger to stability in the Middle East and world peace than cite the current government of Iran.[62] A poll conducted in October 2006 found that citizens

in the United Kingdom considered George Bush second only to
Osama bin Laden as a threat to world peace. Bush was considered a greater threat to world peace than the leaders of North
Korea, Iran, and Hezbollah. More than two-thirds of Britons (69
percent) think that U.S. policy has made the world less safe since
2001. Majorities in Mexico and Canada shared that view.[63]

Such attitudes have serious consequences for U.S. security. In
Turkey, for example, overwhelming public opposition to the
Iraq War forced the government to deny U.S. forces access to its
territory to launch a northern attack against Iraq, despite considerable economic incentives from the United States. Brent
Scowcroft, President George H.W. Bush's national security adviser, has argued that our approach to Iraq has "given us an
image of arrogance and unilateralism, and we're paying a very
high price for that image. If we get to the point where everyone secretly hopes the United States gets a black eye because
we're so obnoxious, then we'll be totally hamstrung in the war
on terror." [64]

Conservative Yale historian John Lewis Gaddis concurs:

> The rush to war in Iraq in the absence of a "first shot" or a
> "smoking gun" left . . . a growing sense throughout much of the
> world that there could be *nothing worse* than American hege-
> mony if it was to be used in this way. For if Washington could
> go against the wishes of the United Nations and most of its allies
> in invading Iraq, what could it *not* do? . . . Within a little more
> than a year and a half, the United States exchanged its long-
> established reputation as the principal *stabilizer* of the interna-
> tional system for one as its chief *destablizer.*[65]

These negative results flow not from the fact that the war
was launched on the basis of faulty intelligence, nor from the
failure to dedicate more troops or to plan adequately for the aftermath of Saddam Hussein's fall, but from the unilateral use of
aggressive, coercive force to "prevent" a speculative threat. Wars

launched for preventive reasons are especially likely to be viewed as illegitimate and engender resistance. A December 2005 report commissioned by the U.S. Army War College found that the problems confronting the United States in Iraq "flowed from the enterprise itself and not primarily from mistakes along the way."[66] As one senior Middle Eastern diplomat observed, "The war itself was the original sin. When you commit a sin as cardinal as that, you are bound to get a lot of things wrong." He analogized the invasion to a car entering "a one-way street in the wrong direction, no matter which way you turn," things are bound to go awry.[67]

BEYOND IRAQ:
PREVENTIVE WAR AND OTHER ROGUE STATES

While our experience in Iraq provides a strong cautionary tale for advocates of preventive war, one bad result does not necessarily disprove the utility of the doctrine in general. The preventive-war doctrine was designed to deal not just with Iraq, but more generally with nations the Bush administration claimed were "rogue states." But the doctrine has already made matters worse with respect to the other "rogue states" most likely to threaten our national security—North Korea and Iran—and provides virtually no promise for dealing with such states in the future.

The administration's claim that a preventive-war strategy will make us safer rests on three propositions. The first is that we can no longer rely on traditional forms of deterrence. The second is that the threat and use of preventive military power will signal to other rogue states that our threats are credible, thereby deterring them from obtaining weapons of mass destruction. Third, the strategy assumes that preventive attack is a realistic option in dealing with the nations we have labeled rogue states. In fact, none of these propositions is accurate.

The first claim, that containment will not work, conflates the threats posed by terrorists and rogue states; as President Bush stated, "you can't distinguish between al Qaeda and Saddam when you talk about the war on terror."[68] In fact, terrorists and rogue states pose distinct challenges. Unlike terrorists, the leaders of states such as Iran, North Korea, or Syria have territory and a citizenry to defend. Unlike Osama bin Laden, none of these states has attacked us or threatened an imminent attack.

Experience shows that traditional measures of deterrence do work with respect to rogue states' use of weapons of mass destruction. During the Persian Gulf War, our threats of retaliation stopped Saddam Hussein from using his massive stockpiles of chemical and biological weapons.[69] Deterrence also appears to have worked for the twelve years between the Gulf wars, convincing Iraq to destroy its weapons and to desist from attacking its neighbors. By contrast, Iraq's aggressive and risky invasions of Iran and Kuwait occured in the absence of any serious attempt to deter Saddam Hussein. The United States actively supported him in his war with Iran, authorizing the sale of poisonous chemicals and deadly biological viruses such as anthrax and bubonic plague to Iraq at a time when the Iraqis were using chemical weapons against Iran.[70] Prior to Iraq's 1990 invasion of Kuwait, the U.S. ambassador did not warn Saddam Hussein that he would face serious consequences if he attacked Kuwait. Indeed, the ambassador's statements could easily have been interpreted (and apparently were interpreted) to give him the go-ahead to attack.[71]

Similarly, deterrence seems to have had a considerable effect on North Korea. While that country has demonstrated a willingness to flout international agreements, it has not attacked the United States or its allies since the Korean War, despite the fact that it may have had nuclear weapons for a decade. Indeed, according to U.S. government sources, North Korea's support for terrorism is virtually nonexistent and its arms exports have declined substantially.[72]

Deterrence is no panacea. But our experience with rogue

states suggests that there is no reason to abandon this strategy. As Secretary of State Rice wrote in 2000, there "need be no sense of panic about [rogue regimes]. Rather, the first line of defense should be a clear and classical statement of deterrence—if they do acquire WMD [weapons of mass destruction], their weapons will be unusable because any attempt to use them will bring national obliteration."[73] Her view remains as sound after 9/11 as it was before.

The preventive-war doctrine's second premise maintains that the use and threat of preventive war will deter rogue states from developing weapons of mass destruction. Thus far, however, the doctrine seems to have had exactly the opposite effect—encouraging Iran and North Korea to accelerate their weapons development programs in order to deter us from preventively attacking them.

During the run-up to the Iraq War, North Korea did not seem cowed, but rather announced its intention to restart its most advanced nuclear reactor and resume construction of two larger reactors. It removed the International Atomic Energy Agency's safeguard seal at the nuclear research center in Youngbyon, shut down the monitoring camera, ordered IAEA inspectors out of the country, and announced that it would withdraw from the Nuclear Proliferation Treaty—the only country ever to do so.[74] In October 2006, North Korea announced publicly that it had conducted its first nuclear test.[75] Iran has similarly accelerated its efforts to enrich uranium.

The message these and other states seem to have derived from the war in Iraq is that the United States will attack "weak" countries. The preventive-war doctrine perversely motivates these states to seek nuclear weapons as a means of deterring us from launching a preemptive strike against them. As Martin Van Creveld, one of Israel's leading military historians, recently wrote, "Obviously, we don't want Iran to have nuclear weapons and I don't know if they're developing them, but if they're not developing them, they're crazy."[76] Touted as a counterprolifera-

tion tactic, preventive war has in practice fueled nuclear proliferation where we fear it most.

At the same time, the war in Iraq has made it more difficult to
deter other states or terrorists. As one senior administration
diplomat involved in the decision to invade Iraq conceded in
2006, "the decisions we made then narrowed our options
now." [77] A 2006 report by a group of experts headed by former
secretary of defense William Perry found that because of the
military's heavy commitments to Iraq, the United States has
"only limited ground force capability ready to respond to other
contingencies." The overextension of our military forces, the report concluded, "increases the risk that potential adversaries
will be tempted to challenge the United States," weakens "our
ability to deter aggression," and poses "a real risk of breaking the
force." [78]

The war in Iraq has dramatically undermined our ability to
confront Iran in particular. As Joseph Cirincione, director for
nonproliferation at the Carnegie Endowment for International
Peace, put it, "Ironically by invading a country that didn't have
nuclear weapons, we put ourselves in a more difficult position to
deal with a country that's trying to get them." [79] While the administration hoped that our invasion would help neutralize Iran
as a regional force, the opposite has occured.[80] Most Iranian officials see the American presence in Iraq as weakening the United
States' hand.[81] As a Western diplomat based in Tehran put it,
"what was seen as power then may be seen as weakness now." [82]
Iran could respond to any preemptive American attack by urging the Shiite militias in Iraq to escalate their attacks on American forces there, a possibility that the influential Iraqi cleric
Muqtada al-Sadr discussed during a visit to Tehran. These calculations have reduced Iranian fears about proceeding with their
nuclear program.

The Iraq invasion has also impeded our efforts to gain support from the international community for serious sanctions
against Iran. After our false claims about Iraq, many nations do

not trust our assertions about Iran's nuclear weapons program.[83] Our allies also worry about the administration's push to
bring Iran before the Security Council, fearing that we will use
the council in the same way we attempted to use it with Iraq—as
a one-way ratchet toward violent confrontation. A number of
countries "don't want to be part of this trap." [84]

President Bush argues that the Iraq War played a decisive role
in Libya's decision to end its WMD programs in December
2003. In his 2004 State of the Union address, Bush claimed that
"nine months of intense negotiations succeeded with Libya,
while 12 years of diplomacy with Iraq did not." The Iraq War
made the difference because "words must be credible, and no
one can now doubt the word of America." [85]

Most experts, however, disagree. As the *New York Times* reported, "experts agree that the main factors underlying Qaddafi's
decision are not Western resolve in toppling Saddam Hussein,
but 'are more likely to be his disastrous economic policies at
home, the squandering of Libya's bountiful oil resources and a
deepening isolation that threatens any hopes for the country's
future.'" [86] Senior government officials point out that during secret negotiations in May 1999, a Libyan representative stated that
Libya would surrender its WMD programs if the United States
lifted its trade sanctions.[87] The United States demanded that
Libya first admit culpability for the bombing of Pan Am Flight
103 over Lockerbie, Scotland; compensate the victims' families;
and end its support of terrorism. Libya satisfied those demands
by early 2003, *before* the Iraq War, and UN sanctions were lifted.
Libya then approached the United States and Britain to discuss
eliminating the separate U.S. sanctions in return for dismantling
its weapons program. As Flynt Leverett, the senior director for
Middle Eastern affairs at the National Security Council from
2002 to 2003, recalls,

> the Iraq war, which had not yet started, was not the driving force
> behind Libya's move. Rather, Libya was willing to deal because of

credible diplomatic representations by the United States over the years, which convinced the Libyans that doing so was critical to achieving their strategic and domestic goals.[88]

Martin Indyk, former assistant secretary of state, concurs with Leverett's assessment: "Libyan disarmament did not require a war in Iraq." [89]

In fact, the history of our dealings with Libya suggests that sanctions and diplomacy succeeded where military force did not. In 1986, the Reagan administration launched an air strike against Tripoli in response to what it claimed was a Libyan-inspired bombing in Berlin that killed a U.S. Army sergeant and injured fifty American military personnel. U.S. officials subsequently determined that the Lockerbie bombing in 1988 was Libya's response to the Tripoli raid, and that, in the words of a former counterterrorism official, "we [had] just set up the next round of terrorism." [90] After the Lockerbie tragedy, the United States shifted its strategy, focused on law enforcement, and obtained UN sanctions against Libya, which eventually led to Libya's decision to turn over the alleged perpetrators of the Lockerbie bombing to Scottish authorities for trial at the Hague.

In sum, the launching of a preventive war in Iraq, far from having the deterrent impact that Bush administration officials predicted, has had precisely the opposite effect, spurring so-called rogue nations to increase their weapons production while we are otherwise engaged with Iraq. Where we have made progress, it is attributable to negotiations that predated the Iraq War, not to the United States flexing its muscles. Thus, the second proposition underlying the preventive-war doctrine—that it deters other rogue states—is contradicted by the facts on the ground.

The administration's third faulty assumption is that preventive war is a plausible threat against most rogue states. In fact, it is wholly unrealistic against any nation that poses a significant nuclear threat, such as Iran or North Korea. Both regimes learned the lessons of Israel's preventive 1981 strike, which destroyed an Iraqi nuclear reactor at Osirak, and have dispersed and hidden their nuclear facilities, burying at least some of them so far underground that they are virtually impregnable from air attack. At best a preventive attack will temporarily slow, but not derail or destroy, the development of nuclear facilities.

In addition, preemptive strikes require extremely good intelligence regarding the location of nuclear facilities, and we just don't have it. For example, the United States does not know exactly where North Korea is hiding whatever nuclear weapons it has, where its stock of secretly reprocessed plutonium is, or where its alleged uranium enrichment facilities are.[91] As for eliminating Iran's nuclear capabilities militarily, a U.S. Army College report found that "the United States and Israel lack sufficient targeting intelligence to do this. Iran has long had considerable success in concealing nuclear activities from U.S. intelligence analysts and IAEA inspectors."[92] Several years ago, the situation dramatically worsened. In 2004, a CIA officer made a disastrous mistake, electronically sending information to an Iranian double agent that could identify virtually every CIA spy in Iran, with the result that the CIA has been unable to provide adequate intelligence on Iran's nuclear program ever since.[93]

In 2005, President Bush's Commission on the Intelligence Capabilities of the United States Regarding Weapons of Mass Destruction, chaired by former senator Charles Robb and senior circuit court judge Laurence Silberman, offered this sobering assessment: "Across the board, the Intelligence Community knows disturbingly little about the nuclear programs of many of the world's most dangerous actors. In some cases, it knows less now than it did five or ten years ago."[94] As David Kay, the chief of the U.S. team looking for Iraqi weapons of mass destruction after the war, said, "The Achilles' heel of a doctrine of pre-emptive war or bombing strikes is that it requires really sound and complete intelligence, because if you can't precisely locate a target, you can't kill it." [95]

Even a relatively successful preemptive attack on either North Korea or Iran would run substantial risks of retaliation. In addition to creating turmoil in neighboring Iraq, the Iranians also have the capability to launch hundreds of ballistic missiles against Israel or U.S. targets in the region, or to unleash attacks from groups that it supports, such as Hezbollah. It could also turn off its oil taps, sending the price of oil skyrocketing and destabilizing the international economy. For its part, North Korea could respond to a U.S. attack by inflicting massive damage against South Korea and the U.S. troops based there, or by attacking our ally, Japan.[96] A large-scale ground attack against either nation could lead to a costly, protracted, and destructive war. A preemptive strike on Iran would likely inflame public opinion there and unify the nation in its determination to go nuclear. While Vice President Cheney has rejected State Department proposals to engage North Korea or Iran diplomatically, asserting that "we don't negotiate with evil; we defeat it," [97] diplomacy appears to be the only realistic option. In short, preventive military action not only did not work in Iraq, but it is not a viable option against the other two charter members of the "axis of evil."

In 2003, the administration rejected out of hand a proposal from Iran for comprehensive negotiations that might have resolved our concerns about Iran's weapons program,[98] and in 2004 President Bush raised the specter of preemption when he questioned whether Iran had ties to al-Qaeda, stating that the United States was investigating whether Iran played any role in the 9/11 attacks.[99] Nonetheless, the United States subsequently let Iran's negotiations with the European Union proceed, encouraged the Russians to get involved, and most recently developed a joint proposal with the Europeans to present to Iran. The administration has worked to build up support at the IAEA, the very agency U.S. officials so bitterly attacked during the inspection process in Iraq. While administration officials might argue that the threat of preventive attack has aided diplomacy, in truth the opposite has occurred: the failure of preventive military coercion has forced the administration to join in the multilateral diplomatic approach favored by other Security Council members.[100]

The administration still apparently contains a faction that favors preventive war against Iran. In April 2006, Seymour Hersh of the *New Yorker* and reporters for the *Washington Post* reported that the administration was actively studying options for a military strike against Iran.[101] Nonetheless, those reports also underscored the difficulty of actually launching such a preventive strike. For example, because conventional weapons probably could not destroy Iran's deep underground facilities,[102] Pentagon planners contemplated the use of tactical nuclear weapons.[103] Hersh reported that senior officials were considering resigning over such a threatened first use of nuclear weapons and that the Joint Chiefs of Staff were strongly opposed. A senior administration official admitted that an attack could be undertaken only at great political cost, and that because of inadequate intelligence, it might "still not set them back."[104] Moreover, the tactical nuclear weapon that the administration is reportedly contemplating using—the B61-11 bunker buster—cannot penetrate the hard rock under which valuable targets are often buried.[105] Even the United Kingdom, our principal ally in Iraq, strongly opposes an air strike on Iran. In 2005 British foreign minister Jack Straw dismissed military action against Iran as "inconceivable."[106] Straw has insisted that Britain would not support preemptive military action against Tehran and that there is no basis on which anybody would claim authority for such military action.[107]

The United States has similarly recognized that a preventive military strike against North Korea is unrealistic and has focused instead on negotiation. In September 2005, North Korea agreed in principle to a verified abandonment of its nuclear weapons program in exchange for security guarantees and economic aid from the West. In February 2007, North Korea agreed to freeze its nuclear program in exchange for fuel aid. The main elements of these deals are similar to one nearly concluded at the very end of the Clinton administration, which Bush and Cheney disavowed upon taking office.[108] After almost five years of preventive-war rhetoric, the administration is negotiating, urging patience, and rejecting as unacceptably risky suggestions that it launch a precision strike against North Korea's missile launching pads.[109]

The preventive-war strategy is also inapplicable to the nation that may well present the most dangerous threat of providing terrorists with weapons of mass destruction: Pakistan. Pakistan is already a nuclear power and has enough material for thirty to fifty nuclear weapons. While it is now a U.S. ally, Pakistan has an unstable government, a strong Islamic fundamentalist opposition movement, and a multitude of armed fundamentalist groups. In the past, Pakistan has been the worst proliferator of nuclear weapons technology and materials. We still do not know whether the network run by Pakistani nuclear scientist A.Q. Khan, which sold nuclear technology and scientific knowledge to countries such as Libya and North Korea, has been fully disassembled.

Preventive-war proponents often point to Israel's 1981 attack on Iraq's nuclear reactor at Osirak as a preventive military strike that successfully eliminated a real threat. Israel's military strike was unanimously condemned as unlawful by the UN Security Council because Iraq had neither attacked Israel nor threatened an imminent attack. British prime minister Margaret Thatcher denounced the raid, stating that "armed attack in such circumstances cannot be justified. It represents a grave breach of international law." [110] The Reagan administration invoked the Arms Export Control Act, which requires that arms supplied to Israel be used for defensive purposes only, and delayed the delivery of arms it had previously contracted to sell to Israel.[111] But preventive-war advocates claim that if Israel had declined to knock out the Iraqi reactor, Saddam Hussein might have already had a nuclear bomb by the time he invaded Kuwait.

The attack did succeed in destroying Iraq's nuclear reactor before it went on line, and undoubtedly set back Iraq's nuclear program in the short term. However, Iraq salvaged about 25 kilograms of bomb-grade uranium from the rubble and then accelerated its efforts to develop a nuclear weapon. Within several years of the strike, Iraq had up to twenty thousand technical workers, including as many as seven thousand scientists and engineers, working on its nuclear weapons program, and was reportedly spending between $4 billion and $8 billion on the project.[112] Iraqi nuclear scientist Khidir Hamza said that the Israeli strike created "a much larger danger in the longer range."[113] Another Iraqi nuclear scientist, Imad Khadduri, claimed that the Osirak strike sent Iraq's nuclear weapon program into "overdrive" and convinced the leadership to replace the relatively small facility that Israel had bombed with a more massive, full-fledged nuclear program.[114] By 1988, after its war with Iran ended, Iraq embarked on building a new array of nuclear facilities, but this time dispersed and concealed to frustrate another quick air strike. Indeed, the Osirak raid led every nation seeking nuclear weapons to disperse and conceal its operations, prompting one military analyst to conclude that "the days of Osiraq-type raids on a single, easily located and above-surface nuclear facility are over."[115] We now know that Iraq, despite the Israeli raid, was perilously close to building a nuclear bomb in 1990. What prevented it from doing so was not the Osirak raid, but Hussein's miscalculation in invading Kuwait.

The preventive-war strategy, in short, has been a failure from a security standpoint. It has embroiled us in a quagmire in Iraq that has inspired, armed, and trained a new generation of terrorists, alienated our friends and inspired our enemies, sacrificed tens of thousands of lives, and diverted billions of dollars from more effective security measures. It has emboldened Iran and North Korea, encouraging them to develop weapons of mass destruction in order to deter us from acting preventively against them. And it has done lasting damage to the legitimacy of our cause, by unilaterally employing war in circumstances that most of the world found unjustified and that international law deemed illegal.

The rules governing war in international law reflect a judgment that the risks of modern warfare are so enormous that nations must not have unilateral authority to launch wars to prevent gathering dangers but only to defend against attacks or imminent attacks. The Bush administration claims that that risk assessment has become untenable in dealing with rogue states and terrorists seeking weapons of mass destruction; in the administration's calculus, the cost of failing to act may outweigh the danger of military action. The Iraq War strongly supports the judgment of international law and the world community. We would have done far better if we had adhered to the law, desisted from attacking Iraq, focused our energies on those who actually threaten us, and deployed our scarce resources on shoring up our defenses against those who might attack us in the future. In this case, the best defense would have been a good defense, not an offensive war.

7. LESSONS OF HISTORY

Despite the Bush administration's claims to have discovered a new paradigm, the idea of preventive war is not new. Like preventive detention, preventive war has often been deployed in the past, generally with calamitous consequences. The history of Western civilization is filled with major wars commenced for preventive reasons: Sparta's Peloponnesian War against Athens, Carthage's preemptive attack on Rome, the preventive war declared by Germany against Russia that initiated World War I, or Japan's attack on the American fleet at Pearl Harbor, to name just a few. A brief review of this history illustrates that the Iraq War is not atypical; preventive wars have often proved disastrous for those who launched them.

It was in view of this history that the framers of the UN Charter sought in 1945 to limit sharply a nation's discretion to use force against perceived dangers. At the founding conference in San Francisco, the U.S. delegation introduced language allowing for a right of self-defense only "if an armed attack occurs." In response to concerns that this might limit too severely the right of self-defense, Governor Harold Stassen, a leader of the American delegation, replied that "this was intentional and sound. We did not want exercised the right of self-defense before an armed attack had occurred."[1]

PREVENTIVE WAR IN EUROPE

The UN Charter's prohibition on the use of force for any reason other than self-defense stemmed most immediately from the experience with preventive war during World Wars I and II. As political scientist David Hendrickson observes, "Repugnance for preventive war became deeply embedded in the world community because the use of that doctrine in the 20th century led to results nearly fatal to civilization."[2]

Many historians view World War I as a preventive war. On June 28, 1914, Archduke Francis Ferdinand of Austria was assassinated by a Serb revolutionary in the Bosnian capital of Sarajevo. Five weeks later, the major European powers were at war, a war in which 10 million people were ultimately killed, more than twice as many as had died in all the wars of the previous two centuries. The war brought chaos and disorder to Europe, and ultimately led to the dissolution of three great empires—the Russian, the Austro-Hungarian, and the Ottoman empires.

An important cause of the war was the increasing turn toward preventive-war reasoning by the great powers in the first two decades of the twentieth century. This development, in part a product of increasing fears wrought by the rapid pace of technological and social change, was nowhere more pronounced than in Germany.[3] Forty years before World War I, the German chancellor, Otto von Bismarck, had strongly argued against preventive war. No dove, Bismarck led Germany during three wars for German unification and believed that great political questions would be decided "by blood and iron."[4] Nonetheless, throughout the 1870s and 1880s Bismarck consistently rejected arguments for preventive war urged by German military leaders, and instead counseled caution and patience. Bismarck characterized preventive war as committing "suicide from fear of death."[5] "I would . . . never advise Your Majesty to declare war forthwith, simply because it appeared that our opponent would begin hostilities in the near future," he told Kaiser Wilhelm I. "One can never anticipate the ways of divine providence securely enough for that."[6]

By the turn of the twentieth century, however, Bismarck had been forced to resign, and German military leaders had concluded that preventive war was essential to the country's security. Germany's generals came to believe that war with France and Russia was inevitable, and that time was not on Germany's side. Russia's modernization of its armed forces would soon render Germany incapable of defeating France and Russia. As German chief of staff Helmuth von Moltke told Kaiser Wilhelm in December 1912, "war is inevitable, and the sooner the better." [7]

By the spring of 1914, Germany's military and civilian leaders concluded that the time was right to wage a preventive war. Moltke calculated that Germany had only "two or three years" before Russia's developing national railway network would make it impossible for Germany to prevail against an alliance of France and Russia.[8] On the eve of war, German chancellor Bethmann-Hollweg's secretary wrote in his diary that "Russia's military power [is] growing rapidly; with the strategic extension [of Russian railways] into Poland the situation is intolerable." The climate of apprehension was summed up by Germany's foreign secretary on May 29, 1914:

> In two to three years . . . [our] enemies' military power would then be so great that [Moltke] did not know how he could deal with it. Now we were still more or less a match for it. In his view there was no alternative but to fight a preventive war so as to beat the enemy while we could still emerge fairly well from the struggle. The Chief of Staff therefore put it to me that our policy should be geared to bringing about an early war.[9]

The Serbian assassin's bullet provided the excuse—in Moltke's words, "an effective slogan"—for the preventive war Germany sought. Chancellor Bethmann-Hollweg took what he admitted was "a calculated risk," a "leap in the dark." [10] In fact, there was little evidence that Russia and France had designs on attacking Germany first.[11] The Germans' decision to go to war proved catastrophic, not only for Germany but also for all of Europe.

Hitler also justified Germany's launching of World War II in preventive terms. In August 1939, he told an assembly of his top military commanders that "we are faced with the hard alternative of either striking or the certainty of being destroyed sooner or later. I am only afraid that some Schwenekind may submit a mediation plan at the last moment." [12] German attacks on Norway, Denmark, Holland, Belgium, and eventually the Soviet Union were all justified by Hitler as preventive moves. After the war, in their testimony before the Nuremberg tribunals, the top German military commanders argued that Germany's invasion of Russia was "undeniably a purely preventive war," undertaken "in order to prevent a definite aggression on the part of the adversary," and "the only way out" of the great threat posed by the Soviets." [13]

Japan's military strike on Pearl Harbor was also said to be preventive. The Japanese felt cornered by President Roosevelt's freezing of Japanese assets and imposition of an oil embargo. [14] They believed that war with the United States was inevitable, and that only by launching a preemptive strike could they avoid defeat. Admiral Yamamoto, commander in chief of the Japanese fleet, wrote that "in the event of outbreak of war with the United States, there would be little prospect of our operations succeeding unless, at the very outset, we can deal a crushing blow to the main force of the American fleet in Hawaiian waters." [15] For six months after the Pearl Harbor attack, the Japanese military had unparalleled success; less than four years later, however, 2 million Japanese were dead and Japanese cities lay smoldering in ruins. [16]

Preventive wars launched to forestall "gathering threats" have ancient roots. The Peloponnesian War from 431 to 404 B.C., for example, was launched preemptively by Sparta because of its fear of Athenian power. Sparta faced no immediate threat from Athens. Rather, the eminent historian Thucydides writes, "what made war inevitable was the growth of Athenian power and the fear which this caused in Sparta." [17]

The Spartan debate over whether to launch a preventive war has a surprisingly modern resonance. Sparta's ally, Corinth, chided the Spartans for their defensive mindset. The Corinthians claimed that the Spartans were the only Greek peoples who "do nothing in the early stages to prevent an enemy's expansion; you wait until your enemy has doubled his strength."[18] The Corinthians argued that Athens presented a new paradigm, a strategic environment "completely different" from anything Sparta had faced before, and warranted preventive warfare.[19]

Sparta's king, Archidamus, urged caution, because "it is impossible to foresee the course that the war will take."[20] He argued that "as for being slow and cautious—which is the usual criticism made against us—there is nothing to be ashamed of in that."[21] He accurately predicted that the war would not "likely be small scale," and would not "soon be over."[22] Arguing that "it is impossible to calculate accurately events that are determined by chance,"[23] Archidamus suggested that Sparta take a diplomatic course because a preemptive attack would have been illegal.[24]

Archidamus's speech was answered by a Spartan leader, Sthenelaidas, who passionately argued that "this is not a matter to be settled by lawsuits and by words." Sthenelaidas called for quick action in support of Sparta's allies, concluding, "Do not allow the Athenians to grow still stronger."[25] The Spartans overwhelmingly followed Sthenelaidas's call for preventive war, despite the fact that Athens represented no immediate threat.[26] Sparta's allies also voted for war, but not by a large majority. As one scholar observes, "among the allies, therefore, we may deduce that not everyone thought the war inevitable, not everyone thought it was just, not everyone thought it would be easy and successful; not everyone thought it was necessary."[27] Historians generally agree that the dissenters had it right.[28] The resulting war lasted almost thirty years.

The war between Carthage and Rome in the third century B.C. also "closely follows the preventive logic of the Greek case."[29] Facing the rise of Rome's power, Carthage decided to launch a preventive war. Carthage wound up losing and was largely destroyed. One study concludes that virtually all of the major wars in Europe between the sixteenth and the twentieth centuries were propelled by preventive motivations, in which a powerful but declining state "engaged in a desperate race against time" to defeat a growing danger.[30] Another study found that between 1848 and 1918, "every war between Great Powers started as a preventive war."[31] All but one "brought disaster on their originators."[32] Yet another analysis of centuries of European warfare agreed that "preventive logic . . . is a ubiquitous motive for war."[33] In 1760, Edmund Burke concluded that the military policy of preventing emerging threats had been the source "of innumerable and fruitless wars" in Europe.[34]

Many of these conflicts were caused by exaggerated suspicions about other nations' motives.[35] Preventive-war theory permits nations to act based on the suspicion that an attack is inevitable in the unspecified future. Often, such suspicions turn out to be ill-founded. One prominent scholar of the history of warfare concluded that the "chief source of insecurity in Europe since modern times . . . lies in the national tendency to exaggerate the dangers they face, and to respond with counterproductive belligerence."[36] Rome during the height of its power always perceived itself as in danger of "being attacked by evil-minded neighbors, always fighting for breathing space,"[37] and launched numerous wars motivated by fears and insecurity. The Athenians launched a disastrous Sicilian expedition in 415 because they believed that their security required preventively attacking others to avoid "being subjected to the rule of another party."[38] The great Swiss jurist Vattel concluded his discussion of the war commenced by Great Britain and its allies against what they believed was King Louis XIV's "design" to dominate Europe on a sobering note: "It has since appeared that the [allies'] policy was too suspicious."[39]

While one must be cautious about drawing conclusive lessons from contested history, the evidence supports the decision of the drafters of the UN Charter to reject preventive war.[40] First, the preventive rationale has often been a pretext masking an aggressive intent. The Nazis' reliance on preventive-war thinking, for example, was plainly a pretext for aggression.

Second, the preventive rationale has often led countries to be overeager to initiate what have turned out to be "fruitless" military campaigns. Many preventive wars have been launched on the deeply felt but often erroneous perception that war was inevitable, and that a new threat had created a new strategic environment requiring bold, decisive action. While some preventive wars may have been necessary, and sometimes nations should have fought when instead they waited for the threat to materialize, a prominent scholar of the history of warfare, Columbia professor Robert Jervis, concluded that, "on balance, it seems that states are more likely to overestimate the hostility of others then to underestimate it."[41]

Third, many preventive wars have been initiated, like the Iraq War, under the illusion that they would be short. That illusion fundamentally skews the cost-benefit analysis that a nation undertakes in deciding whether to launch a war. Rather than leading to quick, relatively costless victories, most preventive wars have had disastrous results. War is of course always costly, in lives and resources, but a preventive war is at least potentially an avoidable war. If the aggressor nation miscalculates and the nation it attacks was not in fact preparing to attack it, then the war is unnecessary. Wars undertaken in self-defense, by contrast, are almost by definition unavoidable.

COLD WAR AND PREVENTIVE WAR: THE AMERICAN DEBATES

The ink was barely dry on the UN Charter when the world irrevocably and dramatically changed. Truman's decision to drop atomic bombs on the Japanese cities of Hiroshima and Nagasaki created a "paradigm shift" in which government officials faced an unprecedented challenge not anticipated by the framers of the Charter. As a result, U.S. policy makers throughout the Cold War repeatedly grappled with arguments for preventive war remarkably similar to those made today. But, to their credit and our benefit, U.S. officials resisted launching a preventive war against either the Soviet Union or China.

Between 1945 and 1949, the United States maintained a monopoly on atomic weapons, but the Soviet Union was determined to break that monopoly. A number of high-level officials in the Truman administration, particularly within the military, favored preventive war.[42] They argued that we should strike first because the Soviets were led by a brutal, paranoid, and aggressive dictator bent on world domination, and that upon reaching atomic parity, the Soviets would inevitably launch a surprise attack against us. As early as January 1946, General Leslie Groves, the wartime head of the Manhattan Project, raised the desirability of preventive war. "If we were ruthlessly realistic," he wrote, "we would not permit any foreign power with which we are not firmly allied, and in which we do not have absolute confidence, to make or possess atomic weapons. If such a country started to make atomic weapons we would destroy its capacity to make them before it had progressed far enough to threaten us."[43] General Orville Anderson, of the Air War College, agreed with Groves that the changed nature of war meant that a country committed an "overt act of war" when it built weapons "intended for our eventual destruction" and that therefore destroying those weapons "before launched or employed is defensive action and not aggression."[44] Some military officials made the identical argument that Rumsfeld later made in the war on terror, namely, that the new "complexion of atomic war reemphasizes the old cliché that the best defense is a good offense and alters it somewhat: the best defense is the *first* offense in force."[45]

Civilian leaders similarly maintained that war with the Soviets was inevitable and that sooner was better than later. Many agreed with William L. Lawrence, the science correspondent for the *New York Times* and the nation's leading writer on nuclear issues, when he wrote in 1948 that the Soviet "insistence on an atomic armament race . . . must inevitably lead to war," and that "it would be to our advantage to have it while we are still the sole possessors of the atomic bomb."[46] Lawrence argued that we should present the Soviets with an ultimatum to dismantle their atomic plants, and if they refused, we should destroy their plants before the bombs could be produced. Senator Brian McMahon, the chairman of the Joint Committee of Atomic Energy, also favored the idea, arguing that "almost nothing could be worse than the current atomic armaments race." Influential intellectuals such as Bertrand Russell and the physicist Leo Szilard supported preventive-war arguments, as did John Williams, a leading figure at the RAND Corporation, and John von Neumann, the founder of game theory. As von Neumann put it, "If you say why not bomb them tomorrow, I say why not today? If you say today at five o'clock, I say why not one o'clock?"[47]

In August 1950, Secretary of the Navy Francis Matthews openly urged the United States to adopt a "character new to a true democracy—an initiator of a war of aggression—it would win for us a proud and popular title—we would become the first aggressors for peace." "The United States should be willing to pay any price to achieve a world at peace," Matthews proclaimed, "even the price of instituting a war to compel cooperation for peace."[48] Matthews's speech, which was believed to be a trial balloon launched at the behest of his boss, Defense Secretary Louis Johnson,[49] was followed less than a week later by an even more explosive public statement by General Orville Anderson of the Air War College:

> Give me the order to do it and I can break up Russia's five A-bomb nests in a week. And when I went to Christ, I think I could explain to Him why I wanted to do it now before it's too late. I think I could explain to Him that I had saved civilization. With it [the atomic bomb] used in time we can immobilize a foe [and prevent] his crime before it happened.[50]

President Truman, however, decisively rejected preventive war. He personally chastised Matthews and fired Anderson the day after his remarks were reported.[51] "We do not believe in aggressive or preventive war," Truman said in a radio broadcast the next day. "Such a war is the weapon of dictators, not of free democratic countries like the United States." [52]

By 1950, the Soviets had exploded their first atomic weapon, which, in the words of Secretary of State Dean Acheson, "changed everything." [53] The Truman administration undertook a comprehensive review of U.S. military policy. The results were set forth in NSC-68, which portrayed the Soviets as driven by "a new fanatic faith" that "seeks to impose its absolute authority over the rest of the world." [54] NSC-68 rejected the views of George Kennan, who advocated negotiations with the Soviets, in favor of a rapid military buildup of both conventional forces and new, superatomic hydrogen bombs. It called for massive military spending theretofore unseen in peacetime.

Despite its militaristic recommendations, NSC-68 rejected preventive war for three reasons. First, it would not work. A U.S. atomic attack "would not force or induce the Kremlin to capitulate and . . . the Kremlin would still be able to use the forces under its control to dominate most or all of Eurasia." Second, a preventive attack "would be repugnant to many Americans," leading to domestic opposition. Third, U.S. allies, particularly in western Europe, would also oppose such a war, harming U.S. relations with them and making it "difficult after such a war to create a satisfactory international order." [55] The conclusion was that the United States should not launch an attack unless it was attacked or facing imminent attack: "These considerations are no less weighty because they are imponderable, and they rule out an attack unless it is demonstrably in the nature of a counterattack to a blow which is on its way or about to be delivered." [56]

Notwithstanding the NSC-68's rejection of preventive war, many U.S. generals and other high-level military officials continued to support the concept in private. Within several years, the Eisenhower administration revisited the issue. In an August 1953 memorandum to the Joint Chiefs of Staff, General Twining, Air Force chief of staff and later chairman of the Joint Chiefs, argued for a preventive war prior to the Soviet's attainment of nuclear forces sufficient to destroy us: "We must recognize this time of decision, or, we will continue blindly down a suicidal path and arrive at a situation in which we will have entrusted our survival to the whims of a small group of proven barbarians."[57]

In 1954, the Joint Chiefs of Staff criticized what they viewed as an overly reactive and defensive U.S. military policy.[58] As the JCS chairman explained to the National Security Council, victory in a nuclear war could be guaranteed only if war occurred "prior to Soviet achievement of atomic plenty."[59] The JCS Advance Study Group briefed President Eisenhower on a proposal that the United States consider "deliberately precipitating war with the USSR in the near future, before Soviet thermonuclear capability became a 'real menace.'"[60]

Like Truman before him, President Eisenhower decisively rejected preventive war. Eisenhower's Army chief of staff, Matthew Ridgeway, denounced the policy as "contrary to every principle upon which our Nation had been founded" and "abhorrent to the great mass of American people."[61] Secretary of State John Foster Dulles argued that containment was working, adding sarcastically, "even if it hasn't got us into a war."[62] While Eisenhower himself had raised in a 1953 private memo to Dulles the thought that the continued arms race "forc[ed] us to consider whether to *initiate* war at the most propitious moment that we could designate,"[63] he ultimately rejected preventive war. "All of us have heard this term 'preventive war' since the earliest days of Hitler. . . . A preventive war, to my mind, is an impossibility today . . . I don't believe there is such a thing; and frankly, I wouldn't even listen to anyone seriously that came in and talked about such a thing."[64]

When asked later by *Washington Post* journalist Chalmers

Roberts whether he was opposed to preventive war only for "military reasons," Eisenhower responded that "there are all sorts of reasons, moral and political and everything else, against this theory, but it is so completely unthinkable in today's conditions that I thought it is no use to go any further." [65]

An updated Basic National Security Policy approved by Eisenhower in late 1954 and early 1955 stated unequivocally that "the United States and its allies must reject the concept of preventive war or acts intended to provoke war." [66] The rejection of preventive war remained official U.S. policy throughout the Cold War. As Professor Bernard Brodie, the preeminent national security scholar of the 1940s and 1950s, wrote, "The people of the United States have obviously made a decision, with little overt debate but quite remarkable unanimity, against any form of preventive war." [67] Even future secretary of state Henry Kissinger concurred, dismissing the idea of preventive war in 1955 with the comment that "there has always been an air of unreality about a program so contrary to the sense of the country and the constitutional limits within which American foreign policy must be conducted." [68]

The closest the United States ever came to launching a preventive war against the Soviet Union or its allies came in the Cuban missile crisis. The Bush administration has since invoked President Kennedy's handling of that crisis as precedent for its policy of preventive war. "Think of John F. Kennedy in the Cuban missile crisis," Rumsfeld has argued. "He didn't sit there and let Soviets put missiles in Cuba and fire a nuclear missile at the United States; he decided to engage in preemptive action, preventive action, anticipatory self-defense, call it what you wish. And he went out and blockaded them. . . . And prevailed because he did take preventive action." [69]

Rumsfeld's invocation of Kennedy is inapt, however, for two reasons. First, Kennedy explicitly *rejected* the option of a preventive military strike against Cuba, despite its recommendation by the Joint Chiefs of Staff and many of his civilian advisers. Instead, Kennedy authorized a minimal use of force—the quarantine or blockade of Cuba—with the goal of seeking a diplomatic solution. That diplomatic resolution involved substantial concessions, including an agreement not to invade Cuba. Second, while a blockade is technically a hostile act of war, Kennedy refused to justify the blockade on preventive grounds, and instead argued that it had been collectively authorized by the Organization of American States. Kennedy therefore did not assert the right to decide unilaterally to engage in a hostile act toward Cuba.

The Cuban missile crisis began with the type of strategic threat that had led to many a preventive war in the past: action by an inferior military power, in this case the Soviet Union, to challenge the United States' overwhelming dominance in intercontinental range nuclear weapons by placing nuclear weapons ninety miles from U.S. territory. The Joint Chiefs of Staff and many civilian advisers—including Dean Rusk, McGeorge Bundy, Max Taylor, former secretary of state Dean Acheson, and Treasury Secretary Douglas Dillon—argued for immediate air strikes to destroy the nuclear missile sites in Cuba, followed by preparations for invasion. At first, the president appeared to lean toward quick military action. U.S. nuclear and conventional military supremacy in the Caribbean meant that there was little chance that the Soviets or the Cubans could defend the island.

Nevertheless, such military action could easily have led to all-out war, and the president instead sought an option that "lessens the chances of a nuclear exchange which obviously is the final failure."[70] The president reportedly found persuasive Under Secretary of State George Ball's argument: a preventive attack would be akin to the Japanese attack on Pearl Harbor, and therefore, "contrary to our traditions . . . directly athwart [what] we have stood for during our national history," and perhaps, most tellingly, would "condemn us as hypocrites in the opinion of the world."[71] In various meetings Robert Kennedy referred to the Pearl Harbor analogy, passing a note to his brother at the very first executive meeting discussing a preemptive air strike. "I now know how Tojo felt when he was planning Pearl Harbor."[72] At a crucial meeting on September 19, 1962, Robert Kennedy made what historian Donald Kagan views as a "decisive intervention" in the debate.[73] The young attorney general made clear that the president rejected the air-strike option, stating that he had spoken with him that morning and "he thought it would be very difficult indeed for the President if the decision were to be for an air strike, with all the memory of Pearl Harbor and with all the implications this would have for us in whatever world there would be afterward. For 175 years we had not been that kind of country."[74] When President Kennedy met with his advisers the next day, he confirmed that he had decided on the blockade and had ruled out immediate military action, calling it "the only course compatible with American principle."[75]

In the end, Khrushchev backed down and removed the missiles from Cuba, but only with the public promise from the Kennedy administration not to invade Cuba, and a secret, private agreement to remove U.S. missiles from Turkey. As Abram Chayes, a State Department official during the crisis, later noted, the trade of Cuban for Turkish missiles meant that the crisis was resolved by a decision to "in part, buy 'em out," a fact "less talked about . . . because of the power of the Munich stigma and because it sounds a lot less courageous."[76] McGeorge Bundy, one of the hawks in Kennedy's inner circle, said immediately after the resolution of the crisis that "this was the day of the doves."[77] Air Force chief Curtis LeMay, a strong supporter of preventive war, angrily called the agreement "the greatest defeat in our history."[78] The Cuban missile crisis, then, provides no support for advocates of preventive invasions of the sort launched against Iraq.

President Kennedy's actions during the Cuban missile crisis expose the false dichotomy between action and inaction that permeates so much of the Bush administration's rhetoric in support of preventive war. As Robert Kennedy argued, the choice was not between a preemptive strike and inaction. Kennedy "favored action" to demonstrate U.S. determination to get the missiles out of Cuba, but it was action that left room for a diplomatic solution as opposed to launching a war.[79] In hindsight it is difficult to see how the United States would be safer if Kennedy had followed the urgings of the Joint Chiefs and launched a preventive attack.

The second important difference between Kennedy's approach and Bush's position is that Kennedy did not seek to justify the blockade by appealing to a concept of preventive self-defense. Instead, the Kennedy administration rejected reliance on self-defense, despite the urgings of former secretary of state Dean Acheson and Deputy Attorney General Nicholas Katzenbach that international law could be read in the atomic age to permit a self-defense justification.[80] The administration rested its argument for the quarantine on the approval of the Organization of American States, which Robert Kennedy later said transformed the U.S. position "from that of an outlaw acting in violation of international law into a country acting in accordance with twenty allies legally protecting their position."[81] Whether this was correct as a legal matter has been disputed; what is indisputable is that President Kennedy, like Truman and Eisenhower before him, eschewed the doctrine of preventive self-defense.

The Kennedy and Johnson administrations also briefly considered preventive war against China in the 1960s. President Kennedy and his national security adviser, McGeorge Bundy, believed that China's possession of nuclear weapons would be intolerable because Mao Tse-tung would be emboldened to commit blackmail and aggression.[82] Kennedy reportedly felt that a successful Chinese nuclear test was likely to be "the most significant and worst event of the 1960s."[83] The influential columnist Stewart Alsop argued in the *Saturday Evening Post* that the "madness of Mao Tse Tung" required military action against Beijing's nuclear program, which he characterized as a "technically easy problem" that could be accomplished with a "few rather small bangs."[84] The *National Review* argued that a preemptive strike at Chinese nuclear installations could be warranted in the future, "as a unique response to a unique situation not yet covered by international law."[85] Nonetheless, President Kennedy did not authorize preventive war, and President Johnson similarly rejected proposals for preventive strikes against China.[86]

Finally, in several instances involving Libya and North Korea, the United States threatened military action against facilities that it believed could produce chemical or nuclear weapons, but ultimately refused to take the step of preventive military action.[87] President Clinton's top military and civilian advisers decided against actually launching such an attack in the event that North Korea did not back down. Their reasoning was that although the immediate objective of destroying the North Korean nuclear facilities could have been easily achieved, a preemptive attack might well have triggered a second Korean war, in which hundreds of thousands of lives might have been lost.[88] In any event, both North Korea and Libya backed down, and in none of these instances did the threat materialize.

To be sure, not all preventive wars are failures.[89] For example, in the eighteenth century Frederick the Great's preventive wars propelled the rise of modern Germany. Caesar's preventive wars were viewed by many Romans as having been undertaken on slight or no provocation, but were enormously successful.[90] While the historical record does not prove that preventive war is never useful, beneficial, or even necessary, it does highlight the dangers of permitting such wars.

Administration defenders often point to the 1938 Munich Pact, in which British prime minister Neville Chamberlain sought to appease Hitler by abandoning Czechoslovakia, as evidence that the risks of inaction sometimes outweigh the risks of preventive war. Condoleezza Rice and Donald Rumsfeld have argued that millions are dead because Britain and France failed to take preventive military action to thwart the gathering Nazi threat in the 1930s. But Britain and France did not need a doctrine of preventive war to use military force to stop Hitler's military actions against the Rhineland, Austria, or Czechoslovakia. In that instance, they would have been acting to stop armed attacks or imminently threatened attacks, not speculative gathering dangers that might (or might not) eventuate in the future. The real lesson of Munich is the lack of political will in Britain and France to forge a strong alliance with the Soviet Union to stand up to Hitler, which might have avoided war and led to Hitler's downfall within Germany. Indeed, such a strong defensive alliance, not preventive war, was the policy Churchill unsuccessfully advocated in the 1930s.[91]

President Bush has said that today "we face a threat with no precedent,"[92] and therefore history is less relevant. But history shows that nations that launch preventive wars often believe that they face an unprecedented threat that will destroy them unless decisive, forceful action is taken immediately. The hazardous character of that judgment is no less true today. In their day Stalin and Mao were viewed as no less paranoid or dangerous than Saddam Hussein in 2003. Nevertheless, the U.S. government wisely rejected what we now know would have been unnecessary and undoubtedly devastating preventive wars.

It may be that the primary reason that Truman, Eisenhower, Kennedy, and Johnson refused to launch preventive strikes against the Soviet Union or China was not moral, ethical, or legal, but because there was a real danger of triggering nuclear destruction or a major war. But if so, that only underscores the bankruptcy of the preventive-war doctrine. The greater the threat another nation poses, the more dangerous a preventive war will be. Thus, the doctrine is least likely to be used where its use would be most theoretically justified—against those countries that most threaten us. The risks presented by such a conflict will generally eliminate preventive war as an option.

That the United States rejected the preventive-war doctrine

during the Cold War is not to suggest that our government always followed international law during that era. The United States and the Soviet Union repeatedly violated the UN Charter's prohibitions on the use of force; the Soviet invasions of Hungary, Czechoslovakia, and Afghanistan and the U.S. invasions of Nicaragua, the Dominican Republic, Grenada, Libya, and Panama are just a few examples. Nonetheless, both the United States and the Soviet Union maintained a formal fealty to the principle that force not be used unilaterally except in self-defense to an attack or imminent attack. While both nations sought to expand the self-defense exception, defining the concept of armed attack broadly to include aid a state provides to insurgents in an allied nation, or asserting an expansive right to protect nationals abroad, both superpowers had an interest in the stability of the formal rules stemming from World War II. Neither desired the destabilizing effects that openly challenging the Charter rule would bring.

The demise of the Soviet Union has left us with enormous, unchallenged power. It is in significant part the privilege of that position that made it possible for the Bush administration to adopt preventive-war strategies that were repeatedly rejected during the Cold War. As conservative columnist Charles Krauthammer points out, what is "new is what happened not on 9/11 but ten years earlier on December 26, 1991: the emergence of the United States as the world's unipolar power." [93] That dominance is likely to keep preventive war as a policy option for future administrations—whether they be Democratic or Republican. [94]

But we should resist that option. By threatening to attack countries that have neither attacked us nor threatened an attack, the Bush administration has ignored the historical dangers of preventive wars, dangers that simultaneously undermine the rule of law and our security. We would do far better to resurrect the view of President John Quincy Adams, who proclaimed in 1821 that the United States "goes not abroad in search of monsters to destroy." [95]

8. TICKING TIME BOMBS
AND SLIPPERY SLOPES

When President Bush sought to justify going to war against Saddam Hussein, he invoked the specter of a nuclear attack: "America must not ignore the threat gathering against us. Facing clear evidence of peril, we cannot wait for the final proof—the smoking gun—that could come in the form of a mushroom cloud." [1] When *Washington Post* columnist Charles Krauthammer argued in favor of using torture to extract information from suspects in the war on terror, he invoked the ticking time bomb scenario: a suspect is known to have planted a time bomb in a building, and the only way to find the bomb before it explodes and kills thousands of people is to torture the suspect. [2] When commentators as disparate as Heritage Foundation scholar Paul Rosenzweig, Yale law professor Bruce Ackerman, and Homeland Security Secretary Michael Chertoff have argued in favor of preventive detention, they have all invoked doomsday scenarios. [3] And when federal judge Richard Posner recently defended the constitutionality of a sweeping variety of preventive measures, including preventive detention, coercive interrogation, and making it a crime for newspapers to publish leaked classified information, he, too, invoked the threat of catastrophic terrorist attacks. [4] The move has become a familiar one: envision a truly horrific attack, and then argue that surely a little preventive government coercion is preferable to being blown to smithereens by a terrorist.

The preventive paradigm is premised on a claim that ordinary cost-benefit calculations are not appropriate when the potential risks are catastrophic. Thus, while in ordinary times we generally accept that it is preferable to let ten guilty persons go free than to convict one innocent, some suggest that we cannot sustain that balance where the risk is that one of the ten who go free may get his hands on a weapon of mass destruction. Preventive-paradigm advocates suggest replacing the rules applicable in normal times with a more ad hoc approach attuned to the exigencies of emergencies, in which preventive coercive action may be deemed the lesser evil necessary to avoid catastrophic harm.[5] As Professor Ruth Wedgwood has put it,

> we tolerate multiple acts of individual and social violence as the cost of safeguarding our privacy and liberty, demanding that the government meet an extraordinary standard of proof before it can claim any powers over our person, acting with retrospective rather than anticipatory glance. But now the stakes seem different. . . . The deliberate temperance and incompleteness of criminal law enforcement seem inadequate to the emergency, when the threat to innocent life was multiplied by orders of magnitude.[6]

The argument that the potential for catastrophic harm requires discarding or modifying traditional legal rules has intuitive appeal. It is only common sense, after all, that the degree of certainty the law should require for coercive government action should vary inversely with the potential severity of the harm the action is designed to prevent. As the Supreme Court noted in a case involving the degree of suspicion required for brief street searches, "We do not say, for example, that a report of a person carrying a bomb need bear the indicia of reliability we demand for a report of a person carrying a firearm before the police can constitutionally conduct a frisk."[7] Similarly, First Amendment doctrine governing the regulation of subversive speech once employed a balancing approach, in which the greater the harm advocated by the speaker, the sooner official suppression of the speech would be permitted.[8] The administration's preventive-war doctrine follows the same logic, maintaining that the increased threat posed by weapons of mass destruction warrants action on less clear evidence of a future attack.

Social science research, however, suggests that we should be skeptical about such an ad hoc balancing approach for at least two reasons. First, emotional factors are likely to cause us to overestimate risks based on vivid, emotionally laden events, such as terrorist attacks, and to underestimate costs and risks that are abstract, statistical, and likely to arise in the long term. Second, the phenomenon of the slippery slope suggests that once authorities are freed of clear rules in order to respond to emergency situations, they are increasingly likely to employ those powers in nonemergency situations. Rule-of-law regimes that promote accountability by setting forth clear rules and instituting checks and balances may temper the risks of overreaction and the slippery slope. At the very moments we intuitively think it most appropriate to permit extreme coercive measures, it is therefore especially important that we adhere to the rule of law.

We do not mean to suggest that emergencies never justify extraordinary responses or that recalibration of existing rules in the face of changing threats is never appropriate. Rather, we only suggest that for reasons of psychology as well as history, we should be hesitant to authorize highly coercive official actions without clear rules and proper accountability, especially where emotional fears of terrorism are likely to be at play.

WORST-CASE SCENARIOS AND SOCIAL SCIENCE

The worst-case scenarios invoked to defend the preventive paradigm inevitably hypothesize a narrow set of circumstances in which it seems justified to depart from the normal rule or procedure. The narrowness of the hypothetical is crucial to its potential acceptance. No one would contend, for example, that the U.S. military should torture every suspected terrorist or Iraqi insurgent that we capture simply because he or she may have information that could prevent future attacks. The ticking time bomb argument is only persuasive—if it is persuasive at all—if the bomb is actually ticking and the suspect is likely to be able to disclose its whereabouts.

By their nature, worst-case scenarios are highly unlikely to come to pass. They are, after all, *worst*-case scenarios. The ticking bomb hypothetical, for example, posits that the bomb is planted and about to go off, that officials know it, that they know they have captured the man who either planted the bomb or knows where it is planted, that there is no other way to get the information, and that the suspect will tell the truth if tortured. In the real world, these conditions will seldom if ever be met, and are frequently unknowable.[9] Nevertheless, because the potential harm from the explosion is catastrophic, preventive-paradigm advocates argue that we must modify or discard the normal rules of law prohibiting torture to address this worst-case scenario.

We do not dispute that in the abstract it may make sense to tolerate more false positives (such as jailing innocent people) when the risk of a false negative (letting a guilty terrorist go free) is potentially catastrophic. But the emotional aspects of human decision making lead ordinary people and politicians to exaggerate fears of catastrophe, often resulting in irrational and unjust trade-offs. For example, Americans living on the West Coast after Pearl Harbor feared that some Japanese nationals or Japanese Americans might act as spies or saboteurs for Japan. But the roundup of more than one hundred thousand Japanese nationals and Japanese Americans was clearly a disproportionate response to a risk that was wildly exaggerated by emotional decision making and racism.

Modern social science suggests that such historical examples are not aberrations. If people could rationally calculate the risks of catastrophic harm and of false positives, in both the short and long term, it might make sense to discard the rules that guard against emotional and irrational decision making. But it makes little sense to do so if emotional factors in these situations systematically lead people to exaggerate the risk of catastrophic harm, and therefore to tolerate many more false positives than a rational calculation would warrant. In addition, where, as is so often the case, the costs of a preventive measure are selectively borne by a minority group, the majority's calculus is likely to be further skewed by the sense that the majority's liberties are not directly threatened.[10] And people tend to focus on short-term, highly vivid, and accessible costs, while discounting dangers that are more abstract and long-term.

Widespread preventive detention without adequate safeguards, for example, creates long-term risks that some of those detained will be radicalized by their treatment and become terrorist sympathizers, that Arab and Muslim communities will grow increasingly distrustful and be less likely to cooperate in tracking down terrorists, and that al-Qaeda will use our actions to recruit more terrorists. If one could rationally calculate the total long-term costs, these coercive preventive actions may very well *increase* the risk of a terrorist attack, especially given the low yield of actual terrorists that mass roundups have generally produced. But the fears of the moment make such a calibration inevitably skewed.

Decision making is often based on emotive, affect-based mental processes that tend to diverge from rational cognitive assessments of risk.[11] When faced with a potential catastrophe that has a small chance of eventuating, emotional factors frequently lead people either to ignore or to exaggerate the risk.[12] At times, to be sure, we may discount risks that would warrant more forceful action: consider the failure to confront global warming. Particularly where worst-case scenarios evoke vivid, emotionally laden images, reinforced by recent events, however, people are much more likely to overreact than underreact. As University of Chicago professor Cass Sunstein has noted, "worst case scenarios have a distorting effect on human judgment, often producing excessive fear about unlikely events."[13]

Because they are vivid, immediate, and potentially catastrophic, terrorist incidents are particularly likely to provoke this tendency to overreact. A study of one thousand Americans across the country, conducted a few weeks after 9/11, found that the average person believed that he or she faced a 20 percent chance of being injured in a terrorist attack within the next year. In fact, statistically speaking, Americans would not have faced that degree of risk even if a terrorist attack of the same magnitude as the 9/11 attacks took place every day for an entire year.[14]

When people are asked how much they will pay for flight insurance to cover losses resulting from terrorism, they agree to pay more than when asked what they would pay for flight insurance to cover losses from all causes (which would by definition include terrorist causes).[15] Specifically mentioning terrorism evokes vivid images of disaster, leading people to act irrationally and overestimate the risks they actually face. For the same reasons, Canadians, having recent vivid examples of persons afflicted with the SARS virus in their country, evaluated their risk of contracting the disease as much higher than did Americans, despite the fact that citizens of both nations faced statistically identical risks of infection.[16]

In short, when strong emotions are triggered, people tend to overestimate the risk of disaster.[17] As Sunstein argues,

> in the context of terrorism, the implication is clear. The risks associated with terrorist attacks are highly likely to trigger strong emotions, in part because of the sheer vividness of the bad outcome and the associated levels of outrage and fear. It follows that even if the likelihood of an attack is extremely low, people will be willing to pay a great deal to avoid it.[18]

Indeed, the perceived risks posed by terrorist threats may be so extreme that they are not quantifiable. Insurance experts and psychologists distinguish between "risk," a probability that is capable of being estimated, and "uncertainty," a probability that is unquantifiable. The threats posed by terrorists generally fall in the latter category.[19] As Judge Richard Posner, one of the country's leading exponents of cost-benefit analysis in law, acknowledges, cost-benefit analysis of counterterrorist measures "is exquisitely difficult" because we simply cannot estimate the probability of terrorist attacks, or for that matter, the costs of counterterrorism measures, which include adverse effects on personal and political liberty, privacy, and potentially, even political stability.[20] Sunstein similarly acknowledges that "when national security is threatened, cost-benefit analysis is far less promising, because the probability of an attack usually cannot be estimated."[21]

These distorting effects impede the ability of anyone to balance rationally the costs and benefits in response to a terrorist attack. But these skewing effects are likely to be even more extreme for politicians. First, the necessity to run for reelection means that politicians have extraordinarily powerful institutional incentives to favor short-term over long-term considerations. The costs of President Bush's war on terror will be borne by Americans long after he has left office. Second, politicians know that the political costs associated with allowing a terrorist to go free dramatically outweigh the costs of infringing on the rights of innocents, especially if the innocents are foreign nationals who have no voice in the political process.[22] Third, the costs of a false negative (failing to lock up a terrorist) are often much more visible than the costs of a false positive (locking up an innocent). The prosecutor who fails to seek pretrial detention of a suspect who subsequently commits a terrorist act will pay a high, and highly visible, price. The prosecutor who "errs on the side of caution" by detaining an individual who in fact possess no risk of danger will pay no price—because one will never know whether, if released, the detainee might have committed a terrorist act. In the former situation, the error is dramatically manifest. In the latter, the error is hidden and indeed inherently speculative.

Thus, for reasons of human psychology and political reality, government officials are far more likely to overreact than underreact to perceived threats of terror. These considerations do not mean that there is no case for changing the rules in the face of new threats, but it does suggest that any new rules that we adopt should preserve substantive and procedural restraints on discretion in order to offset the systemic bias toward overreaction. The rule of law, which favors clear rules and fair procedures for the imposition of harshly coercive measures and insists on checks and balances to ensure accountability, is critical in guiding government responses to the fear of terrorist attacks.

THE SLIPPERY SLOPE

The difficulties of preventive ad hoc balancing are compounded by the inability in practice to limit highly coercive preventive measures to the actual worst-case scenarios invoked to justify them in the first place. Because we tend to exaggerate the possibility of catastrophic harm, measures created to deal with the worst case will inevitably be extended to less-than-worst-case circumstances. If it is legal to torture a terrorist who we know has planted a bomb somewhere in New York City, why shouldn't it be legal to torture someone whom we suspect is a terrorist who may know of future terrorist plots? When the U.S. government permitted coercive interrogation in response to concerns about ticking bombs, the use of cruel and inhumane treatment became almost routine, as accounts from Abu Ghraib and Guantánamo attest. Once the government is permitted to detain suspected terrorists without fair proceedings to determine whether they pose a threat, it is likely that it will detain people who pose no risk, as the small numbers of actual terrorists in the Guantánamo population and the domestic roundups after 9/11 illustrated. Without clear lines, escalation becomes the rule, not the aberration, and a wide range of perceived threats become occasions for abuse.

Indeed, in the absence of clear rules, abuse may arise even without an explicit authorization for harsh treatment in extraordinary circumstances, as the Stanford Prison Project illustrates. Male student volunteers, chosen after interviews and a battery of psychological tests to ensure they were normal, average, and healthy, were randomly divided into two groups simulating inmates and guards in a mock prison. The prisoners were booked at a real jail, then blindfolded and driven to a makeshift prison on Stanford's campus. The guards were given uniforms, told that their job was to maintain law and order, and to use their billy clubs as symbols of authority only, not as actual weapons. They were otherwise given no rules.[23] Within days, the guards began to abuse the prisoners to such an alarming degree that the experiment was halted prematurely. The researchers drew the following conclusion:

> The use of power was self-aggrandizing and self-perpetuating. The guard power, derived initially from an arbitrary label, was intensified whenever there was any perceived threat by the prisoners and this new level subsequently became the baseline from which further hostility and harassment would begin. . . . The absolute level of aggression as well as the more subtle and "creative" forms of aggression . . . increased in a spiraling function.[24]

Stanley Milgram's experiment on people's willingness to inflict pain on others in obedience to authority further illustrates the importance of clear rules. Milgram's experiment suggests that people are more likely to impose escalating forms of abuse once seemingly less objectionable forms of abuse are accepted. When Milgram asked subjects to administer a potentially lethal shock to another person, most of them initially refused. When subjects were instead initially asked to administer only a minor shock, and then given a series of escalating requests to increase the voltage, most eventually administered shocks they thought to be potentially lethal.[25]

The same spiraling function is likely to occur with preventive coercion, especially if coercion is expressly authorized for extraordinary situations. Authorization to use coercive interrogation tactics for ticking time bomb situations is likely to bleed into less compelling circumstances, and the green light to use some coercive tactics is likely to lead interrogators, through a Milgram- or Stanford-like process of dehumanization and shifting baselines, to employ increasingly cruel measures.

Judge Posner, who generally favors permitting expansive preventive measures to respond to the risk of a catastrophic terrorist attack, nonetheless considers these slippery-slope concerns weighty enough to support a categorical legal ban on torture.[26] Posner argues that once legal rules are promulgated that allow torture in narrowly defined circumstances, officials will want to explore the outer bounds of the permission, "and the practice of torture, once it was thus regularized by judicial demarcation of those bounds, would be likely to become regular within them, ceasing to be an exceptional practice and setting the stage for further extension."[27] It is then, Posner explains, a short ride down the slippery slope.

> One begins with the extreme case—the terrorist with plague germs or an A-bomb the size of an orange in his Dopp kit, or the kidnapper who alone can save his victim's life by revealing the victim's location. So far so good; but then the following reflections are invited: if torture is legally justifiable when the lives of thousands are threatened, what about when the lives of hundreds are threatened, or tens. And the kidnap victim is only one. By such a chain of reflections one might be persuaded to endorse a rule that torture is justified if, all things considered, the benefits, which will often be tangible (lives, or a life saved), exceed the costs, which will often be nebulous.[28]

Although Posner fails to acknowledge the point, the same argument can be made for each of the coercive preventive measures at the heart of the Bush administration's response to terrorism. If we know a brutal dictator is developing weapons of mass destruction with the intention of giving them to terrorists to use against us, that no alternative means of deterrence are available, and that we have a very good chance of eliminating or radically reducing the threat with a limited surgical strike, the case for preventive military action seems compelling. But the real world is filled with ambiguities—if Iraq teaches anything, it is that we often cannot know with any degree of certainty the dictator's weaponry, his intentions, his susceptibility to deterrence, the terrorists' intentions and capabilities, or the long-term or short-term costs of military action. Once the normal boundaries are shifted, it is highly unlikely that preventive wars will be confined to the narrowly drawn hypotheticals used to justify the departure in the first place. The result will be an increase in unjustified and costly violence.

So, too, without clear rules to limit it, preventive detention, justified by reference to a worst-case scenario, almost inexorably expands. Judges and prosecutors will "err on the side of caution" by keeping people locked up even where they lack solid evidence of dangerousness. Prisoners detained at Guantánamo Bay were said to be the "worst of the worst," who had to be held to forestall future catastrophic attacks. But we now know that only about 5 percent of those held there over the course of the conflict are even said by the government to be al-Qaeda or Taliban fighters, that many were wrongfully detained, and that hundreds have been released.

The Supreme Court of Israel recently addressed the tendency of exceptions to expand once the government is given discretion to invoke them. The case challenged an Israeli military rule that permitted soldiers surrounding a house of an alleged terrorist to ask a local Palestinian to enter the house and request the fugitive to surrender. The rationale for the rule was that the fugitive would be less likely to attack, and more likely to talk to, a local Palestinian emissary than an Israeli soldier. Israeli army rules permitted this option only where all possibilities other than armed attack have been exhausted, and required that the Palestinian's consent be "genuine." On its face, this narrow exception might seem reasonable. Yet the court declared the practice illegal. Two senior judges in the majority explained that even if the procedure would be legal if consent was genuine, "the danger of slipping into the prohibited practice [of coercion] is inherent in the means it allows.[29] They expressed great "concern that the special and rare will become regular and routine."[30]

The court's conclusion was likely influenced by Israel's experience with torture. In 1987, the Landau Commission, chaired by Moshe Landau, former president of Israel's Supreme Court, concluded that moderate coercive interrogation of Palestinian terrorist suspects was legal under Israeli law so long as the lesser evil of force is necessary to get information that would prevent the greater evil of a loss of innocent lives.[31] The government then authorized moderate coercive interrogation in certain limited situations. In practice, Israeli investigators routinely disregarded the limits on torture that the Landau report attempted to preserve; some commentators claim that the Israeli Security Services tortured as many as 85 percent of detained Palestinians.[32] Against the backdrop of this record, the court ultimately barred all such tactics, rejecting the notion that the ticking bomb scenario provided legal authority for even moderate physical coercion.[33] The court did recognize that there might be occasions in which interrogators who applied physical coercion in a ticking bomb scenario could avail themselves of a necessity defense if criminally indicted for their actions, but refused to allow invocations of necessity to provide advance legal authorization of coercive methods.

The traditional legal rules prohibiting torture, preventive detention without hearings, or unilateral preventive war reflect not merely moral and ethical norms but a considered judgment that ad hoc balancing in certain situations is likely to produce unjustified governmental actions. The U.S. Supreme Court ultimately replaced its balancing approach toward subversive speech, mentioned above, with a bright-line rule that categorically bars the punishment of speech advocating criminal conduct except where the speech is both intended and likely to produce imminent illegal conduct.[34] While one can certainly imagine cases where the benefit of prohibiting subversive speech that falls short of such a bright line would be great, and where the costs of the prohibition would seem minimal, the Court does not trust government officials to reach the optimal cost-benefit judgment, so it has imposed a highly protective bright-line rule. More generally, social science and historical experience suggest the critical importance of protecting fundamental human rights with clear procedural and substantive safeguards to guard against the dangers inherent in unrestrained, ad hoc balancing in times of crisis.

It may well be that the potentially catastrophic dangers posed by al-Qaeda and other terrorist groups shift the cost-benefit analysis. But the highly emotional climate created by the fear of terrorism also makes the likelihood of balancing error even greater than before. On matters of terrorism and in times of emergency or crisis, ad hoc balancing left to political representatives—executive or legislative—is likely to overestimate the benefits of preventive measures and to downplay or ignore altogether the long-term costs to both liberty and security. For this reason, it is essential that we preserve the safeguards associated with the rule of law, such as fair processes, clear rules, and judicial review. They build in a measure of accountability that might cause political actors to think more carefully before acting.[35] As Professor Sunstein argues, the adoption of bright lines to protect liberty "merely recognizes that our balancing is likely to go wrong in practice—and that we need to develop safeguards against our own bad balancing, especially when public fear will predictably lead us astray."[36]

Judge Posner has argued that American officials have repeatedly and disastrously *underestimated* the dangers to our nation's security, ignoring, for example, the risk of a Japanese attack on the United States in 1941 or of an al-Qaeda attack in September 2001.[37] Without doubt, government officials have sometimes ignored dangers that might have been avoided by better precautionary measures. But Posner's argument ignores the evidence of social science and history, which shows that when a nation confronts a recent attack that has triggered strong emotions— precisely the point at which proposals will be considered to change the law, eliminate the bright lines, and expand government discretion—people are much more likely to overreact than underreact. That insight should not lead to government inaction or business as usual in confronting new threats. As we demonstrate in the next part, government can and should take preventive measures to protect against the threat of terrorism. But especially where the measures the government takes are highly coercive or violent—torture, assassination, war, or detention—the likelihood that government officials will exaggerate the need for such action and underestimate their costs argues for retaining, not abandoning, the legal restraints that protect against erroneous decision making.

The psychological evidence, the historical record, and the failure of recent coercive preventive measures to make us more secure cannot provide definitive proof that such measures never work or are always unjustified. At the same time, social science, history, and contemporary experience all point in the same direction, strongly suggesting the grave dangers inherent in the preventive paradigm. This evidence should give us pause before we abandon either the legal procedures or the rules that normally protect our liberty and security. The available evidence shows that the Bush administration's preventive paradigm has failed to make the United States—or the world—more safe from terrorism. On the contrary, it has made us more vulnerable by shoring up al-Qaeda's support. The war on terror and the Iraq War have both backfired, largely because the preventive measures that lie at their core lack the legitimacy that comes from following legal rules. The administration has portrayed itself as willing to make the difficult sacrifices necessary in order to make us more secure, but in fact it has sacrificed not only the principles for which we stand but also our very security.

PART III

AN ALTERNATIVE
PREVENTIVE STRATEGY

9. NONCOERCIVE STRATEGIES

The goal of reducing the risks of terrorism is a perfectly legitimate one, but the preventive paradigm is neither an effective nor a normatively acceptable means to that end. Rejecting the preventive paradigm, however, does not mean abandoning the goal of preventing terrorism. More effective prevention is achievable through a variety of measures, most involving little or no coercion. Because these measures generally do not implicate fundamental civil liberties and are less likely to be selectively targeted at vulnerable groups, they avoid many of the costs associated with the Bush administration's preventive paradigm.

In this section, we propose a four-part alternative preventive strategy. First, we should erect safeguards that reduce the likelihood of future harm without employing controversial and harshly coercive methods; there are many such options available, but the Bush administration has neglected them in favor of its coercive preventive paradigm. Second, we should reshape our foreign policy to address the root causes rather than merely the symptoms of terrorism. Third, we should eschew unilateral assertions of power for multilateral security strategies. In particular, if we are to repair the damage to U.S. standing in the world that the preventive paradigm has done, we must commit ourselves to be truly accountable to international law, and especially international human rights law. Finally, where coercive force is necessary—and surely it is sometimes necessary—we should treat the rule of law as an asset rather than an obstacle in responding to terrorist threats.

We are not the first to propose many of the initiatives discussed here. Many security experts have united behind these ideas. The Bush administration itself has already adopted some, though by no means all of them. Our aim is simply to demonstrate that alternatives to unilateral exercises of anticipatory violence exist, and that these alternatives could provide protection without doing damage to the United States' reputation in the world at large, or to its character at home. Playing by the rules, in other words, by no means requires a nation to surrender to terrorists. A sound counterterrorism program within the rule of law is not "a suicide pact."

In thinking about counterterrorism strategies, we would do well to learn from other settings where prevention has long been a principal policy goal. When doctors and health care professionals seek to prevent disease, for example, they generally prescribe low-cost, low-risk, and unobtrusive measures. Stopping smoking, eating healthier foods, and obtaining regular checkups reduce the incidence of cancer, heart attacks, and other life-threatening diseases and are generally preferable to more intrusive and risky surgical measures. Similarly, maintaining a clean water supply, washing hands regularly, and using condoms are all ways to limit the spread of communicable diseases. Good health care and nutrition for pregnant mothers reduces the risk of infant mortality. Even where disease is not life-threatening, low-cost preventive measures are the better approach. Brushing teeth is infinitely preferable to root canal work.

The same is true for fighting crime. Providing afterschool care to at-risk youth may prevent children from getting involved in juvenile delinquency and crime in the critical hours after school lets out and before their parents get home. Job training and employment assistance to prisoners in prison and upon release reduce rates of recidivism. Community policing initiatives, which seek to build trust between the police and the communities they serve, can make the police more effective in preventing crime. Public education itself is preventive, as those armed with a decent education are less likely to turn to crime as a way of supporting themselves. And drug abuse prevention and treatment have been shown to be more effective and efficient than incarceration in curbing illegal drugs and the criminal activity often associated with them.[1]

What is true in fighting disease and crime is also true in fighting terrorism. There are many low-risk, noncoercive, or mildly coercive initiatives that can make us safer, without triggering the substantial costs associated with the harshly coercive features of the Bush administration's preventive paradigm. While a counterterrorism strategy should not rule out coercion, it should generally prefer noncoercive measures to high-cost, risky, and harshly coercive initiatives. The recommendations of the bipartisan 9-11 Commission are largely of this type: safeguarding nuclear material so that it does not fall into the hands of terrorists; protecting dangerous targets such as chemical plants; improving information sharing between law enforcement and intelligence agencies; ensuring that first responders are adequately trained and equipped in order to reduce the damage from the next terrorist attack; and improving screening at airports, borders, and shipping ports.[2] The 9-11 Commission pointedly did not advocate rendition to torture, disappearance and coercive interrogation of suspects, ethnic profiling, mass roundups, or preventive war. It did address preventive detention of terrorists, but only to encourage the Bush administration to develop a multilateral coalition standard for detention and prosecution of captured terrorists, noting that the administration's unilateral approach to the subject has generated broad criticism and undermined efforts to forge necessary transnational alliances. Other experts have offered similar policy prescriptions; few recommend the kinds of coercive strategies that have come to dominate the Bush administration's approach.[3]

To its credit, the Bush administration has adopted some of these noncoercive or less coercive measures. It has increased security at borders and airports. It has directed more resources toward antiterrorism intelligence gathering, investigation, and analysis. It has reorganized the intelligence and security bureaucracies to improve coordination. And it has conducted surveillance on and placed informants in organizations suspected of planning terrorist crimes.

The Bush administration's record in these areas is mixed at best. In December 2005, the 9-11 Commission issued a report assessing the administration's progress on each of its forty-one specific recommendations for how to protect against the threat of terrorist attacks.[4] The assessment, issued in the form of a report card, is the kind no parent would ever want their child to bring home. The commission gave the administration five Fs, twelve Ds, eight Cs, several incompletes, and only one A–. Among the measures that received either an F or a D are some of the most basic steps toward homeland security: assessing critical infrastructure vulnerabilities (D); securing weapons of mass destruction (D); prescreening of airline passenger lists for potential terrorists (F); screening checked luggage and cargo for explosives (D); information sharing (D); developing common coalition standards for detention and prosecution of terrorist suspects (F); providing adequate communications for first responders (F); and supporting secular education in Muslim countries (D). These failures, in our view, are a direct consequence of the misplaced priorities of the preventive paradigm. Preferring to act tough, the Bush administration has not only run roughshod over the rule of law but also disregarded less dramatic though potentially more effective forms of prevention.

Consider, as one example, the administration's failure to confront the threat posed by the existence of poorly secured nuclear material around the world, especially in the former Soviet Union. The administration claims it went to war against Iraq to prevent it from obtaining nuclear weapons and giving them to terrorists. Yet most experts believe that the greatest danger of nuclear terrorism comes from nuclear theft rather than from a state providing nuclear bombs to terrorists. A January 2001 report issued to the incoming Bush administration by a bipartisan panel chaired by Howard Baker, former chief of staff to President Reagan and majority leader of the Senate, and Lloyd Cutler, who served as counsel to Presidents Carter and Clinton, stated that "the most urgent unmet national security threat to the

United States today is the danger that weapons of mass destruction or weapons-usable material in Russia could be stolen, sold
to terrorists or hostile nation-states and used against American
troops abroad or citizens at home."[5] It urged the government to
secure or eliminate all usable nuclear weapons materials located
in Russia within eight to ten years. Yet as of the end of 2004,
enough highly enriched uranium or plutonium remained in
unsecured Russian storage facilities to make 44,000 nuclear
weapons.[6] In late 2005, the Russian interior minister claimed
that in recent years "international terrorists have planned attacks against nuclear and power industry installations," attempting to "seize nuclear materials and use them to build
weapons of mass destruction for their own political ends."[7]

President Bush has said that "the nations of the world must
do all we can to secure and eliminate nuclear and chemical and
biological radiological material," but his actions have not
matched his rhetoric.[8] In giving the administration a D on this
issue, the 9-11 Commission found that "countering the greatest
threat to America's security [weapons of mass destruction] is
still not the top national security priority of the President and
the Congress."[9]

Here, as in other preventive areas, there is no shortage of ideas
about what to do, but a lack of commitment to implement the
ideas effectively. For fifteen years, the United States has had a
plan for securing, controlling, and destroying nuclear warheads
and materials around the world, named the Nunn-Lugar programs after the two senators who sponsored bipartisan legislation on the matter in 1991.[10] While President Bush has called for
expanding these programs, the amount spent on them has held
steady for the past several years, despite the Baker-Cutler task
force's call for tripling that funding.[11]

Because of insufficient funding and lack of executive leadership, achievement of the goals set forth by the Baker-Cutler task
force is likely to take until at least 2020—more than a decade beyond the target date the task force set.[12] Meanwhile, thousands

of nuclear weapons and materials in Russia remain unsecured. In 2006, a giant secure-storage facility for nuclear weapons materials built with U.S. funds at Mayak, Russia, still stood empty two and a half years after completion.[13] A chemical-weapons destruction facility is less than 40 percent complete, and reportedly may not be open by 2009.[14] A February 2007 Government Accountability Office report criticized the administration for making only "limited progress in securing many of the most dangerous sources" of radioactive materials in Russia. It warned that many nuclear waste disposal sites and abandoned nuclear generators across Russia, each with enough material for several "dirty bombs," remain vulnerable to theft.[15]

Building secure facilities is not enough. A building is ultimately only as secure as the people who guard it. Russian military and security forces are notoriously corrupt and suffer from low pay, poor conditions, and low morale. The pervasiveness of the problem is illustrated by the 1997 conviction of Admiral Igor Khmelnov, commander of the Russian Pacific fleet, for selling sixty-four decommissioned ships, including two aircraft carriers, to South Korea and India and pocketing the proceeds.[16] An internal Russian audit concluded that when submarines arrived at a Murmansk facility to be dismantled, 50 percent of their electronic components had already been stolen.[17] On a visit to a facility whose security had been upgraded with U.S. assistance, the Government Accountability Office found the gate to the central storage facility housing nuclear materials wide open and unattended.[18] A prank by a resident of the closed nuclear city of Lesnoy, site of a major nuclear weapons facility, exposed the ineffectiveness of Russian nuclear security guards. Dressed in combat fatigues and employing a forged identification badge with the name and photograph of Chechen terrorist leader Salmon Raduev, the resident was allowed to pass through three guarded checkpoints and gain access to the closed city.[19] While these lapses of security are primarily Russian responsibilities, it is critical to U.S. security that we help improve training for those who guard Russia's nuclear stockpile.

The Russian supply is by no means the only cache of nuclear materials vulnerable to theft. In March 2004, the *New York Times* reported on the U.S. government's lack of urgency in ensuring the security of highly enriched uranium (HEU) that it had provided to forty-three countries under President Eisenhower's Atoms for Peace program.[20] Enough HEU remains at these research reactors to build over a thousand nuclear weapons.[21] A 2004 Department of Energy review expressed particular concern about HEU stored in Iran, Pakistan, Israel, and South Africa, each in sufficient quantities for at least one bomb.[22] A mid-2005 investigation by *ABC News* disclosed inadequate security at most of twenty-six university-based research reactors in the United States (several of which possess HEU), varying from sleeping guards to security doors propped open with books.[23]

Pakistan poses an especially grave danger. Until 2004, Pakistan was involved in a surreptitious black market in nuclear materials that the head of the IAEA termed a "Wal-Mart of private sector additional proliferation."[24] It is now building a powerful new plutonium reactor that will produce enough fuel to make forty to fifty nuclear weapons a year. The Institute for Science and International Security has warned that "South Asia may be heading for a nuclear arms race that could lead to arsenals growing into the hundreds of nuclear weapons, or at minimum, vastly expanded stockpiles of military fissile material."[25] Yet the White House has done virtually nothing to deter Pakistan from completing this reactor.

Pakistan's rival, India, also poses real risks, and here, the administration has exacerbated the dangers. In 2005, the administration concluded an agreement to transfer U.S. nuclear fuel to India for civilian use, a transfer that some experts believe will dramatically increase India's capacity to build nuclear weapons.[26] It did so without insisting that India open its military nuclear reactors to inspection and comply with safety and security standards. Thus, while it fails to do enough to help Russia secure or eliminate its nuclear weapons, Washington seems to be enabling India and Pakistan to build many more.

The Global Threat Reduction Initiative, launched by the Bush administration in 2004, has the laudable goal of a global cleanout of nuclear materials from vulnerable research reactors and the conversion or closure of reactors that use weapons-grade HEU.[27] The initiative has had some success, but the timelines for implementing its goals stretch out to 2014 and 2019, meaning that even without inevitable delays, terrorists have more than a decade to attempt to obtain weapons-grade uranium from unsecured sources. The major obstacles to a shorter timeline are inadequate staffing and financing, limited incentives for conversions, and virtually no program to get countries to close older, unneeded reactors.[28]

In sum, our national security and the security of the globe desperately need a well-funded, high-priority preventive program to ensure that terrorists cannot gain access to the current stock of weapons-grade nuclear material. Scholars, experts, and task forces have outlined in detail how to do just that.[29] While the administration has acknowledged the problem of unsecured nuclear material, its focus on coercive preventive measures—especially the war in Iraq—has diverted resources, energy, and political capital that could be directed to the one preventive program that most experts agree should be our highest priority.

What is true of securing nuclear material is also true of many other widely recommended counterterrorist initiatives. Instead of pursuing a national campaign of ethnic and religious profiling at home and abroad and denying basic rights to Arab and Muslim detainees in the war on terror, we should be working to develop positive ties with Arab and Muslim communities here and around the world. Just as community policing has been shown to be effective in preventing crime, so, too, developing positive ties with Arab and Muslim communities would help us obtain the intelligence and expertise we need to find the jihadist terrorists who threaten us. It would also help to isolate al-Qaeda from its potential bases of support, a critical element of an effective counterterrorism strategy.[30]

Instead of spending hundreds of billions of dollars digging itself into a quagmire in Iraq, the administration should have focused its resources on shoring up defenses at home. The Iraq War costs more each month than all homeland security expenses combined.[31] In 2005, Congress appropriated $7.6 billion to improve security at military bases, but gave the Department of Homeland Security only $2.6 billion to "protect all the vital systems throughout the country that sustain a modern society."[32] According to *Foreign Policy in Focus*, Bush's 2007 budget would spend eight times as much on the military as on homeland security and all other forms of nonmilitary security programs combined.[33]

We should be spending more on radiation detectors for container cargo at shipping ports. As of 2006, we inspected only about 5 percent of containers coming into the country.[34] As the London and Madrid bombings demonstrated, we need to provide much greater security on our mass transit systems, which are extremely vulnerable to attack. And as we cannot possibly prevent all attacks, we need to prepare for the inevitable and minimize the consequences of the next attack by providing sufficient resources and training to first responders. First-responder initiatives have the benefit of providing protection not only against terrorist attacks but also against natural disasters, such as Hurricane Katrina, or outbreaks of communicable disease, such as bird flu or SARS. But here again, the Bush administration has devoted insufficient attention and resources to the problem.

These are not the glamorous or aggressive shock-and-awe initiatives that the Bush administration favors. They require instead the slow and painstaking work of assessing vulnerabilities, collecting and analyzing information, shoring up our defenses, building coalitions, and working to reduce the social factors that contribute to the dangerous ideological migration from fundamentalist Islamic beliefs to terrorist action. Such measures don't make for presidential photo ops in bomber jackets or sound bites pulled from old westerns, but they also don't lead to photo ops for the opposition, such as Abu Ghraib and Guantánamo. Most importantly, they would make us safer without incurring the considerable costs of the preventive paradigm.

10. A PREVENTIVE FOREIGN POLICY

One cannot fight terrorism without understanding its roots. President Bush has claimed that al-Qaeda commits terrorist acts because they "hate our freedoms."[1] Osama bin Laden refuted the charge, responding that if that were so, "let him explain to us why we don't strike Sweden, for example."[2] In 2004, a Defense Department advisory board sided with bin Laden, concluding that "Muslims do not 'hate our freedom,' but rather they hate our policies."[3] So too, University of Chicago professor Robert Pape's study of suicide bombers found that most are driven not by a hatred of democracy, but by what they perceive as foreign domination.[4] Pape found that "every suicide campaign from 1980 to 2001 has had as a major objective—or as its central objective—coercing a foreign government that has military forces in what they see as their homeland to take those forces out."[5]

An effective preventive strategy to combat terrorism must seek to eradicate or at least reduce the root causes of terrorism. We must understand the motivations of our enemy, for only such understanding can allow us to counteract the conditions that spawn terrorists in the first place. Empty rhetoric that terrorists attack us because they hate our freedoms only leads us astray.

First, our foreign policy must deemphasize military "solutions." The 9-11 Commission recommended "a preventive strategy that is as much or more, political as it is military."[6] To date, our strategy has been predominantly military and coercive. As Anne Marie Slaughter, dean of Princeton University's Woodrow Wilson School of Public and International Affairs, put it, "we are losing the war on terror because we are treating the symptoms and not the cause."[7] Because terrorists are so often motivated by resentment of foreign occupation or intervention, we should emphasize diplomacy and reinforcement of our defenses at home rather than projecting military power abroad.

In the wake of the Cold War, however, we have increased rather than decreased our reliance on military force. During the entire Cold War era, spanning almost forty-five years, there were six large-scale U.S. military actions abroad. Yet the eighteen years since the end of the Cold War have already seen at least eight U.S. military interventions, a number that does not include innumerable lesser military actions, such as President Clinton's cruise missile attacks or the intermittent bombing of Iraq during the 1990s.[8] The Bush administration's global war on terror and preventive-war doctrines have escalated this trend toward militarism.

A preventive foreign policy would start by untethering the goal of defense from the goal of maintaining global dominance reflected in the 2002 National Security Strategy.[9] One concrete step would be to reduce American reliance on overseas military bases. That initiative would in turn deprive terrorists of one of their most powerful recruiting arguments, namely, opposition to the U.S. military presence abroad. It would also allow us to devote more resources to homeland security and encourage our allies to take a greater role in defending themselves.

As of September 2001, the Department of Defense publicly disclosed at least 725 American military bases outside the United States in some forty countries.[10] There are actually many more; the department does not report many of the bases that currently exist. For example, the Pentagon's Base Structure Report for 2003 makes no mention of any U.S. military presence in Iraq, Kuwait, Afghanistan, Uzbekistan, or the Horn of Africa, even though we have a significant military presence in each.[11]

In many foreign nations, the predominant American presence is not diplomatic but military. Many of these bases cause significant tensions with local populations, who see them as representing not legitimate American defensive needs but U.S. military domination of their nation or region. One of bin Laden's principal grievances was the stationing of thousands of U.S. troops in Saudi Arabia, an objection reportedly shared by 95 percent of Saudi society.[12] In a 1998 fatwa calling on his followers to kill Americans and their allies, bin Laden asserted that "for over seven years the United States has been occupying the Lands of Islam in the holiest of places, the Arabian Peninsula, plundering its riches, dictating to its rulers, humiliating its people, terrorizing its neighbors, and turning its bases in the Peninsula into a spearhead through which to fight the neighboring Muslim peoples."[13]

U.S. military bases abroad have become prime terrorist targets. In 1996, terrorists detonated a powerful truck bomb at Khobar Towers, the headquarters of the U.S. Central Command in Saudi Arabia, killing nineteen American servicemen and injuring hundreds. After that attack, a Defense Department science board report concluded that "historical data show a strong correlation between U.S. [military] involvement in international situations and an increase in terrorist attacks against the United States."[14]

After the fall of Baghdad, Rumsfeld announced that American combat troops would be withdrawn from Saudi Arabia. That withdrawal, however, is unlikely to have much effect on terrorist recruitment, given the deployment of over 130,000 American troops in Iraq and the construction of what are widely seen as permanent military bases there, as well as the U.S. bases in neighboring Kuwait, Bahrain, and Qatar. In April 2003, immediately after the fall of Baghdad, the *New York Times* reported that senior Bush administration officials were planning "a long-term military relationship with the emerging government of Iraq, one that would grant the Pentagon access to military bases and project American influence into the heart of the unsettled region."[15] In May 2006, the Bush administration requested hundreds of millions of dollars to expand four huge, heavily fortified bases in Iraq, suggesting, at a minimum, plans for a long-term presence in that country.[16] The White House has refused to state unequivocally whether we plan to have permanent bases in Iraq. Yet an overwhelming majority of Iraqis believe that we do, and that perception contributes to the almost daily violence against American military personnel.[17]

American military bases in Kuwait, Bahrain, and Qatar far exceed any legitimate defensive need the United States might require in the region, particularly given that the navy is capable of deploying up to five carrier battle groups in nearby international waters—each of which includes approximately seventy-five aircraft, cruise missiles and atomic weapons, destroyers, cruisers, and a submarine.[18] Military analysts argue that many of our foreign bases serve only marginal defense interests.[19] The Senate Foreign Relations Committee observed as early as 1970 that "once an American base is established it takes on a life of its own. Original missions may become outdated but new missions are developed, not only with the intention of keeping the facility going, but often to actually enlarge it."[20] If we want to reduce terrorist attacks against U.S. targets, we should reduce our military presence throughout the world except where such presence is truly necessary.

If we were to cut the military budget, we could then redirect some of the money saved toward diplomatic and educational efforts to counteract terrorism. At present, 93 percent of U.S. budgetary allocations dedicated to international affairs goes to the military and only 7 percent goes to the State Department.[21] A 2006 survey of foreign policy experts across the political spectrum found that 86 percent agreed that to succeed against terrorism we must increase the budget of the State Department. On no other single counterterrorism proposal was there such widespread agreement.[22]

Yet the Bush administration has done little or nothing to reduce military spending or increase State Department spending. Its goal of maintaining military dominance has meant maintaining a military establishment that dwarfs all others. According to some estimates, the United States spends almost as much on national defense as all other nations in the world combined.[23] We could drastically reduce that amount without appreciably harming our real defense needs. Harvard professor and foreign policy expert Stanley Hoffman proposes cutting military expenditures by half.[24] A recent task force of security experts identified nearly $62 billion in cuts that could be made without undercutting our national defense, mostly for weapons systems that have scant relevance to the threats we face today.[25] Military analyst Andrew Bacevich claims that we could save tens of billions of dollars per year if we simply reduced our defense spending to the combined total of the next ten largest military powers, a total still far in excess of any remotely plausible defense need.[26]

Meanwhile, while we are the unrivaled world leader in defense spending, the United States ranks virtually at the bottom of industrialized countries in its per capita foreign aid to developing countries.[27] The potential upside of increased foreign aid is illustrated by one side-effect of the U.S. effort to provide relief to Indonesia after the tsunami of December 2004.[28] Surveys show that after the Iraq invasion, the percentage of Indonesians who viewed the United States favorably plummeted to 15 percent. However, after the United States played an important role in the tsunami relief effort, favorable views of the United States there rose to 38 percent, and popular support for combating terrorism more than doubled, from 23 percent in 2003 to 50 percent in 2005.[29] While these poll reversals may prove temporary, they suggest that the anti-Americanism that helps sustain terrorist recruitment could be turned around if we were to engage in more interventions of assistance rather than of domination.

We also need to do much more to improve relations with Muslims worldwide, the vast majority of whom are potential allies in the struggle against extreme jihadists. Our success ultimately turns on isolating al-Qaeda by appealing to those who might become but are not yet sympathetic toward it. That goal has been radically undermined by the double standards and ethnic and religious profiling of the preventive paradigm. We need to resist the temptation to rely on double standards, but we must also devote substantial resources and energy to public diplomacy, foreign exchange, and support of secular education in the Muslim world. In October 2004, the U.S. Advisory Commission on Public Diplomacy reported that public diplomacy was "absurdly and dangerously underfunded." [30] Educational and cultural exchanges with Muslin nations received only slightly more funding in the 2004 budget than in the pre–September 11 budget, and the number of exchange students from those countries is woefully small. [31] The 9-11 Commission gave the administration D grades for both its development of scholarship, exchange, and library programs with Middle Eastern societies and its support of secular education in Muslim countries. [32]

A good part of our vulnerability to terrorists can be traced to our dependence on oil. Our dominant presence in the Middle East and our support of repressive governments there is largely attributable to the fact that we consume 25 percent of the world's oil but possess only 3 percent. As a result, we are heavily dependent on the Middle East, and many of our priorities and policies are skewed by that fact of economic life. As a blue-ribbon committee sponsored by the Century Foundation noted, "the greater our dependence on foreign oil, the greater our exposure to the will of other nations and terrorists." [33] Thus, reducing our use of oil and dramatically investing in the development of energy alternatives would not only serve important environmental needs but also might give us the flexibility to avoid some of the foreign policy choices we make that spur so much anti-American sentiment in the Middle East.

As British prime minister Tony Blair has argued, resolution of the Israeli-Palestinian conflict is absolutely critical to reducing tensions in the Middle East and eliminating one of the most powerful rallying cries of Islamic terrorists. While it has long been noted that bin Laden focused on Palestine only belatedly, it can hardly be denied that that conflict plays a central role in fueling anti-American and pro-jihadist feeling around the world today. As many have recommended, the United States and its partners should push Israel to negotiate with the Palestinians for a two-state solution, in which the Palestinians would get a viable state in the land occupied by Israel since 1967, not truncated and divided by Israeli settlements and roads, or walled in by Israeli fences. The Palestinians in turn should be pressured to recognize Israel, renounce terrorism, and give up their right to return. While the outlines of such a settlement have been clear for many years, the parties to the conflict cannot reach a durable peace without outside intervention, much of which must come from the United States. Thus far, however, the Bush administration has given Israel an essentially free rein in dealing with the Palestinians and done little to resolve the dispute.

Finally, the United States must withdraw its troops from Iraq and seek a multilateral resolution of the Iraq War. As virtually every expert now concedes, our intervention there has backfired in virtually every sense, leading to massive loss of innocent life, dangerous instability, widespread anti-American resentment, and increased terrorism in the region and around the world. We have a responsibility to minimize the damage we have done. An orderly withdrawal seems absolutely essential, but we must also help Iraq achieve a peaceful society and stable government. While the path to peace is not obvious, one thing is clear: keeping U.S. troops there is not helping the situation. It fuels violence, makes the troops themselves targets of insurgents, and feeds the proliferation of terrorist groups. While a withdrawal might spark even more bloodshed in the short term, keeping our troops there virtually ensures that the civil war will continue to escalate. What is needed is the orderly, phased, but relatively quick withdrawal of U.S. troops, combined with genuine multilateral diplomacy with Islamic nations such as Iran, Saudi Arabia, and Syria, as well as with European countries and the United Nations to develop a framework for long-term reconstruction of

Iraq under multinational auspices. The Iraq War has been devastating for the security of Iraqi and U.S. citizens alike, and President Bush's approach is simply making a bad situation worse.

Even the most enlightened foreign policy would not eliminate the threat of terrorism. But it is our foreign policy that is often at the root of terrorist grievances, and therefore we would be foolish not to look to foreign policy as a partial solution. If we can eliminate or mitigate some of the conditions that fuel anti-American resentment and terrorist recruitment, we will be less dependent on the harshly coercive measures that have thus far backfired. To recognize that terrorism has root causes is not to condone it, nor to say that we should give in to terrorist demands. It is to say that an honest, self-critical review of what we do around the world to trigger so much resentment might help us reduce the threat that we now face.

11. MULTILATERAL SOLUTIONS TO A TRANSNATIONAL PROBLEM

When Democratic presidential candidate John Kerry suggested during a 2004 presidential debate that the United States should think about how its actions are perceived by other nations, President Bush immediately derided the idea as an unacceptable "global test." In keeping with that attitude, the Bush administration has projected a go-it-alone attitude hostile to international law almost from the day it took office.[1] In doing so, it has either ignored or undermined a number of multilateral avenues that offer promising ways to advance our preventive interests without triggering a counterproductive backlash.

The terrorist threat we face is distinctively transnational. We must now worry about threats emanating from virtually every corner of the globe. To address the threat effectively, we have no choice but to work with other nations to further the collective interests of many. Moreover, if we are to recover the standing we once had as a human rights leader, it will not be enough to halt the illegal practices that have come to symbolize the preventive paradigm. We must abandon our hostility to the notion that international human rights standards might bind us, and instead embrace those standards fully, as have so many other nations in the modern era. As examples of how a multilateral approach might help to prevent terrorism, we will discuss, in turn, the proliferation of nuclear weapons, the use of international tribunals to hold terrorists accountable, the role of the United Nations in regulating preventive war, and the importance of making a meaningful commitment to human rights and humanitarian law.

NUCLEAR WEAPONS

One of the most direct ways to reduce the likelihood that terrorists will obtain nuclear weapons is to reduce nuclear proliferation itself. The problem of proliferation involves many nations, and therefore the solution must as well. Indeed, that is the animating idea behind the Treaty on the Non-proliferation of Nuclear Weapons (NPT), which has been credited with limiting proliferation of nuclear weapons over the past three decades. The treaty was negotiated in the 1960s, when only five nations possessed nuclear weapons. At that time, the U.S. government predicted that within the next decade, fifteen to twenty more states would obtain nuclear weapons. Independent experts put the figure as high as fifty.[2] Largely because of the NPT, as of 2006 only four other nations (Israel, India, Pakistan, and North Korea), are known to have joined the small club of nuclear weapon states. Many other nations that were beginning nuclear weapons programs—Argentina, Brazil, Canada, Sweden, and Taiwan—accepted the NPT and voluntarily dismantled their programs. Yet the Bush administration, rather than seeking to strengthen a treaty that has demonstrably contributed to our security, has instead undermined it.

Despite the NPT's relative success, the current crises with Iran and North Korea have led some observers to warn that the treaty is in danger of collapse. Most experts believe, however, that the current problems could be corrected if there were strong international leadership to negotiate necessary reforms. U.S. leadership in particular could make an enormous difference in strengthening what heretofore has been a relatively effective legal mechanism for preventing nuclear proliferation. Regrettably, President Bush has failed to play that role.

At the heart of the NPT is a bargain. Nations that do not have nuclear weapons agreed to forgo the development of such weapons, and to subject their nuclear energy programs to international inspection by the IAEA, in exchange for gaining access to nuclear technology and nuclear power for nonmilitary purposes. In addition, the nuclear weapons states agreed to reduce their arsenals and negotiate in good faith toward nuclear disarmament.

In return for agreeing not to develop nuclear weapons, the NPT gives nonweapon states the "inalienable right" to develop nuclear technology for peaceful purposes. But as recent events illustrate, the same technology is often capable of both military and nonmilitary uses. Countries like Iran can assert their right to enrich nuclear fuel for what they claim are peaceful purposes, and thereby develop technology that is the key to making both reactor-grade fuel and bomb-grade material. Once Iran or any other country produces enough bomb-grade uranium to make nuclear weapons, it could withdraw from the treaty and within months or years have a nuclear bomb.

One solution is to limit the right of nonweapon states to produce their own nuclear fuel in return for guaranteeing those states access to internationally controlled fuel. In 2004, a special UN panel composed of former high-level officials from numerous countries (including the first President Bush's national security adviser, Brent Scowcroft) proposed that the IAEA act as the guarantor for the supply of nuclear material for civilian nuclear uses.[3] IAEA director general Mohamed ElBaradei has also proposed an international agreement to place the manufacture and export of enriched uranium under multinational control.[4] Such measures would not prevent rogue states from attempting to violate the treaty but would undermine the claims of nations such as Iran that they have sovereign right to enrich their own uranium.[5]

President Bush has instead proposed that the enrichment and sale of uranium fuel be placed under the control of the countries that already produce nuclear fuel—presumably led by the United States. But Iran and many other non–nuclear weapons states have strongly resisted subjecting themselves to the control of the weapons-producing countries.[6] As ElBaradei has noted, this selective approach is bound to be perceived as unfair: "the representative of South Africa is going to say, how can we accept that Pakistan, India and Israel, which are rogue states so far as the NPT is concerned, are in and we are out"?[7] By refusing to accept true international control, the Bush administration has blocked progress on reconstituting an effective nonproliferation regime. Kofi Annan has termed the failure "a disgrace."[8]

Another major problem is that the nuclear weapon states have been slow to reduce their own nuclear arsenals. In 2000, they committed to taking thirteen concrete steps toward nuclear disarmament—yet by 2004 these efforts were all but renounced.[9] The United States continues to spend $4 billion annually on nuclear weapons research and development, modernizing nuclear missiles, and deploying and developing new tactical nuclear weapons.[10] Even more ominously, nuclear weapon states have reneged on their pledge not to use or threaten to use nuclear weapons against nonnuclear states.[11] The United States, for example, in its 2002 Nuclear Posture Review, declared that it had a right to use nuclear weapons against any country with *any* weapons of mass destruction.[12]

The failure of the nuclear weapon states to abide by their disarmament commitments makes it difficult to deter proliferation by others. In 1998, for example, India justified its development of nuclear weapons by pointing to the refusal of nuclear weapons nations to move toward disarmament.[13] As the UN panel stated, "lackluster disarmament by the nuclear weapon states weakens the diplomatic force of the nonproliferation regime and thus its ability to constrain proliferation."[14] Why should other nations comply with the treaty's obligations when the nuclear powers themselves have disregarded their commitments? As a study by the Carnegie Endowment for International Peace points out, the only way to strengthen the nonproliferation regime is "to enforce compliance universally, not selectively, including the obligations the nuclear states have taken on themselves."[15]

The U.S. approach has been to stem nuclear proliferation crisis by crisis, on an ad hoc basis. What is needed is a reliable system of international inspection and enforcement applicable to all: in other words, an effective multilateral legal framework. As the CIA's George Tenet stated in a related context, "We race from threat to threat to threat. . . . There was not a system in a place to say, 'You've got to go back and do this and this and this.' . . . The moral of the story is, if you'd taken those measures systemically over the course of time . . . you might have had a better chance of succeeding." [16]

INTERNATIONAL CRIMINAL JUSTICE

As the first five years of the war on terror have illustrated, it is not enough to capture terrorists. If we do not eventually bring them to justice international pressure will compel us to release them. It is crucial, moreover, that when we bring terrorists to justice, we do so through means widely accepted as neutral and fair. If we are seen as dispensing a biased form of victor's justice, we may simply turn terrorist defendants into martyrs, thereby sparking the recruitment of still more supporters to the terrorists' cause.

Here, too, a multilateral approach could play an important role in ensuring that terrorists and war criminals are brought to justice with widely accepted legitimacy. We need not limit ourselves to international tribunals, but an effective multilateral legal regime for trying such international criminals could make it easier to bring terrorists to justice, and might deter dictators from engaging in or supporting terrorist acts in the first place. The International Criminal Court could provide such a forum, but the United States has done everything in its power to sabotage this potential ally in the struggle against terrorism.

In 1998, 160 nations negotiated a treaty in Rome to establish an International Criminal Court (ICC) with jurisdiction to prosecute war crimes, crimes against humanity, and genocide. Over one hundred nations have ratified the treaty, including every member of the European Union and virtually all of the United States' traditional allies.[17] The court officially opened for business in March 2003. Alleged crimes arising out of the conflicts in the Darfur region of Sudan, in northern Uganda, the Central African Republic, and the Congo have been referred to the prosecutor for investigation. But the future of the ICC is in serious question.

The biggest single obstacle to the ICC's success is the hostility of the United States. At the root of that hostility is our reluctance to be bound by the rules that apply to everyone else. Our opposition predates the Bush administration, but has become much more entrenched and aggressive under Bush. The Clinton administration supported the call for the ICC in the mid-1990s, but sought to make U.S. citizens immune from prosecution. President Clinton argued that the United States had considerably larger military commitments abroad than any other country and therefore faced a substantially greater risk of having its soldiers prosecuted. He proposed that the court would have jurisdiction only over cases referred to it by the UN Security Council—where the United States exercises a veto power.

Other nations properly rejected that proposal, fearing that the inclusion of such a double standard—effectively immunizing members of the Security Council from accountability—would undermine the court's legitimacy. The treaty that emerged included safeguards to prevent politically motivated prosecutions. But the final treaty provides for criminal jurisdiction over citizens of all countries, including those that have not signed the treaty, a provision deemed crucial to ensure that leaders who committed mass atrocities or war crimes could not escape punishment by not ratifying the treaty. As a result, U.S. military officials could be prosecuted even though the United States has not ratified the treaty.

President Clinton signed the treaty, but stated that his administration would not submit it to the Senate for ratification (where it undoubtedly would have been rejected anyway). By signing the treaty despite continuing objections, the Clinton administration hoped to be part of a process to renegotiate its terms.

When it came to power, however, the Bush administration effectively "unsigned" the treaty and expressed implacable opposition to it.[18] The under secretary for political affairs, Marc Grossman, explained that the administration viewed the ICC as a hindrance to American military power: "With the ICC prosecutor and judges presuming to sit in judgment of the security decisions of States without their assent, the ICC could have a chilling effect on the willingness of States to project power in defense of their moral and security interests."[19] Left unsaid was the fact that the only "security decisions" the ICC can sit in judgment over are decisions to commit war crimes, crimes against humanity, or genocide.

The Bush administration has subsequently taken a series of actions designed to ensure that Americans will never be prosecuted, and in doing so has further undermined the new court. The blueprint was set forth by John Bolton, the administration's first head of its ICC policy team, when he proposed that the U.S. position on the ICC should be termed, "the Three Noes: no financial support, directly or indirectly; no collaboration; and no further negotiation with other governments to improve the Statute." Bolton predicted that "this approach is likely to maximize the chances that the ICC will wither and collapse, which should be our objective."[20]

The Bush administration wasted no time in pursuing Bolton's agenda. In 2002, Congress enacted the American Service Members' Protection Act, which generally prohibits U.S. military assistance to any country that is a party to the ICC. The statute also authorizes the president to "use all means necessary" to free any U.S. national detained by the ICC, a provision some have called the "Hague Invasion Act."[21] The administration has also pressured nations to sign bilateral agreements that would bar them from surrendering an American soldier or U.S. employee accused of war crimes to the ICC. About eighty countries have signed such agreements rather than lose U.S.-funded military training assistance. Others have resisted and as a result have lost needed funds. Over twenty states that are parties to the ICC, including Brazil, Costa Rica, Ecuador, South Africa, and Croatia, refused to sign such bilateral agreements.

These tactics have caused significant tensions with our allies. The European Union has developed a common policy opposing the bilateral agreements the United States is urging countries to sign. In June 2003, the Bush administration warned that the impact on U.S.-EU relations would be "very damaging" if the European Union did not change its stance.[22] The EU did not back down, however, and later that month announced that ten countries soon to become EU members had decided against entering bilateral immunity agreements with the United States.[23] The United States thereupon suspended all U.S. military assistance to Lithuania, Latvia, Estonia, Slovakia, and Bulgaria—some of the first countries to support the administration in the Iraq war.[24]

Shutoffs of programs to train and equip militaries in Kenya, Mali, Tanzania, and Niger over the ICC issue have angered senior U.S. military commanders, who warn that the cuts weaken counterterrorism efforts in places where the threat of international terrorism is believed to be most acute.[25] In 2005, the United States cut off $13 million to Kenya, a nation described by Pentagon officials as a "key partner in our counterterrorism strategy." To these military officers, it makes no sense to seek Kenya's support in fighting terrorism while denying it the funds it needs to carry out that fight.[26]

Richard Goldstone, a South African Constitutional Court justice and chief prosecutor for the UN international criminal tribunals for the former Yugoslavia and Rwanda, has argued that an effective ICC "can be a powerful tool in the fight against terrorism. The important link between peace and prosecution by an impartial court should not be underestimated."[27] Bush administration officials have pointed with pride to "our pioneering leadership in the creation of tribunals in Nuremberg, the Far East, and the International Criminal Tribunals for the former Yugoslavia and Rwanda."[28] In this view, international justice is fine for them but not for us. The United States has failed the challenge set forth by the chief prosecutor at Nuremberg, Supreme Court justice Robert Jackson, who argued that we must be bound by the same rule of law that we apply to others.[29] The vigorous prosecution of terrorists and war criminals requires not simply that we try them ourselves, or that we persuade other nations to create ad hoc tribunals to do so, but that we help create an effective world mechanism for bringing international criminals to justice, to which our own officials are as subject as anyone else. In this area, as in the nonproliferation context, the question is whether U.S. leadership will be brought to bear on behalf of the rule of law—or on behalf of special privileges. We cannot have it both ways.

SEEKING MULTILATERAL APPROVAL
FOR PREVENTIVE WAR

As we have shown above, international law prohibits *unilateral* preventive war, but permits it where the UN Security Council authorizes it. This procedural safeguard ensures that nations will not initiate preventive wars except where there is substantial international consensus that it is truly necessary.

President Bush has insisted that "America will never seek a permission slip to defend the security of our country."[30] But preventive military action would be far less controversial, and far less likely to provoke an anti-American backlash, if we recognized what international law requires: namely, that beyond situations of self-defense, we must seek authorization from the United Nations before using military force against another country. Security Council approval will not be easy to obtain, but given the dangers of preventive war, that is a positive, not a negative, factor. The need to satisfy an international body will both check the temptations to strike unnecessarily and provide much-needed legitimacy to those preventive military enterprises that are necessary.

In 2004, a High-Level Panel on Threats, Challenges and Change appointed by UN Secretary General Kofi Annan to study the issue of preventive war acknowledged that there might be situations that warrant preventive military action against a nonimminent threat, but rejected a rule that would allow unilateral resort to such measures:

> If there are good arguments for preventive military action, with good evidence to support them, they should be put to the Security Council, which can authorize such action if it chooses to. . . . [I]n a world full of perceived potential threats, the risk to the global order and the norm of non-intervention on which it continues to be based is simply too great for the legality of unilateral preventive action, as distinct from collectively endorsed action, to be accepted.[31]

Critics of this approach argue that the United States cannot place its national security at the mercy of an international institution, and especially not the Security Council. As Harvard law professor Alan Dershowitz has put it, "a rule that requires nations to put their own survival in the hands of a potentially hostile international organization will simply not be followed. The concern is not so much with the rule in theory as with the failure to take into account the reality of how the Security Council is constituted and how it makes its decisions."[32] Dershowitz contends that the Security Council "is not a principled institution, with constituent members who vote on the basis of neutral or objective criteria of justice or law." He claims that there is "absolutely no evidence to support the premise that Security Council members vote in accord with *any principle* other than that of self-serving advantage and realpolitik bias."

Admittedly, the Security Council has not been a model of consistency. It was structured as a political institution, after all, not a court, and was expected to make decisions based not only on broad principles but also on state interests. It is also true, as the UN panel found, that council decisions have often been "less than persuasive and less than fully responsive to very real state and human security needs." [33] Nonetheless, it is wrong to say that its members have not voted in accordance with "any principle" other than "self-serving advantage."

In fact, the Security Council and the UN General Assembly have been fairly consistent in condemning the unilateral preventive use of force, but not condemning military responses to imminent threats of attack. When Israel, Britain, and France attacked Egypt in 1956 after Nasser nationalized the Suez Canal, a majority of the Security Council condemned that action, although Britain and France vetoed the resolution. The General Assembly then convened an emergency session to consider a resolution for a cease-fire. Faced with a diplomatic disaster and mounting international pressure, Britain and France withdrew a week later, and eventually the UN arranged for the complete withdrawal of all three nations from Egypt and the placement of UN peacekeepers in the Sinai. As Dershowitz recognizes, the 1956 military action "was largely preventive in nature," and the UN opposed it on that ground. Similarly, when Israel attacked the Osirak nuclear reactor in 1981, the Security Council unanimously condemned it as an unjustified preventive strike. Prime Minister Margaret Thatcher and President Ronald Reagan joined in the criticism, despite their traditional alliances with Israel.

In contrast, when Israel launched the 1967 war against Egypt in response to what it saw as an imminent Egyptian attack, many nations accepted the reasonableness of the Israeli position. The Security Council debated the legality of the Israeli attack, but no resolution was ever voted upon, an outcome that observers interpreted as tacit approval of Israel's actions. The council also declined to condemn Israel's rescue of hostages held in Entebbe, Uganda, who were subject to an imminent threat of injury or death; again, the Security Council's inaction was widely seen as an indication that it did not consider the rescue mission unlawful.[34]

In 1991, the Security Council condemned the Iraqi invasion of Kuwait and authorized nations to use force to remove Iraqi forces from Kuwait. A little more than ten years later, with virtually the same parties involved, the Security Council refused to authorize war against Iraq. The difference in the two votes reflects the principle that the use of force is justified only in self-defense unless the Security Council finds military force necessary to deal with a serious threat to peace. The council correctly perceived that force was not necessary to deal with the threat Iraq posed in 2003.

The United Nations is certainly beset with difficulties. During the Cold War, the Security Council was virtually paralyzed. Civil war has been the main form of post–World War II warfare, and the UN has not developed an effective mechanism to address internal conflicts. The Security Council has largely unchecked discretion in deciding whether to intervene or authorize force to deal with threats to peace, and such broad discretion creates the risk of inconsistent results. The veto power of the five permanent members is an ever-present obstacle to effective collective security action.

Nonetheless, the end of the Cold War has seen the Security Council become much more effective in addressing international threats to peace. The average annual number of resolutions the council has passed has increased fourfold since 1989.[35] Over 90 percent of all the council's resolutions dealing with threats to international peace have been adopted since 1989.[36] Before 1989, the council imposed sanctions against a nation only twice; since then it has applied sanctions fourteen times, and sanctions have in some instances helped to produce negotiated agreements. Since the end of the Cold War, there has been a rapid growth in UN activity in civil wars.[37] At the same time, since 1992, the number of civil wars has steadily declined, dropping more than 40 percent by 2003.[38]

The Security Council's veto is undoubtedly a potential problem. A future U.S. government would face a real dilemma if it had reliable evidence that another country was developing nuclear weapons and would give them to al-Qaeda, and one member of the Security Council unilaterally vetoed a resolution authorizing the use of military force. In such a case, where the overwhelming majority sentiment on the Security Council favored the use of force, the United States might invoke an alternative mechanism: the UN General Assembly can take action by majority vote under the Uniting for Peace Resolution adopted in the 1950s.[39]

The Security Council has shown itself willing and able to address the specific threat of terrorism. On September 12, 2001, it condemned the attacks of 9/11 and unanimously enacted Resolution 1368, "recognizing the inherent right of individual or collective self-defense in accordance with the Charter," [40] a position it reaffirmed two weeks later. While such a right of self-defense might seem self-evident to most Americans, this was the first time that a nation's right to attack another nation in response to terrorist violence was explicitly endorsed by an international body.[41]

Two weeks later, on September 28, 2001, the Security Council unanimously adopted Resolution 1373, which required all states to criminalize terrorist acts, to prevent and suppress the financing of terrorists, to freeze the financial assets of anyone involved in terrorist acts, and to prohibit anyone within their jurisdiction from making assets available to terrorists. It also required states to deny haven or refuge to anyone involved in terrorist acts and to ensure that any person involved in terrorism is brought to justice.[42] The Security Council also established the Counter-Terrorism Committee (CTC) to monitor each nation's implementation of Resolution 1373.[43] In short, the Security Council has been very solicitous in helping the United States protect itself from terrorism.

The Security Council is far from perfect and could use significant reforms. To paraphrase Winston Churchill's view of democracy, the council is the worst form of international governance over war except for all the other forms. In any event, allowing nations to launch preventive wars unilaterally is an unacceptable alternative. As Columbia law professor Louis Henkin, then president of the American Society of International Law, argued, international law cannot permit "unilateral action by a state on its own decision, on the basis of its own finding of undisclosed facts, of its own characterization of those facts, and its own interpretation of applicable legal principle." [44] Here, as elsewhere in the struggle to make ourselves free from the threat of transnational terror, we have no choice but to pursue multilateral strategies.

BRINGING HUMAN RIGHTS HOME

The United States today is widely viewed as a systematic human rights violator—at Guantánamo, at Abu Ghraib, in secret CIA detention centers, and on the streets of the many countries in which U.S. agents have kidnapped suspects for rendition. If we have any hope of reversing or even reducing the tide of anti-Americanism that these practices have generated, we need to take dramatic and affirmative steps to send a different message about the United States' attitude toward international law, and particularly human rights. The depths to which the United States has fallen in the eyes of the world—and the recognition that this is a long-term disaster for our security interests—makes this a propitious moment for reform. Just as the abuses of World War II led to the birth of international human rights, and abuses during the Vietnam War led to reforms in laws governing domestic surveillance and executive powers, so the abuses of the war on terror call for equivalent reforms.

A critical first step would be to repeal the 2006 Military Commissions Act's provision barring enforcement of the Geneva Conventions in suits against the U.S. government or its officials in federal courts. The Geneva Conventions set forth basic, agreed-upon protections for prisoners of war and civilians during military conflicts. They protect our own military when it fights abroad and—at least until the "war on terror"—the United States had long agreed to be bound by the Conventions' requirements. When President Bush sought to try alleged terrorists in military commissions that violated the Conventions, the Supreme Court declared the commissions illegal. But the president convinced a Republican-majority Congress to, in effect, insulate future military commissions and other government measures from challenges that they violate the Geneva Conventions by specifically barring invocation of the Conventions against the U.S. government in U.S. courts. Such legislation sends exactly the wrong message, suggesting that we are unwilling to live up to our international humanitarian law commitments. It needs to be repealed if we are to begin to undo the damage that has been done to the United States' image abroad.

More broadly, the United States should follow Great Britain's lead and "bring human rights home," [45] by making human rights conventions not just symbolic hortatory statements but enforceable legal obligations, as they are in most other developed nations of the world. The United States has signed and ratified a number of important human rights treaties, including the International Covenant on Civil and Political Rights, but we have done so in ways that render those treaties virtually meaningless vis-à-vis U.S. official action. Congress has routinely adopted "reservations" and "declarations" that deny individuals any right to sue for their violation in U.S. courts, and that reject any obligations on government officials beyond those already imposed by the U.S. Constitution. As a result, international human rights have been rendered redundant and symbolic as a matter of domestic law.

A Congress committed to restoring the U.S. role as a human

rights leader could enact a statute making international human rights treaties directly enforceable in our own courts—much as the United Kingdom did in 1998 when it adopted the Human Rights Act, which empowered domestic courts to adjudicate claims that government action is incompatible with the European Convention on Human Rights. Alternatively, the Senate should repeal the declarations that make these human rights treaties unenforceable in the United States and the substantive reservations that make the international human rights treaties redundant of constitutional obligations. If the International Covenant on Civil and Political Rights prohibits a particular government action, that action should be invalid even if the conduct would not independently violate the Constitution.[46] Virtually all of the countries in the European Union have written constitutions, but they are also obligated to abide by the European Convention on Human Rights. While there may be rare situations where specific international rules actually contravene constitutional guarantees, there is otherwise no reason that the United States cannot abide by the same basic human rights as the rest of the civilized world.

In addition to making the human rights treaties that we have signed and ratified independently enforceable in domestic courts, the United States should accede to the jurisdiction and oversight of the Inter-American Court of Human Rights and ratify the American Convention on Human Rights. Just as European countries have agreed to be bound by the decisions of the European Court of Human Rights, the United States should affirm that it is willing to be bound by the judgments of the Inter-American Court of Human Rights. That commitment acknowledges that international human rights are just that—international—and that they should not be captive to domestic interpretation and enforcement. We have been willing to be bound by the judgments of international tribunals in the economic arena.[47] We also ought to be willing to subject ourselves to international oversight and enforcement in the area of human rights.

The United States has a long way to go to repair its image as exceptionalist, unilateral, and dismissive of international laws and standards. But if we are to succeed in protecting ourselves against international terrorism, it is absolutely essential that we do so. The measures we suggest here would send a dramatic message that we are willing to live within the same fundamental rules that govern other nations, and that we acknowledge that we are just one nation among the community of nations, committed to a *collective* enterprise of security, liberty, and human rights for all. Until we make that commitment clearly and unequivocally, the claims of al-Qaeda and its sympathizers that the United States is arrogant, dominating, untrustworthy, and unjustly powerful will continue to resonate in many parts of the world.

12. THE RULE OF LAW AS AN ASSET, NOT AN OBSTACLE

Coercion, including military force, is undoubtedly sometimes a necessary and proper response to a terrorist threat. We do not maintain that a state must always limit itself to noncoercive measures or traditional criminal sanctions. But we do insist that when the state deploys harsh coercive measures, it must do so within the bounds of the rule of law. Proponents of the "everything has changed" school often overlook the fact that the rule of law, while by definition a constraint on state coercion, in fact provides the state a wide range of tools adequate to protect its people in all but the most extreme situations. For the most part, the deficiencies that contributed to the failure to thwart the 9/11 attacks were not deficiencies in the available legal authority, but in the ways that the authority had been deployed (or not deployed). And in those instances where existing law was insufficient, it could have been changed within the constraints of the rule of law. Unilateral extralegal executive action, the administration's preferred mode, was unnecessary.

When an armed group brutally murders thousands of innocent people in a single act of terror, the rule of law should be on the side of the victims and the state that seeks to hold the wrongdoers accountable. The law, after all, imposes basic obligations of mutual respect for human beings in order to ensure relative peace and tranquility. Terrorism is a heinous crime, first and foremost, and the rules of every civilized society permit its perpetrators to be brought to justice and punished harshly for their wrongdoing. In some circumstances, terrorism may also be an act of war, as the world generally acknowledged in the wake of the attacks of 9/11. But here, too, terrorism is a war *crime*, because above all else, the laws of war absolutely preclude the terrorists' tactic of targeting innocent civilians. Thus, whether terrorism is viewed through the prism of domestic criminal law or international humanitarian law, it is a sanctionable wrong, fully justifying the state in employing force, coercion, and violence to respond. Moreover, under conspiracy and attempt laws, the state need not wait until after the bomb has exploded, but can act preventively, holding people responsible for their intended actions so long as they have taken some concrete step toward a criminal end. To avoid the very backlash that terrorists hope to trigger, however, the state must carefully adhere to the limits of law when it resorts to such coercion.

To comply with the rule of law is not only the right thing to do but also will serve our security needs. When a nation overreacts to a terrorist attack and disregards basic rights, it fulfills the terrorist's goal. The Irish Republican Army gained sympathy and support each time British authorities abused the rights of alleged IRA activists. The same is true for Palestinians vis-à-vis Israel. Terrorism succeeds not so much by its direct effects—murder, destruction, and the spread of fear—but through its indirect effects in provoking nations to overreact. A nation that resists the temptation to overreact will be much more difficult to demonize and much more likely to be seen as acting legitimately to redress the wrongs it has suffered at the terrorists' hands.

As we have seen, the preventive paradigm puts tremendous pressure on the rule of law—so much so that it has led the Bush administration to dismiss it, in the 2005 National Defense Strategy, as a "strategy of the weak," on a par with terrorism itself, used by the enemy to challenge "the strength of the nation-state." That attitude, and the measures it has spawned, have in turn strengthened al-Qaeda's hand on the battlefield of hearts and minds.

Defenders of the Bush administration often argue that these are new and dangerous times, that the old rules are no longer appropriate, and that given the nature and gravity of the threat, the administration had no choice but to respond in the way it did.

But the choice between whether to protect national security or follow the rule of law is almost always a false one. The rule of law equips a nation with powerful tools to fight terrorism, on the home front and in the international arena. And adhering to the rule of law itself furthers national security, because by taking the high road, a nation deprives the terrorists of what they want most—to undermine its very legitimacy.

GUANTÁNAMO: A DIFFERENT VISION

Consider what Guantánamo might look like today had the administration chosen to conform its actions to the laws of war, even though al-Qaeda obviously does not. As of December 2006, our Guantánamo policies have brought not a single terrorist to justice, have reportedly developed little useful intelligence, and have locked up hundreds of people who by the government's own determination are not fighters for "the enemy." Meanwhile, along with Abu Ghraib and the war in Iraq, Guantánamo has probably been one of al-Qaeda's best recruiting tools; the image of the United States arbitrarily locking up hundreds of Muslim men, insisting that they have no rights or access to courts, denying them any hearings, and treating them with utter disrespect for their human dignity reinforces the picture that al-Qaeda wants to paint of the United States.

This situation was entirely avoidable. The laws of war permit a nation to detain the enemy for the course of the conflict—and would thereby permit us to hold those fighting with al-Qaeda against us. But the laws of war also establish certain minimal protections for those detained during wartime. They require that detainees be provided a prompt initial hearing to ensure that they are in fact properly detainable as the enemy, that they be treated humanely while in custody, and that they be released once the conflict is terminated. Where detainees are "unprivileged belligerents," they are not entitled to the full protections accorded to prisoners of war, and can be tried and punished for war crimes, but according to the Geneva Conventions, only in "a regularly constituted court, affording all the judicial guarantees which are recognized as indispensable by civilized peoples." [1]

Had the administration adhered to these basic principles, the world would have little reason to object to Guantánamo today. No one disputes that in a military conflict it is appropriate to hold the enemy's fighters; indeed, capture and detention is more humane than killing the enemy on the battlefield, which the laws of war also permit. The world's objections have focused not on the fact that we have detained enemies in a military conflict, but on the administration's refusal to give the detainees a prompt and fair hearing to determine whether they were indeed fighting for the enemy, its failure to treat them humanely in interrogations, and its suggestion that they can be held for the rest of their lives, since a conflict defined as a "global war on terror" against all terrorist organizations of potentially global reach will literally never end.

As noted above, while the administration initially took the position that Guantánamo detainees deserved no hearings, it subsequently provided hearings, called Combatant Status Review Tribunals, where detainees may challenge the determination that they are indeed enemy combatants. The sufficiency of those procedures is being litigated in the courts as of this writing. The administration argues that the CSRT proceedings are at least as robust as those traditionally conducted under Article 5 of the Geneva Conventions. Others have disputed that point. [2] But even if the CSRTs are akin to traditional Article 5 hearings, it may be that in a war of this character, where it is especially difficult to identify the enemy, where no end of the conflict is in sight, and where the detainees are far removed from the battlefield, a more substantial hearing is required to justify their continued detention. It stands to reason that the longer the detention, the more certain we should be that the detainee is in fact an enemy combatant. At the end of the day, however, those who are fairly identified as al-Qaeda fighters can be held until the military conflict with al-Qaeda is concluded.

The administration appears to have resisted treating Guantá-namo detainees as prisoners of war principally out of concern that such treatment might inhibit its ability to interrogate them. A prisoner of war need only give his name, rank, and serial number. But this argument is a red herring. Nothing in the Geneva Conventions precludes the interrogation of captured prisoners of war; they merely preclude captors from using torture or coercive or punitive methods to force the prisoner to talk. Moreover, had the administration provided fair hearings for the al-Qaeda detainees at the outset, those properly denied POW status could have been denied the full protections owed to POWs.

As the Supreme Court held in the *Hamdan* case, even if a prisoner is not entitled to the full rights of a POW, he still must be treated humanely under Common Article 3 of the Geneva Conventions, which sets out a minimal baseline of protections applicable to all detainees in wars involving non-state actors. In particular, Common Article 3 prohibits "outrages upon personal dignity" and "humiliating and degrading treatment." The Geneva Conventions, therefore, would have permitted interrogations of Guantánamo detainees so long as the interrogations were conducted humanely—a limitation President Bush claimed to be willing to follow in any event.[3] In short, we did not need to flout the law either to detain or to interrogate Guantá-namo detainees for preventive purposes.

The same lesson applies to the conduct of military trials. Had President Bush not insisted on acting unilaterally and departing from both federal law and the Geneva Conventions, his use of military tribunals would not have occasioned a Supreme Court defeat and the need to start again from scratch nearly five years after 9/11. It is common for a nation in time of war to use military tribunals to try alleged war criminals. Few would have objected if we had established tribunals that complied with the

Geneva Conventions and the laws of war. If these dictates had been followed, the Supreme Court would not likely have intervened until after a trial had been completed—and if it had intervened, it would have upheld the tribunals' results so long as they conformed to the law of war. At least as important, convictions obtained in fair trials would have demonstrated to the world that we are not detaining people arbitrarily. In short, following the rule of law would not have required forgoing detention, interrogation, or military trials of the enemy.

SURVEILLANCE UNDER LAW

Adhering to the rule of law would not have unduly restricted the nation's ability to conduct surveillance of al-Qaeda, including by wiretapping phone calls within and outside the United States. Here, too, the administration need not have violated the law, as is illustrated by its announcement in January 2007 that it would terminate the NSA program and could accomplish its surveillance pursuant to court supervision under the Foreign Intelligence Surveillance Act after all. FISA permits a court to approve electronic surveillance of any person the government has an objective reason to believe is associated with al-Qaeda or any other international terrorist organization. The warrant application process is entirely secret, and FISA does not require the government to inform the target that he has been subject to surveillance unless the government chooses to use the information against him in a criminal trial. Where there is insufficient time to obtain advance judicial approval, FISA permits the attorney general himself to authorize the wiretap on an emergency basis, so long as he seeks the court's approval within seventy-two hours. And FISA permits *unlimited* warrantless surveillance so long as the target is not a U.S. citizen or permanent resident and the tap is not physically located in the United States. Thus, without violating the law as written, the president had wide latitude to conduct electronic surveillance of the enemy.

It may be that even broader authority is justified during wartime. Perhaps, for example, it would be reasonable to reduce the trigger for monitoring those suspected of association with the enemy in a military conflict from "probable cause" to "reasonable suspicion." Reasonable suspicion, a very low threshold of suspicion, is the standard the courts require police to meet in order to conduct a brief stop-and-frisk on the street. It would not generally be sufficient to justify wiretapping, but where the target is thought to be associated with the enemy in a military conflict, that lower threshold might be reasonable. If that was what the administration needed, however, there was a lawful way to achieve it. Congress recognized in FISA that wartime might call for a different approach to national security and foreign intelligence surveillance. Accordingly, it provided that, when Congress declares war, the president may conduct warrantless wiretapping for the first fifteen days of the conflict. The legislative history made clear that if the president wanted any broader authority, that fifteen-day period would allow him to seek it from Congress.[4]

The president did in fact request several amendments to FISA in the days following 9/11, as part of the Patriot Act—and Congress enacted them. But the administration pointedly did not seek legislative authorization for the NSA program, nor did it seek judicial orders authorizing its wiretaps under FISA until five years later, after its unilateral, unchecked program had been ruled unconstitutional. Had it sought to amend FISA, and had the request been reasonably circumscribed, it is virtually certain that Congress would have cooperated. And as long as such a program was limited to the scope and duration of the military conflict and the wiretaps required court orders, the searches would likely satisfy the Fourth Amendment. In short, the notion that the president should be able to spy on al-Qaeda's phone calls in and out of the United States has never been controversial. What is controversial is the idea that the president can *unilaterally* ex-

ercise that authority, without judicial oversight, and in direct violation of a criminal prohibition.

If the president had sought judicial approval or legislative authority for the NSA program, he could have avoided all the un-
toward consequences that have now resulted from the secret
NSA program. There would have been no wall between the NSA
and other intelligence and law enforcement agencies. Because
the NSA program would have been legal, information obtained
from it could then have been used, both to obtain FISA-
approved wiretaps and to convict criminals in court. And the
NSA program would have been far less divisive, as the criticism
of the president turns almost exclusively on his decision to act
unilaterally in violation of a criminal statute. By short-circuiting
the legal process and unnecessarily asserting absolute executive
power, President Bush ignited a controversy where there need
never have been one.

PREVENTIVE DETENTION

After 9/11, the administration often bent the rules to achieve
preventive detention: locking up foreign nationals within the
United States without charges, holding them even after immigration judges had ordered them released, abusing the material witness law to lock up suspects for investigation on less
than probable cause, and denying enemy combatants at home
and abroad any hearings at all until the Supreme Court ruled
otherwise.

Under existing law, however, preventive detention can be imposed in many situations without bending the rules. If an individual faces immigration or criminal charges and is shown to be
a flight risk or a danger to the community, he or she may be detained pending resolution of the charges. The key requirements
are that the government have a basis for a criminal or immigration charge, and that it be able to show that the individual is

dangerous or a flight risk. Without the latter showing, there is no justification for preventive detention, because there is literally nothing to prevent. Similarly, as noted above, the laws of war permit preventive detention of enemy combatants—but again, a hearing must be provided to determine whether the individual is indeed a member of the enemy forces. These laws permit the government to incapacitate virtually anyone as to whom it has solid evidence of involvement with al-Qaeda. Such involvement will almost by definition be grounds for criminal or immigration charges, even apart from invoking the powers of military custody. Thus, consistent with existing law, we should be able to detain those we can show are actually dangerous.

In the wake of 9/11, however, the administration exploited existing legal authorities to detain people when it did *not* have solid evidence that they were dangerous or a flight risk, often on the flimsiest of bases for suspicion. It turned to the material witness law precisely because that law permits detention on a showing that an individual merely may have information relevant to a criminal investigation, without having to show any grounds for believing that the individual himself has engaged in any wrongdoing. And it abused its immigration authority, adopting a range of legally dubious practices and policies in order to avoid having to release Arab and Muslim foreign nationals from immigration detention even when—as was the case for the vast majority of those rounded up—it had no evidence that they were dangerous. The fact that none of the five thousand foreign nationals so detained in the first two years after 9/11 stands convicted of any terrorist crime suggests that lowering the bar for preventive detention in such circumstances does not make us safer.[5]

One can, however, imagine a case in which government officials have credible and reliable evidence that an individual poses a serious danger to the community, but cannot immediately make that evidence public in the sort of hearing that would be required to justify preventive detention under criminal or immigration law. If the individual is also not associated with al-Qaeda, there would be no legal basis under current law for detaining him. Absent some legal charge or serious mental illness, American law does not authorize preventive detention. Moreover, preventive detention generally requires some factual showing of dangerousness, and if the evidence the government has cannot be disclosed, how can such a showing be made?

Such cases are likely to be extremely rare. But could the law be amended, consistent with the Constitution and international human rights, to permit the state to detain in those circumstances? In our view, short-term preventive detention may be constitutionally permissible in narrow circumstances and subject to strong procedural safeguards. Outside the traditional battlefield detention context, however, the liberty of the individual must prevail over the government's interest in not disclosing classified evidence. As the Supreme Court decided in *Hamdi v. Rumsfeld*, even an individual allegedly captured on the battlefield fighting against us in a war has a right to a fundamentally fair hearing to challenge the government's claims that he was fighting for the enemy.[6] The use of classified evidence presented behind closed doors deprives the individual of a fundamentally fair hearing, because one cannot defend against what one cannot see. Thus, here, as in criminal cases every day, the government must choose between disclosing confidential information in order to establish the basis for preventive detention, and allowing the individual to go free. Where it makes the latter choice, however, it is not without options. If it has reason to believe the individual is a terrorist threat, the government will be able to subject him to close monitoring, usually including electronic surveillance, and as soon as it develops admissible evidence that the individual is engaged in or conspiring to engage in wrongdoing, it can arrest him on those charges.

As long as the detainee's opportunity to defend himself is maintained, however, there is no categorical bar in constitutional or human rights law to preventive detention. Many other nations have preventive-detention laws that permit detention of demonstrably dangerous individuals without charges, at least for a limited period of time.[7] Such laws typically require an evidentiary showing to a judge that the individual poses a threat to national security. There is nothing in our Constitution, or in general principles of the rule of law, that would preclude the adoption of such a scheme in the United States—provided that the law placed strict and fairly short time limits on detention, required a prompt evidentiary showing of the necessity for detention before a judge, and gave the individual access to a lawyer and a meaningful opportunity to challenge the basis for his detention in court. Preventive detention should be strictly limited to holding truly dangerous individuals for a brief period of time in emergency situations, and must be tightly regulated so as not to become a routine investigatory tool.

As a policy matter, laws permitting domestic preventive detention without charges, even where tightly circumscribed, may be a bad idea. The history of preventive detention provides ample reason for skepticism. The number of instances that would truly call for preventive detention seems very small. The restrictions on the authority that would be necessary to render preventive detention constitutional would likely make it of relatively little value in most circumstances. And perhaps of greatest concern, the fear of releasing a person the government claims is dangerous, even without good evidence for doing so, may make judges less than reliable protectors of liberty in these settings; judges are likely to err on the side of detention rather than take the heat for releasing an individual who goes on to commit a terrorist act. Thus, rules about burden of proof should be carefully drafted to discourage skewed decision making by judges.

Moreover, it remains unclear that preventive-detention measures are really needed; during World War II, FBI director J. Edgar Hoover, no civil libertarian, argued that preventive detention of Japanese Americans was unwise and unnecessary because the FBI had the capability to place suspected saboteurs

under surveillance and charge them with a crime if it was determined they were truly dangerous.[8] Thus, there is good reason for
skepticism about preventive detention as a policy matter. The
important point, however, is that carefully circumscribed short-
term preventive detention is not necessarily unconstitutional,
nor does it necessarily violate human rights law. If the administration felt that such a power was necessary after 9/11, it should
have asked Congress to enact it, accompanied by necessary safeguards, rather than abuse existing laws for ends they were not designed to serve, against people who posed no danger to anyone.

In fact, the administration did successfully obtain passage of
one new preventive-detention law in the wake of 9/11. The Patriot Act allows the attorney general to lock up a foreign national
without charges based on his determination that the individual
is suspected of terrorist activity as that term is expansively defined in the immigration law.[9] The Patriot Act provision, however, limits detention to seven days unless immigration charges
are actually filed, and provides for immediate review of the detention in federal court. Perhaps because the law included such
safeguards (over the administration's objections), the government has yet to use it. Instead, it found that it could lock up
literally thousands of foreign nationals, none of whom have
been convicted of terrorist offenses, by abusing existing immigration laws, obstructing their access to court, and keeping them
locked up even after judges had ordered their release. That experience suggests that crafting a new strict and narrowly tailored
preventive-detention law would be insufficient to prevent
abuse. It is essential at the same time to preclude resort to other
laws to effectuate mass roundups without the showings of danger or flight risk that preventive detention requires.

In short, whether or not it is a good idea, the rule of law
and the Constitution would permit a carefully circumscribed
preventive-detention power. While the rule of law, properly understood, would preclude widespread sweeps based on undiffer-
entiated fear rather than on evidence of danger, history suggests

that that consequence would enhance our security by deterring the government from overreaching in ways that do little to identify actual terrorists and do a great deal to alienate and radicalize the communities under suspicion.

INTERROGATION: AVOIDING ABU GHRAIB

Playing by the rules would have limited the interrogation tactics we could have employed against al-Qaeda detainees at Guantánamo and elsewhere. Common Article 3 of the Geneva Conventions commands that no detainee be subjected to cruel or degrading treatment,[10] and that term would surely have barred such tactics as waterboarding, extended sleep deprivation, exposure to extreme heat and cold, forced nudity, stress positions, threats of rendition, and the like. President Bush claims that such "alternative" interrogation tactics have enabled us to capture terrorists and disrupt terrorist plots around the world. But as shown in Chapter 4, Bush's claims are highly contestable.

More important, Bush cannot show that any useful information obtained through coercive interrogation could not have been obtained through lawful methods. Police obtain confessions on a daily basis without subjecting suspects to physical harm, threats, forced nudity, or waterboarding. On September 6, 2006, the same day that President Bush publicly defended the CIA's use of "alternative procedures" for interrogation, the army banned all such tactics in its revised field manual. When questioned about the advisability of forswearing such tactics, Lieutenant General John Kimmons, the army's deputy chief of staff for intelligence, directly refuted the president's message:

> No good intelligence is going to come from abusive practices. I think history tells us that. I think the empirical evidence of the last five years, hard years, tells us that. And, moreover, any piece of intelligence which is obtained under duress, through the use of abusive techniques, would be of questionable credibility, and

additionally it would do more harm than good when it inevitably became known that abusive practices were used. And we can't afford to go there. Some of our most significant successes on the battlefield have been—in fact, I would say all of them, almost categorically all of them—have accrued from expert interrogators using mixtures of authorized humane interrogation practices, in clever ways that you would hope Americans would use them, to push the envelope within the bookends of legal, moral, and ethical, now as further refined by this field manual. So we don't need abusive practices in there.[11]

According to the army's own intelligence expert, then, the interrogation tactics President Bush has gone to such great lengths to preserve are not necessary to gather useful intelligence and prevent terrorist attacks. Lieutenant General Kimmons is surely correct that the costs of employing harsh interrogation tactics are enormous—from faulty intelligence, to undermining our legitimacy abroad, to limiting our ability to use evidence to convict terrorists for their crimes, to putting our own soldiers at risk, to demeaning the character of our interrogators and, ultimately, our society.

It is certainly possible that eschewing coercive interrogation would have reduced the amount of intelligence that we obtained. While the general unreliability of coerced testimony has been recognized for centuries, it is certainly possible that some information obtained through coercion may indeed turn out to be accurate and valuable. But even assuming some valuable information is forgone by barring the use of coercion, the costs of permitting coercive interrogation are so substantial that an absolute legal bar makes sense.

THE EXCEPTION THAT PROVES THE RULE

What should a government official do when he finds himself in an actual ticking-bomb situation? The rules outlined above impose certain fundamental constraints on the exercise of coercive power, including an absolute prohibition on torture, and it is conceivable that in some extreme instances, those constraints would disable the government from taking action that could save thousands of lives. As we have noted above, because ticking-bomb hypotheticals are extremely unlikely to arise in the real world, they are a dangerous predicate upon which to build a system of legal rules. But we cannot say that such situations will *never* arise. So what is to be done?

Alan Dershowitz has proposed a system of judicial warrants to approve of torture in advance in those extraordinary situations where torture is justified.[12] Professors Philip Heymann and Juliette Kayyem, also of Harvard, have proposed a scheme for advance approval of "highly coercive interrogation techniques" in specified emergency situations.[13] In our view, we should not create an ex ante exception for torture or other unlawful means, even if we could agree that in some situations we might concede, after the fact, that the illegal conduct was regrettably necessary. Most government officials will never confront anything like a ticking time bomb. Refusing to create an official avenue for exceptional measures will make officials less likely to employ such tactics. After the fact, they may seek mercy from the prosecution, judge, or jury; indemnification from Congress; or even a pardon from the president. But the conduct should remain illegal. The uncertainty that will result is likely to discourage expansive claims of emergency, as officials will not know in advance whether their actions will be recognized as deserving forgiveness—and if they guess wrongly, they will face serious sanctions.[14] By contrast, if one creates a legal regime that formally authorizes torture or "highly coercive interrogation" in specified emergency situations, the moral clarity of the prohibition will be muddied, officials will be likely to interpret "emergency situations" broadly, and emergency powers will be increasingly used in nonemergency situations.

Thus, even if we could agree that it is morally justifiable to inflict severe physical but temporary pain on a suspected terrorist bomber where that appears to be the only way to obtain information that will save the lives of thousands of innocent civilians—and there are reasonable arguments both ways on that question—there is much to be said for maintaining an absolute criminal ban on torture, and requiring government officials who find themselves in that rare situation to bear the risk that if they torture they will be treated as criminals, not heroes. We must resist making the rule of law captive of the extraordinary exception. We adopt the absolute rule, then, not because there are no exceptions imaginable, but because any exceptions will be exceedingly rare, and because a clear rule serves an important and salutary purpose in the great run of cases.

DISRUPTING TERRORIST PLOTS

One of the frequent arguments made in favor of the preventive paradigm is that traditional law enforcement tactics are insufficient to prevent terrorist attacks, precisely because they are backward-looking. It has become accepted dogma that the FBI, for example, is ineffective at preventing terrorism because it is too focused on traditional law enforcement, solving yesterday's crime rather than preventing tomorrow's terrorist attack. This claim, however, rests on a caricature of traditional law enforcement tools. In fact, police, prosecutors, and the FBI routinely employ traditional tools to prevent future crimes. The laws of conspiracy and attempt make this possible, although both require concrete evidence of overt acts, not mere suspicions of future plots. And of course one of the most accepted justifications for criminal punishment is a future-oriented preventive one— that punishing past crimes will deter future ones.

The preventive possibilities of traditional law enforcement tools, including surveillance, informants, and prosecution for conspiracy and attempt, are illustrated by the fact that three of the most apparently serious terror plots to have been disrupted since 9/11 appear to have been disrupted with such traditional tools. All three took place in the United Kingdom, not the United States.

On March 30, 2004, British authorities arrested eight Britons of Pakistani origin in the UK in a series of predawn raids.[15] Police seized 1,300 pounds of ammonium nitrate fertilizer in the raids.[16] Scotland Yard had been surveilling the group for some time, but following the Madrid train bombings, the British authorities decided to arrest the men.[17]

Similarly, in August 2004, British authorities arrested eight men for conspiring to detonate a dirty bomb in London.[18] The men's goal was allegedly to set off a big bomb at a prestigious target—the bombers reportedly considered Heathrow Airport, the Houses of Parliament, and Westminster Abbey.[19] The arrests, however, were not precipitous, but followed a year-long surveillance operation.[20]

In August 2006, British authorities again disrupted a terrorist plot. This one allegedly targeted international flights from Heathrow Airport to the United States, and was to use liquid explosives in carry-on luggage. Again, the individuals had been under extended British surveillance before they were arrested.[21]

In all three instances, British authorities moved in to arrest only when they had developed evidence of wrongdoing and felt that they could wait no longer. As a result, the suspects were caught in possession of substantial incriminating evidence. These cases illustrate that traditional police work can be more effective in disrupting plots than preemptive interventions that frustrate intelligence gathering and make it more difficult to hold suspects accountable. Constitutional and human rights law both recognize the validity of surveillance, searches, informants, and interrogation, not only to investigate past crimes, but also to disrupt ongoing plots and conspiracies.

It should not be surprising that the rule of law offers substantial resources for states to protect themselves from those who target innocent civilians for murder. It is true, of course, that the rules permitting preventive detention, surveillance, and interrogation of suspects; the use of military force; and trials of war criminals also impose limits on governments. But those limits make as much sense in the age of weapons of mass destruction and al-Qaeda as they did during the age of weapons of mass destruction and the Soviet Union. They are largely designed to protect human dignity, privacy, and liberty, and to ensure that the government exercises coercion against those who are actually engaged in wrongdoing, rather than against innocents.

The rules are not static. They have changed over time, and they are susceptible to further change when needed to respond to changed circumstances. We should not assume, however, that the rules are insufficient simply because they were drawn up before 9/11. A case-by-case examination suggests that, in the main, existing rules provide adequate tools for security, while simultaneously insisting on adequate safeguards for individual liberties and human rights. Where changes are necessary, procedures exist that permit changes to be implemented. Short-circuiting those procedures and compromising fundamental principles of the rule of law, treating the law as an obstacle because "everything has changed," has not made and will not make us more secure.

CONCLUSION

In September 2001, as it considered how to respond to the terrorist attacks of 9/11, the Bush administration made the fateful decision to fight a global war on terror, and to thrust aside the rules of the game in so doing. It claimed war powers, but refused to be governed by the laws of war, dismissing the Geneva Conventions as "obsolete" and "quaint." It exploited immigration powers to conduct a massive national campaign of ethnic and religious profiling aimed at Arab and Muslim foreign nationals. And it set about reinterpreting fundamental prohibitions on torture; cruel, inhuman, and degrading treatment; and offensive war. All of this was done in the name of preventing another terrorist attack. "Everything changed" became the mantra of the day, and the administration took this to mean that as the leadership of the most powerful country in the world, it could rewrite the rules. In the wake of such brutal attacks, who would stand in America's way as we sought to bring the perpetrators to justice?

The Bush administration's adoption of a preventive paradigm led a country that was once a leading proponent of the rule of law to compromise the law's most fundamental commitments—to equality, transparency, individual culpability, fair procedures, checks and balances, and fundamental human rights. These sacrifices have deeply troubling normative implications. But they have also proved to be remarkably counterproductive from a security standpoint. The record shows that our sacrifices of fundamental rights have not resulted in the capture and bringing to justice of many actual terrorists, but have deeply eroded trust in the administration and fueled widespread anti-American resentment, thereby increasing the threat of future terrorist attacks.

Rarely noted, however, and at least as remarkable as the extent of the administration's lawlessness, is the fact that the administration has been forced to retreat on so many fronts. The government lost its first three major cases in the Supreme Court, as the Court repeatedly rejected the argument that the president has unilateral, uncheckable power as commander in chief in the war on terror. As Justice O'Connor wrote, "Whatever power the United States Constitution envisions for the Executive in its exchanges with other nations or with enemy organizations in times of conflict, it most assuredly envisions a role for all three branches when individual liberties are at stake."[1] The government has been compelled to hold hearings for those detained at Guantánamo and to provide the detainees with access to lawyers and courts to challenge the legality of those hearings. It has been ordered to disclose the detainees' identities and other pertinent information about them. It has now let hundreds of detainees go.

Disclosure of abuses at Abu Ghraib, Guantánamo, and CIA black sites have compelled the administration to back off from its policy of tolerating what amounts to torture in the interrogation of al-Qaeda suspects. The president's military tribunal rules were declared illegal, and he had to abandon his unilateral approach and seek congressional approval for a new set of procedures more protective than those the president had initially specified. Congress formally rejected the administration's view that the international law prohibition on cruel, inhuman, and degrading treatment does not protect foreign nationals held abroad, and the Supreme Court rejected its view that the Geneva Conventions do not apply to al-Qaeda detainees. And the president was forced to abandon his warrantless wiretapping program, announcing in January 2007 that heretofore he would conduct surveillance subject to court oversight and pursuant to the Foreign Intelligence Surveillance Act.

Meanwhile, the administration has been forced to acknowledge that its claims of victory in the war in Iraq were embarrassingly premature; as the war drags on and on, Iraq seems embroiled in a civil war with no good end in sight. World opinion, which was opposed to U.S. intervention from the outset, has coalesced into even stronger opposition, and virtually all observers, including the bipartisan Iraq Study Group headed by James Baker, now agree that the situation in Iraq is a disaster. The American public expressed its view in the 2006 midterm elections, giving the Democrats a landslide victory and shifting the balance of power in both houses of Congress.

In short, over the past five years, the most powerful nation in the world has been forced to retreat, at least in significant measure, from many of its most grievous assaults on the rule of law. A realist might well have predicted the opposite—namely, that because the United States has no real rival to counter it on the world stage, because international law lacks enforceable bite, and because courts and Congress have so often deferred to the executive in times of crisis, the limits of law would have little purchase in constraining the United States in its response to 9/11. In fact, however, the rule of law has been more powerful, and the United States less powerful, than many would have predicted.

What accounts for these results? In our view, it has become clear that even the most powerful nation in the world needs to be seen as legitimate in order to implement its policies successfully throughout the world. Large segments of world and U.S. opinion—including elite opinion in Congress, the courts, and foreign governments—have come to view the United States' preventive-paradigm policies as illegitimate, precisely because they have been accompanied by a rejection of the values associated with the rule of law.

These reactions, which insist on the importance of fidelity to law, human rights, separation of powers, and judicial review, have been fueled by an increasingly robust and proactive civil society. Nongovernmental organizations have played a crucial role in standing up to the administration, issuing critical reports, holding press conferences, feeding stories to the media, filing lawsuits, mobilizing world opinion, and lobbying Congress.

The civil society sector in human rights is very strong. It includes traditional human rights groups (such as Human Rights Watch, Human Rights First, and Amnesty International), civil liberties groups (such as the American Civil Liberties Union and the Center for Constitutional Rights), immigrants' rights groups (including the National Immigration Forum and the American Immigration Lawyers Association), ethnic groups (such as the American-Arab Anti-Discrimination Committee and the Arab American Institute), religiously identified groups (including the Council on American-Islamic Relations and the Muslim Public Affairs Council), lawyers' professional associations (including the American Bar Association and the National Lawyers Guild), grassroots organizations (such as the Bill of Rights Defense Committee), and privacy groups (such as the Center for Democracy and Technology and the Electronic Privacy Information Center). All of these groups have played a vital role in exposing and counteracting abuses carried out in the name of the war on terror and in bringing to bear on the United States the very shaming tactics that human rights activists have long employed with respect to other law-violating nations.

The work of the nonprofit sector has in turn buttressed the media, which has played an important role in disclosing and criticizing many of the Bush administration's worst abuses—including torture at Abu Ghraib, the CIA's black sites, and the NSA's warrantless wiretapping program. Op-ed pages in leading papers have strongly condemned the administration's intrusions on fundamental rights. And while many media outlets in the United States initially supported the war in Iraq and the claim that Iraq had weapons of mass destruction, the prevailing view now is that the war has been a disaster from the outset.

These reactions have not been limited to the United States. Foreign nongovernmental organizations, the foreign press, high-ranking foreign government officials, and, if polls and demonstrations are an indicator, foreign populations at large have joined in the criticism. Our government's adoption of the coercive preventive paradigm has led to a strong wave of anti-American resentment, a development we ignore at our peril.

All of this has in turn given the courts a stronger backbone than they have ever shown in confronting an executive in a time of crisis on national security matters. The Supreme Court has historically deferred to executive abuses of fundamental rights during wartime, from the imprisonment of war critics during World War I to the internment of Japanese nationals and Japanese Americans during World War II and the anticommunist initiatives of the McCarthy era. The current Supreme Court is very conservative—it is, after all, the Court that intervened to ensure George Bush's victory in the contested 2000 election. Yet as we have seen, the Court has not been reticent about rejecting President Bush's claims of unchecked executive authority in the war on terror. It has insisted on the importance of the rule of law in our response to terror, and in turn on the central role of checks and balances in a healthy democracy.

While the focus of much of this book has been the Bush administration's response to the threat of terrorism, we do not want to suggest that the problem lies exclusively with this particular administration. The temptation to adopt harshly coercive preventive measures in response to terrorist attacks, especially where those measures can be targeted at the most vulnerable, is not specific to this administration or to any particular party. History has shown that other administrations—Democrat and Republican—have made similar mistakes. Thus, the problem will long outlast the Bush administration. Our hope is that a close analysis of the legality and efficacy of the preventive paradigm might lead future administrations to adopt counterterrorism policies that adhere to the rule of law and thus avoid the damaging consequences illustrated here.

The first five years after 9/11 have taught that a unilateral, ex-

ceptionalist approach to fighting terror by jettisoning fundamental commitments to the rule of law in the name of the preventive paradigm is both morally wrong and, as a pragmatic
security matter, counterproductive. We need another way forward if we are to prevail against those who would intentionally
perpetrate mass casualties on innocent civilians in the name of
an ideological cause. We have sought to show that the best way
forward is to favor noncoercive preventive safeguards, to develop multilateral approaches to a decidedly transnational challenge, to address the underlying factors that lead individuals and
groups to adopt terrorist tactics in the first place, and, when
harsh coercion is necessary, to work within the rule of law, not
against it. That route promises prevention without backlash,
and offers the possibility that we can win the struggle for hearts
and minds that is, in the end, the key to success.

NOTES

INTRODUCTION

1. *Minority Report* is based on a short story of the same name by Philip K. Dick, included in Philip K. Dick, *Selected Stories* (New York: Pantheon, 2002).

2. The White House, *National Security Strategy of the United States of America,* September 17, 2002, available at http://www.whitehouse.gov/nsc/nss.all.html.

3. Preventive strategies have become increasingly common in ordinary criminal law enforcement as well, from injunctions against criminal gangs, to commitment of "sexual predators" beyond the service of their criminal sentences, to "three-strikes" laws imposing life imprisonment on repeat offenders. See Paul H. Robinson, "Punishing Dangerousness: Cloaking Preventive Detention as Criminal Justice," 114 *Harvard Law Review* 1429 (2001); Carol Steiker, "The Limits of the Preventive State," 81 *Journal of Criminal Law and Criminology* 771 (1998); Lucia Zedner, "Seeking Security by Eroding Rights: The Side-Stepping of Due Process," in *Security and Human Rights,* ed. B Goold and L. Lazarus (Oxford: Hart, 2007). These developments also raise serious questions about the appropriate role of prevention in criminal law, but the Bush administration's preventive paradigm is qualitatively more extreme.

4. Douglas Jehl, "The Reach of War: Intelligence; Qaeda-Iraq Link U.S. Cited Is Tied to Coercion Claim," *New York Times,* December 9, 2005, A1.

5. Senate Select Committee on Intelligence, Hearing on Current and Projected National Security Threats to the United States, 109th Cong., 1st sess., February 16, 2005 (testimony of Porter Goss).

6. Ibid.

7. Daniel Benjamin and Steven Simon, *The Next Attack: The Failure of the War on Terror and a Strategy for Getting It Right* (New York: Times Books, 2005), 42, quoting Andrew Cordesman, "Iraq's Evolving Insurgency," availabe at http://www.csis.org/features/050512_IraqInsurg.pdf.

8. For updated accounts of fatalities, see http://www.iraqbodycount.org and http://icasualties.org/oif/.

9. Susan B. Glasser, "Global Terrorism Statistics Debated," *Washington Post,* May 1, 2005, A3.

10. David Sands, "Suicide Bombing Popular Terrorist Tactic," *Washington Times,* May 8, 2006.

11. Mark Denbeaux and Joshua Denbeaux, "Report on Guantánamo Detainees: A Profile of 517 Detainees through Analysis of Department of Defense Data," Seton Hall Public Law Research Paper No. 46 (February 2006), available at http://law.shu.edu/news/guantanamo_report_final_2 _08_06.pdf; Corine Hegland, "Who Is at Guantánamo Bay," *National Journal*, February 3, 2006.

12. "Secret FBI Report Questions Al Qaeda Capabilities," *ABC News*, March 9, 2005, available at http://abcnews.go.com/WNT/Investigation/ story?id=566425&page=1.

13. Dan Eggen and Julie Tate, "U.S. Campaign Produces Few Convictions on Terrorist Charges," *Washington Post*, June 12, 2005, A1.

14. See Chapter 4.

15. See David Cole, *Enemy Aliens: Double Standards and Constitutional Freedoms in the War on Terrorism*, 2d ed. (New York: The New Press, 2004), xx–xxiii, 25.

16. *United States v. Rahman*, 189 F.3d 88 (2d Cir. 1999).

17. See Peter Baker and Susan Glasser, "Bush Says 10 Plots by Al Qaeda Were Foiled," *Washington Post*, October 7, 2005, A1; "Mueller: More than 100 Terror Attacks Foiled Worldwide," CNN, March 4, 2003, available at http://www.cnn.com/2003/ALLPOLITICS/03/04/terror.war.congress/; Department of Justice, "Waging the War on Terror," available at http:// www.lifeandliberty.gov/subs/a_terr.htm.

18. Josh Meyer and Warren Vieth, "Scope of Plots Bush Says Were Foiled Is Questioned," *Los Angeles Times*, October 8, 2005, A15; Sara Kehaulani Goo, "List of Foiled Plot Puzzling to Some," *Washington Post*, October 23, 2005, A6; John Diamond and Toni Locy, "White House List of Disrupted Terror Plots Questioned," *USA Today*, October 26, 2005, 4A.

19. Peter Baker and Dan Eggen, "Bush Details 2002 Plot to Attack L.A. Tower," *Washington Post*, February 10, 2006, A4.

20. Josh Meyer and Warren Vieth, "Bush Likens War on Terror to Cold War," *Los Angeles Times*, October 7, 2005, A1.

21. Baker and Eggen, "Bush Details 2002 Plot."

22. Meyer and Vieth, "Bush Likens War."

23. Ibid.

24. Lowell Bergman, Eric Lichtblau, Scott Shane, and Don Van Natta Jr., "Spy Agency Data After September 11 Led F.B.I. to Dead Ends," *New York Times*, January 17, 2006, A1.

25. Matt Brzezinski, "Red Alert," *Mother Jones*, September–October 2004, available at http://www.motherjones.com/news/feature/2004/09/08 _400.html.

26. Avishai Margalit, "The Wrong War," *New York Review of Books* 50, no. 4, March 13, 2003.

27. Memorandum from Donald Rumsfeld to Dick Myers et al., "Re: Global War on Terrorism," October 16, 2003, available at http://www

.globalsecurity.org/military/library/policy/dod/rumsfeld-d20031016sd
memo.htm.

28. Dana Priest and Josh White, "Policies on Terrorism Suspects Come
Under Fire," *Washington Post*, November 3, 2005, A2.

29. Tracy Wilkinson, "Italy Issues Arrest Warrants for 3 CIA Officers
in 'Rendition' Case," *Los Angeles Times*, July 6, 2006; Mark Landler, "German Court Confronts U.S. on Abduction," *New York Times*, February 1,
2007, A1.

30. See Thomas Powers, "Bringing 'Em On," *New York Times*, December
25, 2005, 13 (Osama bin Laden has 65 percent approval rate in Pakistan);
Pew Research Center for the People and the Press, "A Year After Iraq War:
Mistrust of America in Europe Ever Higher, Muslim Anger Persists,"
March 16, 2004, 24 (reporting that only 21 percent of Pakistanis had a favorable opinion of the United States), available at http://people-press
.org/reports/pdf/206.pdf.

31. Department of Defense, *National Defense Strategy of the United
States of America*, March 2005, available at http://www.globalsecurity.org/
military/library/policy/dod/nds-usa_mar2005_ib.htm.

32. Bruce Ackerman, *Before the Next Attack: Preserving Civil Liberties
in an Age of Terrorism* (New Haven, CT: Yale University Press, 2006);
Alan Dershowitz, *Preemption: A Knife That Cuts Both Ways* (New York:
W.W. Norton, 2006).

33. *Public Committee Against Torture v. State of Israel*, HCJ No. 5100/94,
July 15, 1999, 27, available at http://elyon1.court.gov.il/files_eng/94/000/
051/a09/9405100.ao9.pdf.

1. PREVENTIVE LAW ENFORCEMENT AND INTELLIGENCE GATHERING

1. *Report of the Events Relating to Maher Arar by the Canadian Commis-
sion of Inquiry into the Actions of Canadian Officials in Relation to Maher
Arar* (September 18, 2006); Ian Austen, "Canada Will Pay $9.75 Million to
Man Sent to Syria and Tortured," *New York Times*, January 27, 2007, A5.
The authors are co-counsel for Arar, along with lawyers from the Center
for Constitutional Rights. *Arar v. Ashcroft*, 414 F. Supp. 2d 250, 253–57
(E.D.N.Y. 2006).

2. Dana Priest, "Wrongful Imprisonment: Anatomy of a CIA Mistake:
German Citizen Released After Months in Rendition," *Washington Post*,
December 4, 2005, A1; see also *El-Masri v. Tenet*, 437 F. Supp. 2d 530 (E.D.
Vir. 2006) (complaint available at www.aclu.org/safefree/torture/255341
g120060511.html).

3. Dana Priest reports that renditions "played well at the White House,
where the president was keeping a scorecard of captured or killed terrorists." Priest, "Wrongful Imprisonment," A1.

4. *Arar v. Ashcroft,* 414 F. Supp. 2d at 287. The district court dismissed Arar's case without reaching the government's assertion of state secrets privilege, finding that a damages action against federal officials for complicity in Arar's torture should be barred because it might prove embarrassing to our foreign policy. The decision has been appealed.

5. Priest, "Wrongful Imprisonment," A1.

6. Donald Rumsfeld, "Speech to Greater Miami Chamber of Commerce," February 13, 2004, available at http://www.defenselink.mil/speeches/2004/sp20040213-secdef0883.html.

7. Mark Denbeaux and Joshua Denbeaux, "Report on Guantánamo Detainees: A Profile of 517 Detainees Through Analysis of Department of Defense Data," Seton Hall Public Law Research Paper No. 46 (February 2006), 2, 8, available at http://law.shu.edu/news/guantanamo_report _final_2_08_06.pdf; White House, Office of the Press Secretary, "President Discusses Creation of Military Commissions to Try Suspected Terrorists," September 6, 2006, available at http://www.whitehouse.gov/news/re leases/2006/09/20060906-2.html.

8. Dana Priest, "CIA Holds Terror Suspects in Secret Prisons; Debate Is Growing Within Agency About Legality and Morality of Overseas System," *Washington Post,* November 2, 2005, A1; Eric Schmitt, "House Defies Bush and Backs McCain on Detainee Torture," *New York Times,* December 15, 2005, A14.

9. Interview by Julie Etchingham of Sky News with Condoleezza Rice, December 6, 2005, available at http://www.state.gov/secretary/rm/2005/ 57678.htm. On her way to Europe, Rice stated that U.S. cooperation with European allies in intelligence and law enforcement "has helped protect European countries from attack, helping save European lives." Condoleezza Rice, "Remarks upon Her Departure for Europe," December 5, 2005, available at http://www.state.gov/secretary/rm/2005/57602.htm; see also Joel Brinkley, "U.S. Interrogations Are Saving European Lives, Rice Says," *New York Times,* December 6, 2005, A3.

10. White House, Office of the Press Secretary, "President Bush Discusses Creation of Military Commissions to Try Suspected Terrorists," September 6, 2006, available at http://www.whitehouse.gov/news/re leases/2006/09/20060906-3.html.

11. White House, Office of the Press Secretary, "President Bush Signs the Military Commissions Act," October 17, 2006, available at http://www .whitehouse.gov/news/releases/2006/10/20061017-1.html.

12. 18 U.S.C. §2339B; Executive Order 13224, 66 Fed. Reg. 49,079 (September 23, 2006); International Emergency Economic Powers Act, 50 U.S.C. §1701 et seq.

13. *Humanitarian Law Project v. Reno,* 205 F.3d 1130, 1133 (9th Cir. 2001). Stuart Levey, State Department under secretary for terrorism and financial intelligence, explained to Congress that the terror-financing laws

had permitted the government to shut down the Holy Land Foundation, which the government alleges was a source of funding for Hamas, in preventive terms: "the more nimble administrative standard for designations allowed Treasury to intercede swiftly and shut down terrorist financing that was occurring through HLF accounts, thereby potentially preventing future terrorist acts." Stuart A. Levey, "Testimony Before House Committee on Financial Services," August 23, 2004, available at http://www.treas.gov/press/releases/js1869.htm.

14. See generally David Cole, *Enemy Aliens: Double Standards and Constitutional Freedoms in the War on Terrorism*, 2d ed. (New York: The New Press, 2005), 17–56 (describing programs targeted at Arab and Muslim immigrants).

15. Attorney General John Ashcroft, "Prepared Remarks for the U.S. Mayors Conference," October 25, 2001, quoted in U.S. Department of Justice, Office of the Inspector General, *The September 11 Detainees: A Review of the Treatment of Aliens Held on Immigration Charges in Connection with the Investigation of the September 11 Attacks* (April 2003) (released June 2003) ("Inspector General's Report"), ch. 2, available at http://www.usdoj.gov/oig/special/0306/chapter2.htm.

16. Inspector General's Report; Cole, *Enemy Aliens*, 30–33.

17. See USA PATRIOT Act, Pub. L. No. 107–56, §218 (2001) (permitting foreign intelligence surveillance on a showing of less than probable cause of criminal activity in criminal investigations); David Cole, "Section 218: Amending the FISA Standard," in *The Patriot Debates: Experts Debate the USA PATRIOT Act*, ed. Stewart Baker and John Kavanagh (Chicago, IL: American Bar Association, 2005).

18. USA PATRIOT Act, §215.

19. John Poindexter stated, "Total Information Awareness—a prototype system—is our answer. We must be able to detect, classify, identify, and track terrorists so that we may understand their plans and act to prevent them from being executed." John Poindexter, "Remarks at DARPATech 2002 Conference," August 2, 2002, available at http://www.fas.org/irp/agency/dod/poindexter.html.

20. In a radio address following disclosure of the NSA spying program, President Bush argued that "the activities conducted under this authorization have helped detect and prevent possible terrorist attacks in the United States and abroad." George W. Bush, "The President's Radio Address," December 17, 2005, available at http://www.whitehouse.gov/news/releases/2005/12/20051217.html. Richard W. Stevenson and Adam Liptak, "Cheney Defends Eavesdropping Without Warrants," *New York Times*, December 21, 2005, A36.

21. President George W. Bush, "Prepared Remarks for West Point," June 1, 2002, available at http://www.whitehouse.gov/news/releases/2002/06/20020601-3.html.

22. Human Rights First, "Human Rights First's Analysis of Gonzales' Testimony Before the Senate Judiciary Committee and His Written Answers to Supplemental Questions," January 24, 2005, available at http://www.humanrightsfirst.org/us_law/etn/gonzales/statements/hrf_opp_gonz_full_012405.asp (accessed April 5, 2006); "Gonzales Faces Tough Questions at Hearing," *CNN*, January 7, 2005, available at http://www.cnn.com/2005/ALLPOLITICS/01/06/gonzales.hearing/.

23. In a January 21, 2005, letter to the Senate Judiciary Committee, Mr. Sofaer explained that "the purpose of the reservation [to the Convention Against Torture] was to prevent any tribunal or state from claiming that the U.S. would have to follow a different and broader meaning of the language of Article 16 than the meaning of those same words in the Eighth Amendment. *The words of the reservation support this understanding, in that they related to the meaning of the terms involved, not to their geographic application.*" Letter from Abraham Sofaer to Senator Patrick Leahy, January 21, 2005, reprinted in 151 *Congressional Record* S12383 (November 4, 2005) (emphasis added).

24. Mark Danner, *Torture and Truth: America, Abu Ghraib, and the War on Terror* (New York: New York Review Books, 2004); Human Rights Watch, *"No Blood, No Foul": Soldiers' Accounts of Detainee Abuse in Iraq* (July 2006), available at http://hrw.org/reports/2006/us0706/.

25. Senator John McCain, "Statement on Detainee Amendments," October 5, 2005, available at http://mccain.senate.gov/press_office/view_article.cfm?id=135.

26. Elisabeth Bumiller, "For President, Final Say on a Bill Sometimes Comes After the Signing," *New York Times*, January 16, 2006, A11.

27. Andrew Sullivan, "We Don't Need a New King George," *Time*, January 16, 2006, available at http://www.time.com/time/magazine/article/0,9171,1149361,00.html.

28. For development of this point and evidence that it has been a persistent feature of responses to crises in American political history, see Cole, *Enemy Aliens.*

29. See, e.g., Universal Declaration of Human Rights, Preamble (1948).

30. For a detailed and footnoted account of these initiatives, see Cole, *Enemy Aliens,* 17–46.

31. Inspector General's Report.

32. These numbers are based on figures that the federal government itself issued. As of November 5, 2001, the government publicly announced that it had detained 1,192 terrorist suspects. As of May 2003, it had detained another 1,100 Arabs and Muslims in the Absconder Apprehension Initiative, aimed at Arabs and Muslims in the hopes that some terrorists would be apprehended. And as of May 2003, it had arrested another 2,747 foreign nationals in connection with the Special Registration Program,

also aimed at Arabs and Muslims. See Cole, *Enemy Aliens*, 25 (and accompanying notes).

33. See *A(FC) and Others v. Secretary of State for the Home Department*, [2004] UKHL 56 (December 16, 2004).

34. *Detroit Free Press v. Ashcroft*, 303 F.3d 681, 683 (6th Cir. 2002).

35. Priest, "CIA Holds Terror Suspects."

36. See OMB Watch, *Muslim Charities and the War on Terror* (2006), available at http://www.ombwatch.org/pdfs/muslim_charities.pdf.

37. *El-Masri v. Tenet*, 437 F. Supp. 2d 530 (E.D. Va. 2006), *aff'd*, 2007 U.S. App. LEXIS 4796 (4th Cir. March 2, 2007).

38. *Al-Haramain Islamic Found., Inc. v. Bush*, 451 F. Supp. 2d 1215 (D. Or. 2006) (rejecting dismissal on state secrets grounds); *ACLU v. NSA / Central Sec. Serv.*, 438 F. Supp. 2d 754 (D. Mich. 2006) (rejecting state secrets argument, holding NSA spying program invalid); *Terkel v. AT&T Corp.*, 441 F. Supp. 2d 899 (D. Ill. 2006) (dismissing lawsuit on state secrets grounds).

39. Under the initial rules, the defense lawyer appointed from within the military had to be present when protected information was used against a defendant, but he could not share that information with his client or his civilian co-counsel. In June 2006, the Supreme Court ruled that these procedures were invalid, and in October 2006 Congress enacted a new set of procedures in the Military Commissions Act, Publ. L. No. 109–366, 120 Stat. 2600. Under the new rules, classified evidence may not be presented outside the defendant's presence, but summaries of classified evidence may be used.

40. *In re Guantánamo Cases*, 355 F. Supp. 2d 443, 459 (D.D.C. 2005), vacated on other grounds by *Boumediene v. Bush*, 2007 U.S. Dist. LEXIS 3682 (D.C. Cir. February 20, 2007).

41. *Boumediene v. Bush*, 2007 U.S. App. LEXIS 3682 (D.C. Cir. February 20, 2007), *cert. denied*, 2007 U.S. LEXIS 3783 (April 2, 2007).

42. *Scales v. United States*, 367 U.S. 203, 224–25 (1961).

43. See Louis Post, *The Deportations Delirium of Nineteen-Twenty: A Personal Narrative of an Historic Official Experience* (New York: Da Capo Press, 1923, 1970); Robert K. Murray, *Red Scare: A Study in National Hysteria, 1919–1920* (Minneapolis: University of Minnesota Press, 1955); Cole, *Enemy Aliens*, 116–28.

44. Peter Irons, *Justice at War* (New York: Oxford University Press, 1983).

45. Michal R. Belknap, *Cold War Political Justice: The Smith Act, the Communist Party, and American Civil Liberties* (Westport, CT: Greenwood Press, 1977); Ralph Brown Jr., *Loyalty and Security: Employment Tests in the United States* (New Haven, CT: Yale University Press, 1958).

46. Executive Order 13224, 66 Fed. Reg. 49,079 (September 23, 2006).

47. *Humanitarian Law Project v. United States Dep't of Treasury*, 463 F. Supp. 2d 1049 (C.D. Cal. 2006).

48. T.R. Goldman, "Refugees from Oppressive Regimes Kept Out," *Legal Times*, June 12, 2006, 1.

49. *NAACP v. Claiborne Hardware*, 458 U.S. 886, 932 (1982).

50. Inspector General's Report.

51. *Hamdi v. Rumsfeld*, 542 U.S. 507, 509 (2004).

52. The agreement is unenforceable because as a constitutional matter one cannot be compelled to give up one's citizenship, *Afroyim v. Rusk*, 387 U.S. 253 (1967), and because the United States has no authority to stop Hamdi from leaving Saudi Arabia.

53. The findings summarized here are from Mark Denbeaux and Joshua Denbeaux, "No-Hearing Hearings; CSRT: The Modern Habeas Corpus? An Analysis of the Proceeding of the Government's Combatant Status Review Tribuanls at Guantánamo" (2006), available at http://law.shu.edu/news/final_no_hearing_hearings_report.pdf.

54. 18 U.S.C. §2339A; 8 U.S.C. §1189.

55. 8 U.S.C. §§1189(a)(1), (c)(2).

56. *People's Mojahedin Org. of Iran v. U.S. Sec. of State*, 182 F.3d 17, 23 (D.C. Cir. 1999), *cert. denied*, 529 U.S. 1104 (2000)

57. Executive Order 13224, 3 C.F.R. §786 (2001).

58. 50 U.S.C. §1703(c).

59. USA PATRIOT Act, §106, amending 50 U.S.C. §1702(a)(1)(B) and adding 50 U.S.C. §1702(c).

60. As noted above, however, the courts have declared some of the more expansive provisions of both material-support laws unconstitutional, largely because their terms are so vague and broad that they give the executive branch far too much discretion and chill legitimate political activity. See *Humanitarian Law Project v. Gonzales*, 380 F. Supp. 2d 1134 (D. Cal. 2005); *Humanitarian Law Project v. United States Dep't of Treasury*, 463 F. Supp. 2d 1049 (C.D. Cal. 2006). David Cole is counsel for Humanitarian Law Project in these cases.

61. Antonin Scalia, "The Rule of Law as a Law of Rules," 56 *University of Chicago Law Review* 1175 (1989).

62. *Flipside v. Hoffman Estates*, 455 U.S. 489, 495 (1982).

63. Office of Legal Counsel, Memorandum from Jay S. Bybee, Assistant Attorney General, to Alberto R. Gonzales, Counsel to the President, Re: *Standards of Conduct for Interrogation under 18 U.S.C. §§2340–2340A* (August 1, 2002), (hereinafter "August 2002 Torture Memo"), reprinted in Danner, *Torture and Truth*, 115.

64. "Presidential Order on Treatment of al Qaeda and Taliban Detainees," February 7, 2002, available at http://lawofwar.org/Bush_torture_memo/htm.

65. "Responses to Senator Richard Durbin's Written Questions for

Timothy Flanigan, Nominee to Be Deputy Attorney General," quoted in "Mr. Flanigan's Answers," *Washington Post*, September 28, 2005, A20.

66. Ian Fishback, "A Matter of Honor," *Washington Post*, September 28, 2005, A22.

67. 66 Fed. Reg. 48,334 (September 20, 2001) (amending 8 C.F.R. §287.3[d]).

68. Robert Kirsch, "Unclassified Attorney Notes Regarding Hadj Boudella," quoted in Center for Constitutional Rights, *Report on Torture and Cruel, Inhuman and Degrading Treatment of Prisoners at Guantánamo Bay, Cuba* (July 2006).

69. Adam Liptak, "In Terrorism Cases, Administration Sets Own Rules," *New York Times*, November 27, 2005, §1, p. 1 (quoting transcript of oral argument in D.C. Circuit appeal of Guantánamo detainee cases).

70. See "Press Briefing by Attorney General Alberto Gonzales and General Michael Hayden, Principal Deputy Director for National Intelligence," December 19, 2005, available at http:///www.whitehouse.gov/news/releases/2005/12/20051219-1.html.

71. See Charles Black, *The People and the Court: Judicial Review in a Democracy* (New York: Macmillan, 1960).

72. Memorandum from John C. Yoo, Deputy Assistant Attorney General, Office of Legal Counsel, to the Deputy Counsel to the President, Re: *The President's Constitutional Authority to Conduct Military Operations Against Terrorists and Nations Supporting Them* (September 25, 2001), available at www.usdoj.gov/olc/warpowers925.htm (emphasis added).

73. August 2002 Torture Memo, 31.

74. *Rasul v. Bush*, 542 U.S. 466 (2004).

75. Brief for Respondents at 42, 44, *Rasul v. Bush* (Nos. 03-334, 03-343).

76. *Rasul*, 542 U.S. at 506 (Scalia, J., dissenting).

77. *Hamdi v. Rumsfeld*, 542 U.S. 507, 536 (2004).

78. Brief for Respondents at 23, *Hamdan v. Rumsfeld*, No. 05-184 (U.S., filed February 23, 2006), quoting *Ex parte Quirin*, 317 U.S. 1, 25 (1942).

79. *Hamdan v. Rumsfeld*, 126 S. Ct. 2749, 2774 n.23 (2006) (citing the "lowest ebb" passage of Justice Jackson's concurrence in *Youngstown Sheet & Tube Co. v. Sawyer*, 343 U.S. 579, 637 [1952] [Jackson, J., concurring]). In a concurring opinion, Justice Kennedy explained that in creating military tribunals, the president was acting at the lowest ebb of presidential power because he had acted "in a field with a history of congressional participation and regulation," where the Uniform Code of Military Justice had established "an intricate system of military justice." 126 S. Ct. at 2800–2801 (Kennedy, J., concurring, joined by Souter, Ginsburg, and Breyer, JJ.).

80. *ACLU v. NSA/Central Sec. Ser.*, 438 F. Supp. 2d 754 (E.D. Mich. 2006); see also David Cole and Martin S. Lederman, "The National Security Agency's Domestic Spying Program: Framing the Debate," 81 *Indiana Law Journal* 1355 (2006) (reprinting Justice Department letter and memo

defending the NSA program and two letters signed by fourteen constitutional scholars and former government officials arguing that the program appears to be illegal).

81. *Youngstown Sheet and Tube Co. v. Sawyer*, 343 U.S. 579 (1952).

82. Ibid., at 637, 640 (Jackson, J., concurring).

83. *Little v. Barreme*, 6 U.S. (2 Cranch) 170 (1804).

84. Interview by David Frost with Richard Nixon, former President, United States (May 19, 1977), excerpt available at http://www.landmark-cases.org/nixon/nixonview.html.

85. *Hamdan v. Rumsfeld*, 126 S. Ct. at 2795–96.

86. Department of Defense, *Interrogation Log, Detainee 063* (November 23, 2002 to January 11, 2003), available at www.time.com/time/2006/log/log.pdf.

87. Ron Suskind, *The One Percent Doctrine: Deep Inside America's Pursuit of Its Enemies Since 9/11* (New York: Simon & Schuster, 2006); Mark Bowden, "The Dark Art of Interrogation," *Atlantic Monthly*, October 2003.

88. President George W. Bush, "Address to a Joint Session of Congress and the American People," September 20, 2001, available at http://www.whitehouse.gov/news/releases/2001/09/20010920-8.html.

89. "Presidential Military Order on Detention, Treatment, and Trial of Certain Non-Citizens in the War Against Terrorism," November 13, 2001, available at http://www.state.gov/coalition/prs/6077.htm.

90. Senator John McCain, "Statement on Army Field Manual," July 25, 2005, available at http://mccain.senate.gov/press_office/view_article.cfm?id=50.

2. PREVENTIVE WAR

1. The White House, *The National Security Strategy of the United States of America*, September 2002, 15, available at http://www.whitehouse.gov/nsc/nss.pdf.

2. The White House, *The National Security Strategy of the United States of America*, March 2006, available at http://www.whitehouse.gov/nsc/nss/2006.

3. The reports of the Senate Select Intelligence Committee and the Silberman-Robb Commission addressed the intelligence failures prior to the Iraq War and attempted to explain why those failures occurred. Senate Report No. 108-301, *Report of the Senate Select Committee on Intelligence on the U.S. Intelligence Community's Prewar Intelligence Assessments on Iraq* (2004), 14–29; Report to the President of the United States, *The Commission on the Intelligence Capabilities of the United States Regarding Weapons of Mass Destruction* (2005), available at http://www.wmd.gov/report/wmd_report.pdf. The reports do not explore the relationships between those intelligence failures and the administration's National Security Strategy or

its preventive-war policies. A number of prominent and very insightful recent analyses of the war with Iraq and the intelligence failures leading up to the war make virtually no mention of the National Security Strategy or the preventive-war doctrine and contain no discussion of any relationship between the intelligence failures and the administration's preventive policy. See, e.g., Daniel Benjamin and Steven Simon, *The Next Attack: The Failure of the War on Terror and a Strategy for Getting It Right* (New York: Times Books, 2005); James Risen, *State of War: The Secret History of the CIA and the Bush Administration* (New York: Free Press, 2006); George Packer, *The Assassins' Gate: America in Iraq* (New York: Farrar, Straus and Giroux, 2005); Paul R. Pillar, "Intelligence, Policy, and the War in Iraq," *Foreign Affairs*, March/April 2006, 15. One notable exception is Jeffrey Record, *Dark Victory: America's Second War Against Iraq* (Annapolis, MD: Naval Institute Press, 2004), which has an excellent analysis of the administration's preventive war against Iraq.

4. Hans Blix, *Disarming Iraq* (New York: Pantheon Books, 2004), 264.

5. Record, *Dark Victory*, 33 (quoting Scott Peterson, "Can Hussein Be Deterred?" *Christian Science Monitor*, September 10, 2002, World, 1). President Bush said in an October 7, 2002, speech in Cincinnati, Ohio, that "facing clear evidence of peril, we cannot wait for the final proof—the smoking gun—that could come in the form of a mushroom cloud." "Address to the Nation on Iraq from Cincinnati, Ohio," 38 *Weekly Compilation of Presidential Documents* 1716, October 7, 2002.

6. François Heisbourg, "A Work in Progress: The Bush Doctrine and Its Consequences," *Washington Quarterly*, Spring 2003, 76 (quoting Wolfowitz, "Remarks Before the World Affairs Council and the Commonwealth Club," December 6, 2002); transcript available at www.dod.gov/speeches/2002/s2002/s.20021202.depsecdef.html (emphasis added).

7. "Vice President Dick Cheney Discusses 9/11 Anniversary, Iraq, Nation's Economy and Politics 2002," *Meet the Press*, NBC News transcripts, September 8, 2002 (emphasis added).

8. "Interview with Colin Powell," *Fox News Sunday*, Fox News Network, September 8, 2002 (emphasis added).

9. Record, *Dark Victory*, 108.

10. President George W. Bush, "Address to the Nation on Iraq from Cincinnati, Ohio," 38 *Weekly Compilation of Presidential Documents* 1717, October 7, 2002 (emphasis added).

11. Joseph Cirincione, Jessica T. Mathews, George Perkovich, and Alexis Orton, *WMD in Iraq: Evidence and Implications* (Carnegie Endowment for International Peace, January 2004), 29, (hereinafter "Carnegie Report"), available at http://www.carnegieendowment.org/publications/index.cfm?fa=view&id=1435. Powell's statements and the Defense Intelligence Agency assessment are quoted in this report.

12. Ibid., 33.

13. Blix, *Disarming Iraq*, 156.

14. Judith Miller and Julia Preston, "Threats and Responses: The Inspector; Blix Says He Saw Nothing to Prompt a War," *New York Times*, January 31, 2003, A10.

15. Blix, *Disarming Iraq*, 154.

16. The IAEA had jurisdiction to determine whether Iraq was attempting to revive its nuclear weapons program. Hans Blix and the UNMOVIC inspectors were responsible for inspections involving all other weapons prohibited by the UN Security Council after the 1991 war.

17. Mohamed ElBaradei, "The Status of Nuclear Inspectors in Iraq: An Update, Remarks to the UN Security Council," Statement to the United Nations Security Council, March 7, 2003, available at http://www.iaea.org/NewsCenter/Statements/2003/ebsp2003n006.shtml.

18. Steven R. Weisman, "Threats and Responses: United Nations; To White House, Inspector Is Now More a Dead End Than Guidepost," *New York Times*, March 2, 2003, A15.

19. Helena Smith, "Blix: I Was Smeared by the Pentagon," *The Guardian*, June 11, 2003, 1.

20. Secretary Donald Rumsfeld, Interview on ABC, *This Week with George Stephanopoulos*, ABC News, March 30, 2003, transcript available at http://www.defenselink.mil/transcripts/2003/t03302003_t0330sdabcsteph.html.

21. President George W. Bush, "Address to the Nation on War with Iraq," 39 *Weekly Compilation of Presidential Documents* 338, March 17, 2003.

22. Benjamin and Simon, *Next Attack*, 147.

23. Ibid., 164.

24. Eric Schmitt, "Threats and Responses: Intelligence; Rumsfeld Says U.S. Has 'Bulletproof' Evidence of Iraq's Links to Al Qaeda," *New York Times*, September 28, 2002, A9.

25. President Bush's statements can be found in "The President's News Conference," 38 *Weekly Compilation of Presidential Documents* 2007 (November 7, 2002); "The President's Weekly Radio Address," 39 *Weekly Compilation of Presidential Documents* 175 (February 8, 2003); "Remarks Prior to Discussions with President Alvaro Uribe of Columbia and an Exchange with Reporters," 38 *Weekly Compilation of Presidential Documents* 1619 (September 25, 2002). Powell's quote is reprinted in "Threats and Responses; Powell's Address, Presenting 'Deeply Troubling' Evidence in Iraq," *New York Times*, February 6, 2003, A18.

26. Douglas Jehl, "High Qaeda Aide Retracted Claim of Link with Iraq," *New York Times*, July 31, 2004, A1.

27. James Risen, "Threats and Responses: C.I.A.; Captives Deny Qaeda Worked with Baghdad," *New York Times*, June 9, 2003, A1.

28. Douglas Jehl, "Questioning Nearly Every Aspect of the Responses to September 11 and Terrorism," *New York Times*, June 18, 2004, A18; Na-

tional Commission on Terrorist Attacks, "Overview of the Enemy: Staff Statement No. 15" *9-11 Commission: Official Statements by Commission Staff* (January–June 2004), 5; National Commission on Terrorist Attacks, "Outline of the 9/11 Plot: Staff Statement No. 16," *9-11 Commission: Official Statements by Commission Staff* (January–June 2004), 8; Senate Report No. 108-301, 226–27.

29. Carnegie Report, 13.

30. Pillar, "Intelligence," 16.

31. Ibid., 17–18.

32. Blix, *Disarming Iraq*, 202.

33. "Blix Attacks Iraq Weapons 'Spin,'" CNN, September 18, 2003, available at http://www.cnn.com.

34. Carnegie Report, 17.

35. James Risen, *State of War*, 116–17.

36. Christopher Marquis, "The Struggle for Iraq: Diplomacy; Powell Admits No Hard Proof in Linking Iraq to Al Qaeda," *New York Times*, January 9, 2004, A10 (emphasis added).

37. James Risen, David Sanger, and Thom Shanker, "After the War: Weapons Intelligence; In Sketchy Data, Trying to Gauge Iraq Threat," *New York Times*, July 20, 2003, 1.

38. Carnegie Report, 17 (quoting Condoleezza Rice, Interview on ABC, *This Week with George Stephanopoulos*, June 8, 2003; Dick Cheney, Interview on NBC, *Meet the Press*, September 8, 2002).

39. Record, *Dark Victory*, 112.

40. See Colum Lynch, "Allied Doubts Grow About U.S. Strikes on Sudanese Plant," *Boston Globe*, September 24, 1998, A2 (noting assertions by French and Italian foreign ministers, as well as British and German officials, that the evidence is less than convincing and stating that senior British officials reportedly privately expressed "dismay and anger" over the missile strikes). See also "Carter Urges Inquiry into U.S. Raid on Sudan," *New York Times*, September 18, 1998, A4 (noting the assertion of former president Carter that British, German, and other foreign leaders "were increasingly skeptical of American assertions about the [Sudan] factory").

41. See Terry Atlas and Ray Moseley, "'Smoking Gun' for Sudan Raid Now in Doubt," *Chicago Tribune*, August 28, 1998, N1; Colum Lynch, "Sudan Working for Better Ties with U.S.," *Boston Globe*, October 7, 1998, A8; Betsy Pisik, "Pakistan Files Complaint over Attack," *Washington Times*, August 25, 1998, A1; "Sudanese Factory Was Working with Iraq on VX Nerve Agent, U.S. Intelligence Says," *Baltimore Sun*, August 26, 1998, 18A; "Embassy Bombing Suspects Charged in U.S.; Ties to Saudi Exile Asserted; Other Developments," *Facts on File World News Digest*, September 3, 1998, 608; Seymour M. Hersh, "The Missiles of August," *New Yorker*, October 12, 1998, 40; Tim Weiner and Steven Lee Myers, "After the Attacks: The Overview; Flaws in U.S. Account Raise Questions on Strike in Sudan," *New*

York Times, August 29, 1998, A1; Tim Weiner and Steven Lee Myers, "U.S. Notes Gaps in Data About Drug Plant but Defends Attack," *New York Times,* September 3, 1998, A6.

42. Daniel Pearl, "In Sudanese Bombing, 'Evidence' Depends on Who Is Viewing It," *Wall Street Journal,* October 28, 1998, A1. When asked how they "knew" that the plant was run by the Sudanese government's weapons-making arm in which bin Laden purportedly had an interest, a U.S. intelligence official said that they assumed that any chemical weapons plant in Sudan would be run by the government. Ibid.; Paul Richter, "Sudan Attack Claims Faulty, U.S. Admits," *Los Angeles Times,* September 1, 1998, A1. See also Daniel Pearl, "More Doubts Rise over Claims for U.S. Attack," *Wall Street Journal,* August 28, 1998, A8; Tim Weiner and James Risen, "Decision to Strike Factory in Sudan Based on Surmise Inferred from Evidence," *New York Times,* September 21, 1998, A1; see also Vernon Loeb, "U.S. Unfreezes Assets of Saudi Who Owned Plant Bombed in Sudan," *Washington Post,* May 9, 1999, A11 (stating that after the attack, the United States froze Mr. Idris's assets in American banks, claiming that he was connected with bin Laden, prompting Mr. Idris to file suit against the government. Just before the government's response to his lawsuit was due in court, the Treasury Department agreed to release his assets, claiming that it did not want to divulge secret evidence).

43. James Risen, "Question of Evidence: A Special Report to Bomb Sudan Plant, or Not: A Year Later, Debates Ramble," *New York Times,* October 27, 1999, A1; Spencer Ackerman and John B. Judis, "The Operator," *New Republic,* September 22, 2003, 18.

44. See Daniel Benjamin and Steven Simon, "A Failure of Intelligence?" *New York Review of Books,* December 20, 2001, 76. But see Michael Barletta, "Chemical Weapons in the Sudan: Allegations and Evidence," *Nonproliferation Review,* Fall 1998, 116 (finding that "the balance of available evidence indicates that the facility probably had no role whatsoever in [chemical weapons] development"); see also Jules Lobel, "The Use of Force to Respond to Terrorist Attacks: The Bombing of Sudan and Afghanistan," 24 *Yale Journal of International Law* 537, 545–46 (1999) (summarizing the administration claims and doubts of independent observers).

45. See "Carter Urges Inquiry." Both the *New York Times* and the *Washington Post* editorialized that the doubts about the administration's evidence regarding the El Shifa factory required further investigation. See "Eliminating Hidden Weapons: Too Much Secrecy on the Sudan," editorial, *New York Times,* August 28, 1998, A24; "Intelligence Lapse?" editorial, *Washington Post,* September 6, 1998, C6. Abraham Sofaer, while supporting the legality of preemptive strikes, wrote that it is "disturbing . . . that the defense secretary announced (on the basis of erroneous intelligence) that the factory in Sudan did not make pharmaceuticals, and that the Clinton administration has been unwilling to participate in a thorough evalu-

ation of its factual premises concerning the plant." Abraham D. Sofaer, "U.S. Acted Legally in Foreign Raids," *Newsday* (New York), October 19, 1998, A29.

46. See, e.g., Raymond S. Nickerson, "Confirmation Bias: A Ubiquitous Phenomenon in Many Guises," 2(2) *Review of General Psychology* 175 (1998).

47. Charles G. Lord, Lee Ross, and Mark R. Lepper, "Biased Assimilation and Attitude Polarization: The Effects of Prior Theories on Subsequently Considered Evidence," 37 (11) *Journal of Personality and Social Psychology* 2098 (citing Francis Bacon, *The New Organon and Related Writings* [New York: Liberal Arts Press, 1960], 1620).

48. See Pillar, "Intelligence," 19.

49. Risen, *State of War*, 113.

50. Silberman-Robb Report, 87, 162, 169 (emphasis in original) ibid., 115.

51. Risen, *State of War*, 122.

52. Carnegie Report, 17 (quoting Shlomo Brom, "The War in Iraq: An Intelligence Failure," Jaffe Center's *Strategic Assessment* 6, no. 3 [November 2003]).

53. Pillar, "Intelligence," 21–22.

54. Gideon Rose, "'The Connection': Proof," *New York Times Book Review,* September 19, 2004, 19.

55. *Department of Defense Dictionary of Military and Associated Terms,* Joint Publication, 1–02, April 12, 2001 (As amended through June 9, 2004), 415 (emphasis added). For Webster's statement, see "Letter from Daniel Webster to Lord Ashburton" (August 6, 1842), quoted in 2 John Bassett Moore, *A Digest of International Law* 412 (GPO, 1906).

56. Ibid., 419.

57. "Address Before a Joint Session of the Congress on the State of the Union," 39 *Weekly Compilation of Presidential Documents* 115, January 28, 2003.

58. John Yoo, "Using Force," 71 *University of Chicago Law Review* 729, 735 (2004).

59. Ibid., 730, 758–62, 787.

60. Abram Chayes, *The Cuban Missile Crisis* (New York: Oxford University Press, 1974), 65.

61. Ibid.

62. See, e.g., Convention Against Torture and Other Cruel, Inhuman or Degrading Treatment or Punishment.

63. George P. Fletcher, *Basic Concepts of Criminal Law* (New York: Oxford University Press, 1998), 134; see also Jane Campbell Moriarty, "While Dangers Gather: The Bush Preemption Doctrine, Battered Women, Imminence and Anticipatory Self-Defense," 30 *New York University Law & Social Change* 1, 33 n.111 and n.115. While the Model Penal Code attempted

to introduce some flexibility into the concept of "immediate," most states have adhered to the traditional notion of imminence as temporally imminent, and even the states that have interpreted the language liberally have still required that the defendant have a reasonable "perception of imminent harm." Ibid., n.111.

64. M. Elaine Bunn, "Preemptive Action: When, How, and to What Effect?" *Strategic Forum*, no. 200, July 2003, 4 (quoting Condoleezza Rice, Remarks on the President's National Security Strategy, Waldorf-Astoria Hotel, New York, October 1, 2002).

65. Yoo, "Using Force," 750.

66. Ibid., 753–56.

67. Gordon A. Craig, *The Politics of the Prussian Army, 1640–1945* (New York: Oxford University Press, 1955), 255 (quoting Bismarck).

68. Record, *Dark Victory*, 80 (quoting Gwynne Dyer, "Laying on the Old Munich Smear," *Toronto Star*, September 2, 2002, A13).

69. David Luban, "Preventive War," *Philosophy and Public Affairs*, July 2004, 229–30, n.40 (quoting Winston Churchill, *Great Contemporaries* [London: Butterworth, 1937], 225).

70. Henry Kissinger, "The Custodians of the World?" *San Diego Union-Tribune*, September 8, 2002, G2.

71. Luban, "Preventive War," 226–27.

72. Robert Kagan, *Of Paradise and Power* (New York: Alfred A. Knopf, 2003), 74–75 (approvingly quoting British journalist Robert Cooper).

73. Luban, "Preventive War," 242–43 (quoting Kagan).

74. Jonathan Schell, "The Case Against the War," *The Nation*, March 3, 2003, 14.

75. The Bush administration argued that the United States and its allies ("the coalition of the willing") were enforcing prior Security Council resolutions requiring Iraq to disarm. There are many difficulties with this argument. One obvious problem was that the administration relied heavily on Resolution 678, enacted in 1990, which authorized states to use force to expel Iraq from Kuwait, an authorization which by 2003 was obviously no longer relevant. The argument's most fundamental deficiency, however, was that it allowed a state to invoke military means ostensibly to enforce Security Council resolutions where the Security Council itself had rejected such measures. It is hardly surprising that the United States' argument was rejected by most international law scholars, most of the nations of the world, and Secretary-General Annan, who called the attack on Iraq "illegal." John C. Yoo and Will Trachman, "War, International Law, and Sovereignty: Reevaluating the Rules of the Game in a New Century," 5 *Chicago Journal of International Law* 379, 383 (2005).

76. James Madison, *Notes of Debates in the Federal Convention of 1787*, rev. ed. (Athens: Ohio University Press, 1984), 476 (remarks of George Mason).

77. Yoo and Trachman, "War, International Law and Sovereignty," 381.

78. Ibid., 385.

79. "Address to the United Nations General Assembly in New York City," 38 *Weekly Compilation of Presidential Documents* 1532, September 12, 2002; Yoo and Trachman, "War, International Law and Sovereignty," 385.

80. Michael Glennon, "Why the Security Council Failed," *Foreign Affairs*, May–June 2003, 16.

3. COLLATERAL CONSEQUENCES

1. Douglas Jehl and Eric Lichtblau, "Shift on Suspect Is Linked to Role of Qaeda Figures," *New York Times*, November 24, 2005, A1.

2. See, e.g., *Rogers v. Richmond*, 365 U.S. 534 (1961); *Ashcraft v. State of Tennessee*, 327 U.S. 274 (1946) (both ruling that any tactics that override the free will of the suspect and coerce his confession violate due process).

3. White House, Office of the Press Secretary, "President Discusses Creation of Military Commissions to Try Suspected Terrorists," September 6, 2006, available at http://www.whitehouse.gov/news/releases/2006/09/20060906-2.html.

4. Military Commissions Act of 2006, Publ. L. No. 109-366 (2006). See David Cole, "Sanctioning Lawlessness," *The Nation*, October 23, 2006.

5. Memo of Deputy Secretary of Defense, Implementation of Combatant Status Review Tribunal Procedures (July 29, 2004), Encl. 1 pars. G(7) and G(11) (A390) ("There is a rebuttable presumption that the Government Evidence . . . to support a determination that the detainee is an enemy combatant, is genuine and accurate.")

6. Transcript of Oral Argument, 83–87, *Boumediene v. Bush, et al.*, Civ. No. 04-1166 (RJL) (D.D.C. December 2, 2004).

7. See "Brief of *Amici Curiae* Retired Federal Jurists in Support of Petitioners' Supplemental Brief Regarding the Military Commissions Act of 2006," in *Al Odah v. U.S.A.*, Nos. 05-5064, 05-5095 through 05-5116 (D.C. Cir.) (November 1, 2006), 6–14 (quoting from CSRT transcripts).

8. Paul Richter, "U.S. Efforts in Caucasus Underscore Global Fight," *Los Angeles Times*, February 28, 2002, A1. President Bush, "Discussion on Creation of Military Commissions to Try Suspected Terrorists" (September 6, 2006) (speech available at http://www.whitehouse.gov).

9. Bill Dedman, "Can the '20th Hijacker' of September 11 Stand Trial?" MSNBC.com, October 26, 2006, available at http://www.msnbc.msn.com/id/15361462/from/ET/.

10. CNN exit polls (available at http://www.cnn.com/ELECTION/2004/pages/results/states/US/P/00/epolls.0.html). Also see Steve Rosenthal, "Okay, We Lost Ohio—but Why?" *Houston Chronicle*, December 12, 2004, Outlook, 5.

11. "Interview: E.J. Dionne and David Brooks on the Alito Hearings," *All Things Considered*, National Public Radio, January 13, 2006, available at http://www.npr.org/templates/story/story.php?storyID=5157013.

4. THE FAILURE OF PREVENTIVE LAW ENFORCEMENT

1. Bill Fenton, "Taliban Prisoners Are 'Enemy Combatants,'" *Daily Telegraph*, January 12, 2002, available at http://www.telegraph.co.uk/news/main.jhtml?xml=/news/2002/01/12/wtal12.xml (quoting Myers saying, "these are the sort of people who would chew through a hydraulics cable to bring a C-17 down").

2. Katharine Seelye, "Threats and Responses: The Detainees," *New York Times*, October 23, 2002, A14; Katharine Seelye, "A Nation Challenged: Captives; Detainees Are Not P.O.W.s, Cheney and Rumsfeld Declare," *New York Times*, January 28, 2002, A6; Tim Golden, "Voices Baffled, Brash and Irate in Guantánamo," *New York Times*, March 6, 2006, A1.

3. Quoted in Corine Hegland, "Empty Evidence," *National Journal*, February 3, 2006.

4. Tim Golden and Don Van Natta Jr., "U.S. Said to Overstate Value of Guantánamo Detainees," *New York Times*, June 21, 2004, A1.

5. Hegland, "Empty Evidence."

6. Mark Denbeaux and Joshua Denbeaux, "Report on Guantánamo Detainees: A Profile of 517 Detainees Through Analysis of Department of Defense Data," Seton Hall Public Law Research Paper No. 46 (February 2006), 2, 8., Mark and Joshua Denbeaux represent two Guantánamo detainees; however, their report is based not on their clients' or any Guantánamo detainee's allegations, but on the government's own reports.

7. Ibid., 12 (quoting CSRT report).

8. Ibid., 17 (quoting CSRT report).

9. The administration has claimed that a small number of those released have joined (or rejoined) enemy forces against us. But it does not dispute that the vast majority of those released have not done so.

10. Leaflet distributed in Afghanistan, reprinted and quoted in Seton Hall report at 15, 25; see also http://www.psywarrior.com/afghanleaf40.html.

11. Abu Bakker Assim, "The View from Guantánamo," *New York Times*, September 17, 2006, 15; Thomas Eddlem, "Emerging Police State," *New American*, July 24, 2006, 19.

12. Corine Hegland, "Guantánamo's Grip," *National Journal*, February 3, 2006; Department of Defense, Interrogation Log, Detainee No. 063 (November 23, 2002 to January 11, 2003), available at www.time.com/time/2006/log/log.pdf.

13. Hegland, "Empty Evidence."

14. Summarized transcript from Sa ad Ibrahim Sa Ad Al Bidna's Com-

bat Status Review Tribunal, 102–16, available at http://www.dod.mil/pubs/foi/detainees/csrt/Set_47_3130-3248.pdf.

15. See Hegland, "Empty Evidence."

16. Attorney General John Ashcroft, "Prepared Remarks for the US Mayors Conference," October 25, 2001, available at http://www.usdoj.gov/archive/ag/speeches/2001/agcrisisremarks10_25.htm; James Gerstenzang and Edwin Chen, "Response to Terror: Bush Signs Anti-Terror Bill, Calls It Essential Step," *Los Angeles Times*, October 27, 2001, A5.

17. Rachel L. Swarns, "Program's Value in Dispute As a Tool to Fight Terrorism," *New York Times*, December 21, 2004, A26.

18. National Commission on Terrorist Attacks, "Threats and Responses in 2001: Staff Statement No. 10," April 13, 2004, available at http://www.9-11commission.gov/staff_statements/staff_statement_10.pdf.

19. Testimony of Chris Wray, Assistant Attorney General, United States Department of Justice, before the Senate Judiciary Committee, *Aiding Terrorists—An Examination of the Material Support Statute*, May 5, 2004, available at http://judiciary.senate.gov/hearing.cfm?id=1172.

For example, when Mr. Wray stated, "We've charged 310 defendants with criminal offenses as a result of terrorism investigations" and "one hundred and seventy-nine of those have already been convicted," Senator Hatch interrupted and the following exchange took place:

HATCH: How many did you say you've charged?

WRAY: We've charged 310 with criminal offenses that arise directly out of terrorism investigations.

HATCH: About 170 . . .

WRAY: And 179 have been convicted.

HATCH: Actually been convicted . . .

WRAY: . . . thus far

HATCH: . . . of terrorist activities.

WRAY: Yes, sir.

See Senate Judiciary Committee, transcript of May 5, 2004 hearing, 4–5, available at http://www.cq.com. In fact, 179 were not convicted of terrorist activities, but Mr. Wray did not correct the senator's misimpression.

20. U.S. Department of Justice, Office of Inspector General Audit Division, *The Department of Justice's Internal Controls Over Terrorism Reporting* (February 2007), vii–ix.

21. Ibid., v, viii, xiii.

22. Dan Eggen and Julie Tate, "U.S. Campaign Produces Few Convictions on Terrorism Charges," *Washington Post*, June 12, 2005, A1.

23. Scott Shane and Lowell Bergman, "Adding Up the Ounces of Prevention," *New York Times*, September 10, 2006, sec. 4, p. 1.

24. Eggen and Tate, "U.S. Campaign."

25. See Center on Law and Security, New York University, "Terrorist Trials: A Report Card," February 2005, available at http://www.law.nyu.edu/

centers/lawsecurity/publications/terrori sttrialreportcard.pdf. In January 2007, the Center on Law and Security published an updated report, finding that only 15 percent of convictions in "terrorism-related" cases were for federal terrorist crimes, and that "the vast majority of cases turn out to include no link to terrorism once they go to court." Center on Law and Security, New York University Law School, "Terrorist Trial Report Card: U.S. Edition," 2007, available at http://www.lawandsecurity.org/publica tions/TTRCComplete.pdf.

26. See "Criminal Terrorism Enforcement Since the 9/11/01 Attacks," a report issued by the Transactional Records Access Clearinghouse, December 8, 2003, available at http://trac.syr.edu/tracreports/terrorism/report 031208.html.

27. Center on Law and Security, "Terrorist Trial Report Card," 3. U.S. Department of Justice, Bureau of Justice Statistics, *Compendium of Federal Justice Statistics, 2004* (December 2006), 59.

28. Richard Schmitt, "For the Justice Department, A Welcome Conviction; The Government Has Experienced a Series of Missteps and False Starts in Some Terrorism Cases," *New York Times*, April 26, 2006, A15.

29. Tim Padgett and Wendy Malloy, "When Terror Charges Just Won't Stick," *New York Times*, December 19, 2005.

30. The judge presiding over Al-Arian's trial overrode the sentencing agreement and imposed a sentence on Al-Arian that exceeded the government's request. Anthony McCartney, "Al-Arian to Appeal Sentence," *Tampa Tribune*, May 11, 2006. But even under that result, Al-Arian was to be permitted to leave the United States a free man by March 2007—surely not the outcome the government would accept for someone who posed any real threat to the safety of the nation. As of February 2007, however, the administration had subpoenaed Al-Arian to testify before a grand jury, and he had refused. He was cited for civil contempt, raising the possibility that he will be detained in connection with the grand jury investigation for another year or more.

31. James Yee, *For God and Country: Faith and Patriotism Under Fire* (New York: Public Affairs, 2005); Laura Parker, "The Ordeal of Chaplain Yee," *USA Today*, May 17, 2004, A1.

32. Laura Parker, "Airman Says He Did 'A Dumb Thing' but Was No Spy," *USA Today*, September 23, 2004.

33. Shelley Murphy, "Ex-translator Pleads Guilty in U.S. Sentencing Deal," *Boston Globe*, January 11, 2005, B4.

34. Will Dunham, "Army Drops Charges Against Guantánamo Colonel," *Boston Globe*, September 17, 2004.

35. Maureen O'Hagan, "A Terrorism Case That Went Awry," *Seattle Times*, November 22, 2004, available at http://seattletimes.nwsource.com/ html/localnews/2002097570_sami22m.html.

36. Noelle Crombie, "FBI Blamed in Print Error," *The Oregonian*, November 16, 2004, A1. In November 2006, the FBI paid $2 million to settle a lawsuit filed by Mayfield over the incident. James Risen, "The War on Terror, Under New Scrutiny," *New York Times*, December 3, 2006, §4, p. 14.

37. Libby Sander, "2 Men Cleared of Charges of Aiding Hamas Violence," *New York Times*, February 2, 2007, A14.

38. 18 U.S.C. §2339B.

39. David Cole has agreed to consult with Mr. Yousry's attorneys on his appeal.

40. David Cole, "The Lynne Stewart Trial," *The Nation*, March 7, 2005.

41. Michael Powell and Michelle Garcia, "Translator's Conviction Raises Legal Concerns; Trial Transcripts Show Lack of Evidence," *Washington Post*, January 16, 2006, A1.

42. The facts in this account are principally drawn from Matthew Purdy and Lowell Bergman, "Where the Trail Led; Between Evidence and Suspicion; Unclear Danger; Inside the Lackawanna Terror Case," *New York Times*, October 12, 2003, 1; see also "Chasing the Sleeper Cell," *Frontline* (October 16, 2003), available at http://www.pbs.org/wgbh/pages/frontline/sleeper.

43. Deputy Attorney General Larry D. Thompson, Press Conference, September 14, 2002, available at http://www.usdoj.gov/dag/speech/2002/091402dagremarks.htm.

44. *Humanitarian Law Project v. Reno*, 205 F.3d 1130 (9th Cir. 2000); *United States v. Sattar*, 272 F.Supp.2d 348 (S.D.N.Y. 2003); *Humanitarian Law Project v. Reno*, 2001 U.S. Dist. LEXIS 16729 (C.D. Cal. October 2, 2001).

45. Jerry Markon, "Va. Jihad Case Hailed as Key in War on Terror," *Washington Post*, June 8, 2006, A3.

46. Danny Hakim and Eric Lichtblau, "After Convictions, the Undoing of a U.S. Terror Prosecution," *New York Times*, October 7, 2004, A1.

47. David Shepardson, "U.S. Widens Probe of Prosecutor; 2 Drug Cases Added to the Investigation of the Assistant U.S. Attorney Who Ran the Terrorism Case," *Detroit News*, December 3, 2004, A1.

48. Noelle Crombie, "Defendant Admits 'Terrible Mistake,'" *The Oregonian*, June 1, 2005, C9.

49. Robert L. Jamieson Jr., "Ujaama Smoking Gun Goes Up in Smoke," *Seattle Post-Intelligencer*, April 16, 2003, B3.

50. "Secret FBI Report Questions Al Qaeda Capabilities," *ABC News*, March 9, 2005, available at http://abcnews.go.com/WNT/Investigation/story?id=566425&page=1.

51. William K. Rashbaum, "Jury Convicts Pakistani Immigrant in a Plot to Blow Up a Subway Station," *New York Times*, May 25, 2006, A23.

52. Daniel Klaidman, "Al Qaeda in America: The Enemy Within," *Newsweek*, June 23, 2003, available at http://www.msnbc.com/news/926691.asp?0cv=KA01.

53. Robert Ruth, "Al-Qaida Operative; Government Unsealed Case to Stop Rumors," *Columbus Dispatch*, July 10, 2003, C6. See also Department of Justice, "Iyman Faris Sentenced for Providing Material Support to al Qaeda," press release, October 28, 2003, available at http://www.usdoj.gov/opa/pr/2003/October/03_crm589.htm.

54. *Abu Ali v. Ashcroft*, 350 F. Supp. 2d 28 (D.D.C. 2004).

55. "U.S. Man Guilty of Bush Death Plot," BBC News, November 22, 2005, available at http://news.bbc.co.uk/1/hi/world/americs/4461642.stm; *United States v. Abu Ali*, 395 F. Supp. 2d 338,380 (D.C.E. Vir. 2005). See also Jerry Markon, "Al Qaeda Suspect Tells of Bush Plot," *Washington Post*, September 20, 2005, A14 (saying that the plot "never got past the 'idea stage'").

56. Sara Kehaulani Goo, "List of Foiled Plots Puzzling to Some," *Washington Post*, October 23, 2005, A6; Josh Meyer and Warren Vieth, "Scope of Plots Bush Says Were Foiled Is Questioned," *Los Angeles Times*, October 8, 2005, A15; John Diamond and Toni Locy, "White House List of Disrupted Terror Plots Questioned," *USA Today*, October 26, 2005, 4A.

57. Goo, "List of Foiled Plots."

58. Richard Benedetto, "White House: U.S. Allies Have Foiled Terror Plots," *USA Today*, October 6, 2005.

59. Meyer and Vieth, "Scope of Plots."

60. Kenneth R. Bazinet and James Gordon Meek, "We Halt Deadly Plots, W Says," *Daily News* (New York), October 7, 2005, 5.

61. The same is true of most of the plots President Bush cited outside the United States. Two of the other plots cited by President Bush involved alleged plans to attack ships in the Arabian Gulf and the Straits of Hormuz. Counterterrorism officials said that both plots were nowhere close to the execution stage. John Diamond and Toni Locy, "White House List of Disrupted Terror Plots Questioned," *USA Today*, October 26, 2005, 4A; Dana Priest and Glenn Frankel, "Terrorism Suspect Had U.S. Ship Data," *Washington Post*, August 7, 2004, A1. It is not even clear that U.S. authorities had anything to do with disrupting these plots. Bush listed the ten plots as having been disrupted by "the United States and its allies," without distinguishing those we had a hand in disrupting and those we did not.

62. Scott Shane, "FBI Killed Plot in Talking Stage, a Top Aide Says," *New York Times*, June 24, 2006.

63. Eric Lipton, "Recent Arrests in Terror Plots Yield Debate on Preemptive Action by Government," *New York Times*, July 9, 2006, §1, p. 11; Jay Weaver and David Ovalle, "How FBI Moles Snared Terror Suspects," *Miami Herald*, July 16, 2006.

64. White House, Office of the Press Secretary, "President Bush Dis-

cusses Creation of Military Commissions to Try Suspected Terrorists," September 6, 2006, available at http://www.whitehouse.gov/news/re leases/2006/09/20060906-3.html.

65. Dan Eggen and Dafna Linzer, "Secret World of Detainees Grows More Public," *Washington Post,* September 7, 2006, A18; Mark Mazzetti, "Questions Raised About Bush's Primary Claims in Defense of Secret Detention System," *New York Times,* September 8, 2006, A24.

66. See "Bush Lies About Ramzi Bin Al Shibh, Abu Zubaydah and Torture," available at http://www.tnr.com/blog/theplank?pid=36597.

67. Ronald Suskind, *The One Percent Doctrine: Deep Inside America's Pursuit of Its Enemies Since 9/11* (New York: Simon & Schuster, 2006), 100.

68. Ibid., 115–17.

5. THE COSTS OF OVERREACHING

1. Department of State, *Patterns of Global Terrorism Report,* April 29, 2004; Richard Armitage, "Remarks on the Release of the 2003 'Patterns of Global Terrorism' Annual Report," April 29, 2004, available at http://www .state.gov/s/d/former/armitage/remarks/31961.htm.

2. Alan Krueger and David Laitin, "Faulty Terror Report Card," *Washington Post,* May 17, 2004, A21; Raphael Perl, "The Department of State's Patterns on Global Terrorism Report: Trends, State Sponsors, and Related Issues," *CRS Report for Congress,* June 1, 2004, available at http://www.fas .org/irp/crs/RL32417.pdf.

3. Susan B. Glasser, "Global Terrorism Statistics Debated," *Washington Post,* May 1, 2005, A23.

4. National Counterterrorism Center Report, *A Chronology of Significant International Terrorism for 2004,* April 27, 2005, available at http:// wits.nctc.gov/reports/2004nctcchronology.pdf.

5. David Sands, "Suicide Bombing Popular Terrorist Tactic," *Washington Times,* May 8, 2006.

6. "Terrorism Survey," conducted by *Foreign Policy* and the Center for American Progress, March 8–April 21, 2006, available at http://web1.for eignpolicy.com/issue_julyaug_2006/TI-index/2006results.doc.

7. James Fallows, "Bush's Lost Year," *Atlantic Monthly,* October 2004, 68, 71.

8. For a detailed discussion of these initiatives and their failure to serve the ends of security, see David Cole, *Enemy Aliens: Double Standards and Constitutional Freedoms in the War on Terrorism,* 2d ed. (New York: The New Press, 2005), 85–179.

9. This account is drawn from Tom Parker, "Counterterrorism Policies in the United Kingdom," in Philip B. Heymann and Juliette Kayyem, *Protecting Liberty in an Age of Terror* (Cambridge, MA: MIT Press, 2005), 125–27.

10. Peter Taylor, *Provos: The IRA and Sinn Fein* (London: Bloomsbury, 1997), 129–30.

11. Lowell Bergman, Eric Lichtblau, Scott Shane, and Don Van Natta Jr., "Spy Agency Data After September 11 Led FBI to Dead Ends," *New York Times*, January 17, 2006, A1.

12. Carol D. Leonnig, "Secret Court's Judges Were Warned About NSA Spy Data; Program May Have Led Improperly to Warrants," *Washington Post*, February 9, 2006, A1.

13. Jim McGee, "Ex-FBI Officials Criticize Tactics on Terrorism; Detention of Suspects Not Effective, They Say," *Washington Post*, November 28, 2001, A1.

14. Jessica Stern, "Al Qaeda—American Style," *New York Times*, July 15, 2006, A15.

15. Dana Priest and Josh White, "Policies on Terrorism Suspects Come Under Fire; Democrats Say CIA's Covert Prisons Hurt U.S. Image," *Washington Post*, November 3, 2005, A2.

16. Stephen Grey and Don Van Natta Jr., "In Italy, Anger at U.S. Tactics Colors Spy Case," *New York Times*, June 26, 2005, A1.

17. Mark Landler, "German Court Confronts U.S. on Abduction," *New York Times*, February 1, 2007, A1.

18. Karen DeYoung, "Distrust Hinders FBI in Outreach to Muslims," *Washington Post*, February 8, 2007, A1.

19. Pew Research Center, *Americans and Europeans Differ Widely on Foreign Policy Issues* (2002), available at http://pewglobal.org/reports/print.php?ReportID=153.

20. Pew Research Center, *What the World Thinks in 2002* (2002), available at http://pewglobal.org/reports/display.php?ReportID=165.

21. Ibid.

22. See Cole, *Enemy Aliens*, 195–97 (quoting criticism from foreign press and foreign governments).

23. Paul Pillar, *Terrorism and American Foreign Policy* (Washington, DC: Brookings Institution Press, 2001), 186–89; Stansfield Turner, "Address at Center for International Studies Forum," Carnegie Endowment for International Peace, Washington, DC, July 13, 2006.

24. See, e.g., Human Rights Watch, *World Report 2003*, introduction (discussing a "copycat phenomenon" in which other countries cite the United States as justification to infringe human rights in the name of fighting terrorism), available at http://www.hrw.org/wr2k3/introduction.html.

25. President George W. Bush, "State of the Union Address," January 29, 2002, available at http://www.whitehouse.gov/news/releases/2002/01/20020129-11.html.

26. Daniel Benjamin and Steven Simon, *The Next Attack: The Failure of the War on Terror and a Strategy for Getting It Right* (New York: Times Books, 2005), 59–65.

6. THE FAILURE OF PREVENTIVE WAR

1. White House, Office of the Press Secretary, "President Bush Announces Major Combat Operations in Iraq Have Ended," speech made onboard the USS *Abraham Lincoln*, May 1, 2003, available at http://www .whitehouse.gov/news/releases/2003/05/20030501-15.html.

2. Mike Allen, "Bush: We Found Banned Weapons; President Cites Trailers in Iraq as Proof," *Washington Post*, May 31, 2003, A1; "New Team of Experts Searching for Weapons in Iraq; Bush Departs for Visits to Six Nations," Fox News Network, May 30, 2003 (transcript no. 053001cb.254 available on Lexis/Nexis).

3. In September 2006, the UN estimated 48,000 to 52,000 Iraqi civilian deaths attributable to military intervention since March 20, 2003, and criticized the United States for underreporting these fatalities. UN Assistance Mission for Iraq, Human Rights Report, May 1–June 30, 2006, 3, http:// www.uniraq.org/documents/HR%20Report%20Ma y%20Jun%202006% 20EN.pdf.

4. James Fallows, "Bush's Lost Year," *Atlantic Monthly*, October 2004, 73.

5. See "The Terrorism Index," conducted by *Foreign Policy* and the Center for American Progress Report, June 14, 2006, available at http://www .americanprogress.org/issues/2006/06/b1769267.html, also published in *Foreign Policy*, August 2006. A follow-up study published in February 2007 made similar findings.

6. Declassified Key Judgments of the National Intelligence Estimate, "Trends in Global Terrorism: Implications for the United States," dated April 6, 2006, reprinted in the *New York Times*, September 27, 2006, A1.

7. Jessica Stern, "How America Created a Terrorist Haven," *New York Times*, August 20, 2003, A21.

8. James E. Baker III and Lee H. Hamilton, Co-Chairs, *The Iraq Study Group Report*, December 6, 2006, 12, available at http://www.bakerinsti tute.org/Pubs/iraqstudygroup_findings.pdf.

9. Cesar G. Soriano and Steven Komarow, "Poll: Iraqis Out of Patience," *USA Today*, April 29, 2004, 1A (citing a *USA Today/CNN*/Gallup poll finding that 71 percent of Iraqis view the U.S.-led coalition as "occupiers" instead of "liberators").

10. Anthony Shadid, *Night Draws Near: Iraq's People in the Shadow of America's War* (New York: Henry Holt & Co., 2005), 17.

11. Ibid., 287.

12. Brookings Institution, *Iraq Index, Tracking Variables of Reconstruction & Security in Post-Saddam Iraq*, July 10, 2006, 17, 18, available at http://www.brookings.edu/iraqindex; *The Iraq Study Group Report*, 10.

13. Daniel Benjamin and Steven Simon, *The Next Attack: The Failure of*

the War on Terror and a Strategy for Getting It Right (New York: Times Books, 2005), 9–10, 39.

14. Bryan Bender, "Study Cites Seeds of Terror in Iraq," *Boston Globe*, July 17, 2005, A1.

15. Ibid.

16. *Global Intelligence Challenges 2005: Meeting Long-Term Challenges with a Long-Term Strategy*, Hearing Before the Senate Intelligence Committee, 109th Cong. 1st Sess. (February 16, 2005) (statement of Porter J. Goss, director of central intelligence).

17. Benjamin and Simon, *Next Attack*, 42–46.

18. Ibid., 47.

19. Ibid., 46; James Glanz, William J. Broad, and David E. Sanger, "Huge Cache of Explosives Vanished from Site in Iraq," *New York Times*, October 25, 2004, A1.

20. Farah Stockman, "Explosives Were Looted After Iraq Invasion, UN Nuclear Official Cites Security Lapse," *Boston Globe*, October 26, 2004, A1.

21. Dan Rather, "Twenty Percent," *Times Union* (Albany, NY), May 26, 2003, A6; Richard Norton-Taylor, Gary Younge, and Michael Howard, "Iraq: After the War: U.S. Struggles in Country Awash with Weapons," *The Guardian*, November 3, 2003, 13.

22. Elaine Sciolino and Don Van Natta Jr., "June Report Led Britain to Lower Its Terror Alert," *New York Times*, July 19, 2005, A1.

23. Ibid.

24. Naomi Klein, "Terror's Greatest Recruitment Tool," *The Nation*, August 29, 2005, 14.

25. Benjamin and Simon, *Next Attack*, 9–10.

26. Ibid., 31.

27. Stanley Hoffman, "America Goes Backward," *New York Review of Books*, June 12, 2003, 78.

28. Yigal Schleifer, "Sure It's Fiction. But Many Turks See Fact in Anti-U.S. Novel," *Christian Science Monitor*, February 15, 2005, World, 1.

29. Ibid.

30. Pew Reports, *16 Nation Pew Global Attitudes Survey*, June 23, 2005, available at http://pewglobal.org/reports/pdf/247.pdf.

31. Pew Reports, *A Year After Iraq War*, March 16, 2004, available at http://people-press.org/reports/pdf/206.pdf.

32. Ibid. There is unfortunately no reason to think that popular opinion is any better in other predominantly Muslim countries—the Pew Charitable Research Center chose these four as representative.

33. Benjamin and Simon, *Next Attack*, 47.

34. In February 2005, CIA director Porter Goss told Congress that "Islamic extremists are exploiting the Iraq conflict to recruit new anti-U.S. jihadists." *Global Intelligince Challenges 2005: Meeting Long-Term Challenges with a Long-Term Strategy*, Hearing Before the Senate Intelligence

Committee, 109th Cong. 1st Sess. (February 16, 2005) (testimony of Porter Goss). See also Declassified Key Judgments of the National Intelligence Estimate, "Trends in Global Terrorism: Implications for the United States" (April 2006), available at http://www.dni.gov/press_releases/Declassified_NIE_Key_Judgments.pdf.

35. Tod Robberson, "Is Iraq Worth Its Price Tag? Bloodstained Progress Saps Support for Bush Strategy, Analysts Say," *Dallas Morning News*, October 31, 2005, 1A.

36. See, e.g., "Remarks to the Troops in Fort Carson, Colorado," 39 *Weekly Compilation of Presidential Documents* 1684, November 24, 2003; "Address to the Nation on the War on Terror from Fort Bragg, North Carolina," 41 *Weekly Compilation of Presidential Documents* 1079, June 28, 2005.

37. Paul R. Pillar, "Intelligence, Policy, and the War in Iraq," *Foreign Affairs*, March–April 2006, 19.

38. Paul Pillar, e-mail correspondence with Jules Lobel, March 31, 2006.

39. Don Van Natta Jr. and Desmond Butler, "Threats and Responses: Terror Network; Anger on Iraq Seen as New Qaeda Recruiting Tool," *New York Times*, March 16, 2003, A1 (cited in Benjamin and Simon, *Next Attack*, 57).

40. Quoted in Richard Norton-Taylor, "A Boost for Bin Laden," *The Guardian*, September 26, 2006, 34.

41. Max Rodenbeek, "Their Master's Voice," *New York Review of Books*, March 9, 2006, 8 (quoting Peter L. Bergen, *The Osama bin Laden I Know: An Oral History of al Qaeda's Leader*, [New York: Simon & Schuster, 2006]).

42. Leo Shane III, "Poll of Troops in Iraq Sees 72% Support for Withdrawal Within a Year," *Stars & Stripes*, March 1, 2006.

43. Thom Shanker, "Young Officers Leaving Army at a High Rate," *New York Times*, April 10, 2006, A1. For example, the retention rate for the West Point class of 2000 fell to only 65.8 percent, the highest rate of loss over the past sixteen years among West Point officers reaching the five-year mark.

44. "Top General: U.S. Forces 'Stretched,'" CBS News, January 26, 2006, available at http://www.cbsnews.com/stories/2006/01/26/iraq/main1240559.shtml?CMP=ILC-SearchStories.

45. Associated Press, "Report: Army Could Be Near Breaking Point," MSNBC, January 24, 2006, available at http://www.msnbc.msn.com/id/11009829/.

46. Pillar, "Intelligence," 24. See also Fallows, "Bush's Lost Year," 81–82.

47. See note 3.

48. *The Iraq Study Group Report*, 27. Congressional Research Service Report for Congress, "The Cost of Iraq, Afghanistan and Other Global War on Terror Operations Since 9/11" (Amy Belasco, Defense Specialist), April 24, 2006, 8, 16; Shailagh Murray, "Hill Approves Funding for Wars, Storm Relief," *Washington Post*, June 16, 2006, A7.

49. Congressional Research Service Report for Congress, "The Cost of Iraq," October 7, 2005. The Congressional Budget Office estimated total costs under three scenarios: the low figure would put the total cost at over $400 billion, the moderate figure was approximately $500 billion, and the high estimate would put the total cost at over $600 billion.

50. Linda Bilmes and Joseph E. Stiglitz, "The Economic Costs of the Iraq War: An Appraisal Three Years After the Beginning of the Conflict," KSG Faculty Research Working Paper Series RWP06-002, January 2006, 1.

51. Ibid., 5–11.

52. Matthew Brzezinski, "Red Alert," *Mother Jones*, September–October 2004, 94.

53. Ibid.; Brian Bremner, "A Homegrown Solution for Keeping Ports Safe," *Business Week*, March 27, 2006, 38.

54. Brzezinski, "Red Alert."

55. Ibid.

56. Joseph Button, "Increased Security Amidst a Mounting Insurgency: A Close Look at the Afghan Security Paradox," Center for Defense Information, January 17, 2006, available at http://www.cdi.org/program/docu ment.cfm?documentid=3262&programID=39&from_page=../friendly version/printversion.cfm.

57. Eric Schmitt, "Springtime for Killing in Afghanistan," *New York Times*, May 28, 2006, 1; Ivan Watson, "Taliban Enlists Video in Fight for Afghanistan," National Public Radio, December 7, 2006, available at http://www.npr.org/templates/story/stor y.php?storyId=6423946.

58. Rosie Cowan and Richard Norton-Taylor, "Britain Now No. 1 Al-Qaida Target—Anti-Terror Chiefs," *The Guardian*, October 18, 2006, 1.

59. Kim Sengupta and Jerome Taylor, "Into the Valley of Death, UK Troops Head into the Afghan War Zone," *The Independent*, February 13, 2006.

60. Anna Morgan, "Northern Ire, Canadian Politics Are All About America," *Washington Post*, January 8, 2006, B2.

61. The 15 Nation Pew Global Attitude Survey, June 13, 2006, available at http://pewglobal.org/reports/display.php?ReportID=252.

62. 16 Nation Pew Attitude Survey, June 23, 2005, available at http://pewglobal.org/reports/display.php?PageID=801.

63. Julian Glover, "British Believe Bush Is More Dangerous than Kim Jong-Il," *The Guardian*, November 3, 2006, 1.

64. Cited in Jeffrey Record, "Nuclear Deterrence, Preventive War and Counterproliferation," 519 *Policy Analysis* 17 (July 8, 2004).

65. John Lewis Gaddis, *Surprise, Security, and the American Experience* (Cambridge, MA: Harvard University Press, 2005), 100–101.

66. David C. Hendrickson and Robert W. Tucker, *Revisions in Need of Revising: What Went Wrong in the Iraq War*, December 2005, 24, available at http://www.strategicstudiesinstitute.army.mil/pdffiles/PUB637.pdf.

67. Quoted in Larry Diamond, *Squandered Victory: The American Occupation and the Bungled Attempt to Bring Democracy to Iraq* (New York: Henry Holt & Co., 2005), 280.

68. White House, Office of the Press Secretary, "President Bush, Columbia President Uribe Discuss Terrorism," September 25, 2002, at http://www.whitehouse.gov/news/releases/2002/09/20020925-1.html.

69. See James A. Baker III, *The Politics of Diplomacy: Revolution, War and Peace 1989–1992* (New York: Putnam, 1957), 359.

70. Michael Dobbs, "U.S. Had Key Role in Iraq Buildup, Trade in Chemical Arms Allowed Despite Their Use on Iranians, Kurds," *Washington Post*, December 30, 2002, A1.

71. Richard K. Betts, "Suicide from Fear of Death," *Foreign Affairs*, January–February 2003, 39.

72. Michael O'Hanlon, Susan E. Rice, and James B. Steinberg, "The New National Security Strategy and Preemption," Brookings Institution, December 2002, 6; U.S. Department of State Country Reports on Terrorism (2005), ch. 6, April 28, 2006.

73. Condoleezza Rice, "Promoting the National Interest," *Foreign Affairs*, January–February 2000, 61.

74. Robert S. Norris, Hans M. Kristensen, and Joshua Handler, "North Korea's Nuclear Program, 2003," *Bulletin of the Atomic Scientists*, March–April 2003, 74–77.

75. David E. Sanger, "North Korea Says It Tested a Nuclear Device Underground," *New York Times*, October 9, 2006, A1.

76. John Pilger, "The Next War—Crossing the Rubicon," *Truthout*, February 10, 2006, available at http://www.truthout.org/cgi-bin/artman/exec/view.cgi/48/17612.

77. David E. Sanger, "Bush's Shift: Being Patient with Foes, Fresh Rhetoric Amid Standoffs with Iran and North Korea," *New York Times*, July 10, 2006, A9.

78. William J. Perry et al., "The U.S. Military: Under Strain and at Risk," National Security Advisory Group Report, January 2006, 12.

79. Terry Gross, "The New Brinksmanship: Iran's Nuclear Threat," transcript of Terry Gross's interview of Joseph Cirincione, *Fresh Air*, National Public Radio, February 8, 2006.

80. Michael Slackman, "Guess Who Likes the G.I.'s in Iraq," *New York Times*, January 29, 2006, 4 (shortly after Saddam Hussein's downfall, a top aide to L. Paul Bremer III, then the head of American occupation authority in Iraq, explained that Iraq had just become the front line in Washington's effort to neutralize Iran as a regional power).

81. Ibid.

82. Ibid.

83. Gross, "New Brinksmanship."

84. Ibid.

85. President George W. Bush, "State of the Union Address," January 20, 2004, available at http://www.whitehouse.gov/news/releases/2004/01/20040120-7.html.

86. Patrick E. Tyler, "Libyan Stagnation a Big Factor in Qaddafi Surprise," *New York Times*, January 8, 2004, A3.

87. Martin Indyk, "The Iraq War Did Not Force Gadaffi's Hand," *Financial Times*, March 9, 2004, 21; Flynt Leverett, "Why Libya Gave Up on the Bomb," *New York Times*, January 23, 2004, A23.

88. Leverett, "Why Libya Gave Up."

89. Indyk, "The Iraq War."

90. Andrew Marshall, "Strike First, Ask Questions Later; U.S. Policy Is Now to Hit Terrorists Hard, Without Any Legal Niceties," *The Independent*, August 30, 1998, 13; see also Richard T. Newman et al., "Clinton Raises the Stakes in the War Against Terrorism," *U.S. News & World Report*, August 31, 1998, 38 ("The bombing of Pan Am Flight 103 in 1988 is widely believed to have been an act of revenge for the U.S. bombing of Libya in 1986. . . .").

91. Colonel David Bishop, "Dismantling North Korea's Nuclear Weapon Programs," Strategic Studies Institute, April 2005, 5.

92. Henry Sokolski and Patrick Clawson, eds., *Getting Ready for a Nuclear-Ready Iran: Report of the NPEC Working Group* (Strategic Studies Institute, October 2005), 5.

93. James Risen, *State of War* (New York: Free Press, 2006), 193–94.

94. Commission on the Intelligence Capabilities of the United States Regarding Weapons of Mass Destruction, *Report to the President of the United States*, March 31, 2005, 4, available at http://www.wmd.gov/report/.

95. James Kitfield, "National Security—Coercion and Pre-emption," *National Journal*, May 28, 2005, 1625.

96. Philip Saunders, "Military Options for Dealing with North Korea's Nuclear Program," Center for Nonproliferation Studies, January 27, 2003, available at http://cns.miis.edu/research/korea/dprkmil.htm#fn1.

97. Jim Lobe, "Iraq: A Certified Case of 'Chickenhawk Groupthink,'" *Inter Press Service*, May 11, 2004.

98. Flynt Leverett, "The Gulf Between Us," *New York Times*, January 24, 2006, A21.

99. "Bush: U.S. Probes Possible Iran Ties to 9/11," CNN, July 20, 2004, http://www.cnn.com.

100. David Sanger, "Behind the Urgent Nuclear Diplomacy: A Sense That Iranians Will Get the Bomb," *New York Times*, February 6, 2006, A10. (Bush knows, "aides say, that even to hint at military action or deadlines if Iran refuses to suspend enriching uranium, or if North Korea continues to test missiles and make bomb fuel, would probably destroy any chance of getting China and Russia aboard on a common strategy.") See Elaine Sci-

olino and William J. Broad, "Iran Quietly Learns of Penalties in a Nuclear Incentives Deal," *New York Times*, June 15, 2006, A3; Helene Cooper, "U.S. Is Offering Deals on Trade to Entice Iran," *New York Times*, June 6, 2006, A1.

101. Seymour M. Hersh, "The Iran Plans," *New Yorker*, April 17, 2006, 30; Peter Baker, Dafna Linzer, and Thomas E. Ricks, "U.S. Is Studying Military Strike Options on Iran," *Washington Post*, April 9, 2006, A1.

102. Roger Speed and Michael May, "Dangerous Doctrine," *Bulletin of the Atomic Scientists*, March–April 2005, 38.

103. Hersh, "Iran Plans."

104. Baker, Linzer, and Ricks, "U.S. Is Studying."

105. Speed and May, "Dangerous Doctrine"; Benjamin Phelan, "Buried Truths: Debunking the Nuclear Bunker Buster," *Harper's Magazine*, December 1, 2004, 70 (quoting the Defense Department's Nuclear Posture Review for 2001, which states that the B61-11 "cannot survive penetration into many types of terrain in which hardened underground facilities are located).

106. Hersh, "Iran Plans."

107. Tom Baldwin, "It Would Be Nuts to Bomb Iran, Says Britain," *The Times* (London), April 10, 2006, 4; Baker, Linzer, and Ricks, "U.S. Is Studying."

108. Lee Feinstein and Ray Takeyh, "Apply Korea Lessons to Iran Stalemate," *Baltimore Sun*, September 26, 2005, 11A; Madeleine Albright, "The Cost of the Last Six Years, from North Korea to Kosovo: An Interview with Madeleine Albright," *New Perspectives Quarterly*, March 15, 2007, available at http://www.digitalnpq.org/articles/global/161/03-15-2007/madeleine_ albright.

109. David E. Sanger, "Don't Shoot, We're Not Ready," *New York Times*, June 5, 2006, 1.

110. Beth M. Polebaum, "National Self-Defense in International Law: An Emerging Standard for a Nuclear Age," 59 *New York University Law Review* 187, 227 (1984).

111. 22 U.S.C. §2754 (1982) provides that "defense articles . . . shall be sold . . . solely for internal security, for legitimate self defense." See also Polebaum, ibid.

112. R. Jeffrey Smith and Glenn Frankel, "Saddam's Nuclear-Weapons Dream: A Lingering Nightmare," *Washington Post*, October 13, 1991, A1. See also Peter Scott Ford, "Israel's Attack on Osiraq: A Model for Future Preventive Strikes," September 2004 (Thesis, Naval Post Graduate School, Monterey, CA), 51–52.

113. "*Crossfire* Transcript," CNN, February 7, 2003, http://www.cnn .com.

114. Sammy Salama and Karen Ruster, "A Preemptive Attack on Iran's

Nuclear Facilities: Possible Consequences," Center for Nonproliferation Studies, available at http://cns.miis.edu/pubs/week/040812.htm, citing Imad Khadduir, *Iraq's Nuclear Mirage: Memoirs and Delusions* (Toronto: Springhead, 2003), 82; "*Crossfire* Transcript," CNN, February 7, 2003, http://www.cnn.com.

115. Eliot Cohen, quoted in Ford, "Israel's Attack," 51.

7. LESSONS OF HISTORY

1. Minutes of the Forty-Eighth Meeting (Executive Session) of the United States Delegation, San Francisco, May 20, 1945, 1 *Foreign Relations of the United States*, 1945, 813 at 818.

2. David C. Hendrickson, "Imperialism versus Internationalism: The United States and World Order," *Gaiko Forum*, Fall 2002, 35, 36.

3. Dan Moran, "Preventive War and the Crisis of July, 1914," *Strategic Insights*, November 6, 2002.

4. Fritz Stern, *Gold and Iron: Bismarck, Bleichröder, and the Building of the German Empire* (New York: Vintage Books, 1979), 28 (quoting Bismarck).

5. Gordon A. Craig, *The Politics of the Prussian Army 1640–1945* (New York: Oxford University Press, 1955), 268 (quoting *The Memoirs of Prince Bülow* [Boston, 1931], iv, 609); Richard K. Betts, "Suicide from Fear of Death?" *Foreign Affairs*, January–February 2003, 35.

6. Craig, *Politics of the Prussian Army*, 255 (quoting Bismarck).

7. James Joll, *The Origins of the First World War* (New York: Longman, 1984), 87; Craig, *Politics of the Prussian Army*, 291.

8. Moran, "Preventive War."

9. Dale C. Copeland, *The Origins of Major War* (Ithaca, NY: Cornell University Press, 2000), 71.

10.. Donald Kagan, *On the Origins of War and the Preservation of Peace* (New York: Doubleday, 1995), 187, 191.

11. Marc Trachtenberg, *History and Strategy* (Princeton, NJ: Princeton University Press, 1991), 67. Trachtenberg points out that if Germany's goal was to maintain its existing position, that was quite manageable without preventive war. As the German Foreign Secretary admitted in 1912, the British and the French were too committed to peace to ever cause a war, so if Germany did not provoke one "no one else certainly will do so." Ibid. See also Stephen Van Evera, "The Cult of the Offensive and the Origins of the First World War," 9 *International Security* 58, 69 (1984).

12. Quoted in Alfred Vagts, *Defense and Diplomacy: The Soldier and the Conduct of Foreign Relations* (New York: King's Crown Press, 1956), 315.

13. Quoted in Vagts, *Defense and Diplomacy*, 319.

14. Walter Lafeber, *The American Age: United States Foreign Policy at Home and Abroad Since 1750* (New York: W.W. Norton, 1989), 379; James McPherson, "The Fruits of Preventive War," *Perspectives*, May 2003.

15. Donald Goldstein and Katherine V. Dillon, eds., *The Pearl Harbor Papers: Inside the Japanese Plans* (Washington: Brassey's, 1993), 13 (quoting the affidavit of Minoru Genda).

16. See McPherson, "Fruits of Preventive War."

17. Thucydides, *History of the Peloponnesian War* (London: Penguin Books, 1972), 49.

18. Ibid., 75.

19. Ibid.

20. Ibid., 82, 84.

21. Ibid., 84.

22. Ibid., 82–83.

23. Ibid., 84.

24. Ibid., 84.

25. Ibid., 86.

26. Kagan, *On the Origins of War*, 57.

27. Ibid., 58.

28. Kagan, *On the Origins of War*, 58; Copeland, *Origins of Major War*, 211.

29. Copeland, *Origins of Major War*, 211.

30. Ibid., 214–33.

31. A.J.P. Taylor, *The Struggle for Mastery of Europe 1848–1918* (Oxford: Claredon Press, 1954), 166.

32. Ibid.

33. Stephen Van Evera, *Causes of War: Power and the Roots of Conflict* (Ithaca, NY: Cornell University Press, 1999), 76.

34. Burke, quoted in Michael Walzer, *Just and Unjust Wars: A Moral Argument with Historical Illustrations* (New York: Basic Books, 1977), 76.

35. Van Evera, *Causes of War*, 186.

36. Ibid., 192.

37. Joseph A. Schumpeter, *Imperialism and Social Classes*, trans. Heinz Norden (Fairfield, NJ: A.M. Kelly, 1951), 51.

38. Vagts, *Defense and Diplomacy*, 267.

39. Quoted in Walzer, *Just and Unjust Wars*, 79.

40. UN Charter, Preamble.

41. Robert Jervis, "War and Misperception," *Journal of Interdisciplinary History*, Spring 1988, 688.

42. See generally Trachtenberg, *History and Strategy*, 100–53.

43. Jeffrey Record, "Nuclear Deterrence, Preventive War and Counterproliferation," 519 *Policy Analysis* 14 (July 8, 2004) (quoting General Leslie Groves).

44. Gain P. Gentile, "Planning for Preventive War, 1945–1950," *JFQ*, Spring 2000, 71.

45. Ibid., 72 (emphasis in original).

46. Trachtenberg, *History and Strategy*, 103 (quoting William L. Lawrence,

"How Soon Will Russia Have the A-Bomb?" *Saturday Evening Post*, November 6, 1948, 182).

47. Ibid., 103–4.

48. "Matthews Favors U.S. War for Peace," *New York Times*, August 26, 1950, 1.

49. Hanson W. Baldwin, "War of Prevention," *New York Times*, September 1, 1950, 4.

50. Record, "Nuclear Deterrence," 14 (quoting Allen Rankin, "U.S. Could Wipe Out Red A-Nests in Week, Gen. Anderson Asserts," *Montgomery Advertiser*, September 1, 1950).

51. Steven R. Prebeck, "Preventive Attack in the 1990s?" (thesis, School of Advanced Airpower Studies, Maxwell Air Force Base, Alabama, May 28, 1993), 8, 9.

52. "Text of Truman's 'Report to the Nation' on Korean War," *New York Times*, September 2, 1950, 4.

53. Lafeber, *The American Age,* 479.

54. Ibid.

55. Scott D. Sagan, "The Perils of Proliferation: Organization Theory, Reference Theory, and the Spread of Nuclear Weapons," 18 *International Security*, Spring 1994, 66, 78 (quoting NCS-68, in *Foreign Relations of the United States, 1950*, vol. 1, National Security Affairs, 281–82).

56. Sagan, "Perils of Proliferation," 78.

57. Ibid., 80 (quoting "Memorandum by the Chief of Staff, U.S. Air Force, to the JCS on the Coming National Crisis," Twining Papers, series 2, topical series, nuclear weapons 1952–1961 (Colorado Springs, CO: USAF Academy, August 21, 1953).

58. McGeorge Bundy, *Danger and Survival: Choices About the Bomb in the First Fifty Years* (New York: Random House, 1988), 251.

59. Sagan, "Perils of Proliferation," 80.

60. David Alan Rosenberg, "The Origins of Overkill: Nuclear Weapons & American Strategy 1945–1950," 7 *International Security* 3, 34 (Spring 1983).

61. Ibid., 34.

62. Bundy, *Danger and Survival,* 251.

63. "Memorandum by the President to the Secretary of State, September 8, 1953," *Foreign Relations of the United States, 1952–54*, vol. 2, part 1, 461.

64. Dwight D. Eisenhower, "The President's News Conference of August 11, 1954," Public Papers, 192, available at http://www.presidency.ucsb.edu/ws/index.php?pid=9977&st=prevent ive+war&st1.

65. Ibid.

66. "National Security Report, NSC 5501," *Foreign Relations of the United States, 1955–1957*, vol. 19, 33.

67. Bernard Brodie, *Strategy in the Missile Age* (Princeton, NJ: Princeton University Press, 1959), 392.

68. Henry S. Laver, "Preemption and the Evolution of America's Strategic Defense," *Parameters*, summer 2005, 114 (quoting Henry A. Kissinger, "Military Policy and Defense of the Key Areas," *Foreign Affairs*, April 1955, 416).

69. John Shirek, NBC Affiliate WXIA Channel 11, Atlanta, GA, "Interview with Secretary of Defense Donald Rumsfeld," September 27, 2002, quoted in Michael J. Kelly, "Time Warp to 1945—Resurrection of the Reprisal Aid Anticipatory Self-Defense Doctrines in International Law," 13 *Journal of Transnational Law and Policy* 1, 34–35 (Fall 2003).

70. Copeland, *Origins of Major War*, 194.

71. Record, "Nuclear Deterrence," 13–14.

72. Kagan, *On the Origins of War*, 517.

73. Ibid.

74. Ibid.

75. Ibid., 520.

76. Ibid., 543.

77. Ibid., 545.

78. Ibid., 546.

79. Ibid., 517.

80. Abram Chayes, *The Cuban Missile Crisis: International Crisis and the Role of Law* (New York: Oxford University Press 1974), 62–64.

81. Robert F. Kennedy, *Thirteen Days: A Memoir of the Cuban Missile Crisis* (New York: W.W. Norton, 1969), 121.

82. Record, "Nuclear Deterrence," 15.

83. William Burr and Jeffrey T. Richelson, "Whether to 'Strangle the Baby in the Cradle': The United States and the Chinese Nuclear Program, 1960–64," 25 *International Security* 54, 61 (Winter 2000/01).

84. Ibid., 74.

85. Robert M. Lawrence and William R. Van Cleave, "Assertive Disarmament," *National Review*, September 10, 1968, 898, 901.

86. Record, "Nuclear Deterrence," 15.

87. Elaine Monaghan, "Clinton Planned Attack on Korean Nuclear Reactors," *The Times* (London), December 16, 2002, 12.

88. Ashton B. Carter and William J. Perry, *Preventive Defense: A New Security Strategy for America* (Washington, DC: Brookings Institution Press, 1998), 128, 131.

89. Max Boot, "Who Says We Never Strike First?" *New York Times*, October 4, 2002, 27.

90. Vagts, *Defense and Diplomacy*, 268.

91. Ibid., 311; Winston S. Churchill, *The Gathering Storm* (Boston, MA: Houghton Mifflin, 1948), 210; Tuvia Ben-Moshe, *Churchill, Strategy and History* (Boulder, CO: Lynne Rienner Publishers, 1992), 108–9; A.P. Taylor, *Churchill: Four Faces and the Man* (London: Allen Lane, 1969), 28–31.

92. President Bush, "Commencement Address at West Point," June

1, 2002, available at http://www.whitehouse.gov/news/releases/2002/06/
20020601-3.ht ml.

93. Charles Krauthammer, *Democratic Realism: An American Foreign
Policy for a Unipolar World* (Washington, DC: AEI Press, 2004), 18.

94. See, e.g., Ashton Carter and William J. Perry, "If Necessary, Strike
and Destroy: North Korea Cannot Be Allowed to Test This Missile," *Washington Post,* June 22, 2006, A29 (former Clinton administration secretary
of defense and assistant secretary of defense urge a preemptive military
strike against North Korea); David Rieff, "But Who's Against the Next
War," *New York Times,* March 25, 2007, §6, p. 13.

95. John Lewis Gaddis, *Surprise, Security, and the American Experience*
(Cambridge, MA: Harvard University Press, 2005), 28 (quoting John
Quincy Adams, "Address on U.S. Foreign Policy," July 4, 1820).

8. TICKING TIME BOMBS AND SLIPPERY SLOPES

1. President George W. Bush, "Address to the Nation on Iraq from
Cincinnati, Ohio," 38 *Weekly Compilation of Presidential Documents* 1718,
October 7, 2002.

2. Charles Krauthammer, "The Truth About Torture," *Weekly Standard,*
December 5, 2005.

3. See Bruce Ackerman, *Before the Next Attack: Preserving Civil Liberties
in an Age of Terrorism* (New Haven: Yale University Press, 2006); Paul
Rosenzweig and James Jay Carafano, "Preventive Detention and Actionable Intelligence," Heritage Foundation Legal Memorandum #13, November 16, 2003, available at http://www.heritage.org/Research/Homeland
Defense/lm13.cfm (using examples provided by Michael Chertoff in
speech to ABA Standing Committee on National Security and the Law,
April 13, 2004, Washington, D.C.).

4. Richard Posner, *Not a Suicide Pact: The Constitution in a Time of National Emergency* (New York: Oxford University Press, 2006); see David
Cole, "How to Skip the Constitution," *New York Review of Books,* November 16, 2006, 20 (reviewing Posner's book).

5. See, e.g., John Yoo, "Using Force," 71 *University of Chicago Law Review*
729 (2004); Michael Ignatieff, *The Lesser Evil: Political Ethics in an Age of
Terror* (Princeton, NJ: Princeton University Press, 2004).

6. Ruth Wedgwood, "The Law's Response to September 11," 16 *Ethics
and International Affairs* 9 (March 2002).

7. *Florida v. J.L.,* 529 U.S. 266, 273–74 (2000), cited in Richard Posner,
Catastrophe: Risk and Response (New York: Oxford University Press, 2004),
232–33.

8. *Dennis v. United States,* 341 U.S. 494, 548–49 (1950).

9. David Luban, "Liberalism, Torture and the Ticking Bomb," 91 *Vir-*

ginia Law Review 1425, 1441 (2005); Oren Gross, "Are Torture Warrants Warranted? Pragmatic Absolution and Official Disobedience," 88 *Minnesota Law Review* 1481, 1501–3 (2004).

10. See generally, David Cole, *Enemy Aliens: Double Standards and Constitutional Freedoms in the War on Terrorism*, 2d ed. (New York: The New Press, 2005); Jules Lobel and George Loewenstein, "The Substitution of Symbol for Substance in Foreign Policy and International Law," 80 *Chicago Kent Law Review* 1045, 1083–84 (2005).

11. See George Loewenstein, Christopher Hsee, Elke Weber, and Ned Welch, "Risk as Feelings," 127 *Psychological Bulletin* 267 (2001).

12. Posner, *Catastrophe*, 248.

13. Cass Sunstein, *The Laws of Fear: Beyond the Precautionary Principle* (New York: Cambridge University Press, 2005), 105.

14. Jeffrey Rosen, *The Naked Crowd: Reclaiming Security and Freedom in an Anxious Age* (New York: Random House, 2004), 73.

15. Sunstein, *Laws of Fear*, 40 (citing Eric J. Johnson et al., "Framing, Probability Distortion and Insurance Decisions," 7 *Journal of Risk and Uncertainty* 35 [August 1993]).

16. Neal Feigenson, Daniel Bailis, and William Klein, "Perceptions of Terrorism and Disease Risks: A Cross-National Comparison," 69 *Missouri Law Review* 991, 995 (2004).

17. See George Lowenstein et al., "Risk as Feelings," 267; Sunstein, *Laws of Fear*, 79.

18. Cass R. Sunstein, "Terrorism and Probability Neglect," 26 *Journal of Risk and Uncertainty* 121, 122 (2003).

19. Because of the difficulty of estimating risk of catastrophic harm, the private insurance market would not provide insurance at reasonable rates for terrorism, leading Congress to enact the Terrorism Risk Insurance Act of 2002, in which the public in effect insures the insurers against calamitous losses from a terrorist attack. See, e.g., "Safety Solution Terrorism Insurance Program Spreads Risk Around," *Pittsburgh Post-Gazette*, September 13, 2005, E8; Michelle E. Boardman, "Known Unknowns: The Illusion of Terrorism Insurance," 93 *Georgetown Law Journal* 783, 784 (2005).

20. Posner, *Catastrophe*, 262.

21. Sunstein, *Laws of Fear*, 205.

22. Cole, *Enemy Aliens*.

23. Philip G. Zimbardo, Christine Maslach, and Craig Haney, "Reflections on the Stanford Prison Experiment: Genesis, Transformation, Consequences" (2000), available at http://www.prisonexp.org/pdf/blass.pdf.

24. Luban, "Liberalism," 1451.

25. Stanley Milgram, *Obedience to Authority: An Experimental View* (New York: HarperCollins, 2004).

26. For Posner's advocacy of the position that the Constitution be read to permit the use of widespread preventive powers, see Posner, *Not a Suicide Pact.*

27. Posner, *Catastrophe,* 240.

28. Ibid., 240–41.

29. Ron Dudai, "Slippery Slopes and the War on Terror: Lessons from Israel," *Jurist,* April 11, 2006, available at http://jurist.law.pitt.edu/forumy/2006/04/slippery-slopes-and-war-on-terror.php.

30. *Adalah—The Legal Center for Arab Minority Rights in Israel v. GOC Central Command,* 45 ILM 491 (March 2006).

31. *Report of the Commission of Inquiry into the Methods of Investigation of the General Security Service Regarding Hostile Terrorist Activity* (1987), excerpted in 23 *Israel Law Review* 146, 174 (1989).

32. Welsh White and John Parry, "Interrogating Suspected Terrorists," 63 *University of Pittsburgh Law Review* 743, 758 (2002).

33. *Public Committee Against Torture in Israel v. State of Israel,* 38 I.L.M. 1471 (1999). The court prohibited executive-authorized use of coercion, but left open the possibility that the legislature could authorize such measures.

34. *Brandenburg v. Ohio,* 395 U.S. 444 (1969).

35. Christina Wells has argued, based on social science studies demonstrating the benefits of accountability mechanisms, that nondeferential judicial review is a particularly important measure for ensuring accountability among executive decision makers in times of crisis. Christina Wells, "Questioning Deference," 69 *Missouri Law Review* 903 (2004).

36. Sunstein, *Laws of Fear,* 221.

37. Richard Posner, *Law, Pragmatism and Democracy* (Cambridge, MA: Harvard University Press, 2003), 289–99.

9. NONCOERCIVE STRATEGIES

1. See generally David Harris, *Good Cops: The Case for Preventive Policing* (New York: The New Press, 2005); David Cole, *No Equal Justice: Race and Class in the American Criminal Justice System* (New York: The New Press, 1999); Joel A. Egertson, Daniel M. Fox, and Alan I. Leshner, *Treating Drug Abusers Effectively* (Cambridge, MA: Blackwell, 1997).

2. National Commission on Terrorist Attacks upon the United States, *The 9/11 Commission Report* (2004), 367–428, available at http://www.9-11commission.gov/report/911Report.pdf.

3. See, e.g., Clark Kent Ervin, *Open Target: Where America Is Vulnerable* (New York: Palgrave MacMillan, 2006); James Fallows, "Bush's Lost War," *Atlantic Monthly,* October 2004, 68; Richard A. Clarke, *Against All Enemies: Inside America's War on Terror* (New York: Free Press, 2004); Richard A. Clarke et al., *Defeating the Jihadists: A Blueprint for Action* (New York: Century Foundation Press, 2004); Stephen Flynn, *America the Vul-*

nerable: How Our Government Is Failing to Protect Us from Terrorists (New York: Council on Foreign Relations, 2004).

4. 9/11 Public Discourse Project, *Final Report on 9/11 Recommendations*, December 5, 2005, available at http://www.9-11pdp.org; Philip Shenon, "9/11 Panel Issues Poor Grades for Handling of Terror," *New York Times*, December 6, 2005, A24.

5. U.S. Department of Energy, Howard Baker and Lloyd Cutler, co-chairs, Russia Task Force, *A Report Card on the Department of Energy's Nonproliferation Programs with Russia*, January 10, 2001, 25, available at http://www.seab.energy.gov/publications/rusrpt.pdf.

6. Graham Allison, *Nuclear Terrorism: The Ultimate Preventable Catastrophe* (New York: Times Books, 2004), 147.

7. Cited in Matthew Bunn and Anthony Wier, *Securing the Bomb*, Nuclear Threat Initiative, July 2006, 10, available at www.nti.org/securing_the_bomb.

8. "Remarks by the President on Weapons of Mass Destruction Proliferation, Fort Lesley J. McNair—National Defense University," February 11, 2004, available at http://whitehouse.gov/news/releases/2004/02/20040211=4.html.

9. *Final Report on 9/11 Recommendations*, 4.

10. Conventional Forces in Europe Treaty Implementation Act of 1991, HR 3807, Title II.

11. Bunn and Wier, *Securing the Bomb*, ix.

12. Brian Finlay and Andrew Grotto, *The Race to Secure Russia's Loose Nukes: Progress Since 9/11* (Henry L. Stimson Center, New York, September 2005), 1, 53–54.

13. Joanna Wintrol, "News Analysis: The Global Partnership—A Mixed Record," *Arms Control Today*, May 2006.

14. Peter Baker, "U.S., Russia Break Impasse on Plan to Keep Arms from Rogue Users," *Washington Post*, June 20, 2006, A11.

15. Government Accountability Office, "Nuclear Nonproliferation: Focusing on the Highest Priority Radiological Sources Could Improve DOE's Efforts to Secure Sources in Foreign Countries," GAO-07-580T, March 13, 2007.

16. Allison, *Nuclear Terrorism*, 70.

17. Bunn and Wier, *Securing the Bomb*, 11–12.

18. U.S. Congress, General Accounting Office, "Nuclear Nonproliferation: Security of Russia's Nuclear Material Improving; Further Enhancements Needed," GAO-01-312 (Washington, DC, GAO, 2001) February 28, 2001, 12.

19. Bunn and Wier, *Securing the Bomb*, 12.

20. Joel Brinkley and William J. Broad, "U.S. Lags in Recovering Fuel Suitable for Nuclear Arms," *New York Times*, March 7, 2004, A16.

21. Allison, *Nuclear Terrorism*, 154.

22. Ibid.

23. Bunn and Wier, *Securing the Bomb*, 20–21.

24. Allison, *Nuclear Terrorism*, 151.

25. Bob Herbert, "A World Gone Mad," *New York Times*, July 31, 2006, A17 (quoting experts at the Institute for Science and International Security).

26. "Green Light for Bomb Builders," *New York Times*, July 22, 2005, editorial, A18.

27. George Perkovich, Jessica Mathews, Joseph Cirinciae, Rose Gottemoeller, and Jim Wolfsthal, *Universal Compliance: A Strategy for Nuclear Security*, Carnegie Endowment for International Peace, March 2005, 89 (hereinafter "Carnegie Report").

28. Carnegie Report, 28; Bunn and Wier, *Securing the Bomb*, 23.

29. Allison, *Nuclear Terrorism*, 140–209; Carnegie Report; Bunn and Wier, *Securing the Bomb*, 8.

30. See Louise Richardson, *What Terrorists Want* (2006).

31. Fallows, "Bush's Lost Year," 72.

32. Stephen E. Flynn, "The Neglected Homefront," *Foreign Affairs*, September–October 2004, 20.

33. Miriam Pemberton and Lawrence Korb, "A Unified Security Budget for the United States," *Foreign Policy in Focus*, May 3, 2006, 1.

34. See Ervin, *Open Target*, 117–35, 221.

10. A PREVENTIVE FOREIGN POLICY

1. See, e.g., President George W. Bush, "Address to a Joint Session of Congress and the American People," September 20, 2001, at http://www.whitehouse.gov/News/releases/2001/09/20010920-8.html.

2. "Full Transcript of bin Laden's Speech," Al-Jazeera, November 1, 2004, available at http://english.aljazeera.net/NR/exeres/79C6Af22-98FB-4A1C-B21f-2B C36E87F61F.htm; see also "Excerpts from Bin Laden's Video Statement," *Chicago Tribune*, October 30, 2004, C25.

3. Madeline Albright, *The Mighty and the Almighty: Reflections on America, God, and World Affairs* (New York: HarperCollins, 2006), 187.

4. Robert A. Pape, *Dying to Win: The Strategic Logic of Suicide Bombers* (New York: Random House, 2006), 21, 242–43.

5. Robert A. Pape, "The Strategic Logic of Suicide Bombers," 97 *American Political Science Review* 343, 348 (August 2003).

6. National Commission on Terrorist Attacks upon the United States, *9/11 Commission Report: Final Report of the National Commission on Terrorist Attacks upon the United States* (New York: W.W. Norton, 2004), 364.

7. "The Terrorism Index," Center for American Progress Report, June

14, 2006, at 2, available at http://www.americanprogress.org/site//pp.asp, also published in *Foreign Policy*, August 2006.

8. Andrew J. Bacevich, *The New American Militarism: How Americans Are Seduced by War* (New York: Oxford University Press, 2005), 19.

9. White House, *National Security Strategy of the United States* (September 2002), available at http://www.whitehouse.gov/nsc/nss.pdf.

10. Chalmers Johnson, *The Sorrows of Empire: Militarism, Secrecy and the End of the Republic* (New York: Metropolitan Books, 2004), 4.

11. Bacevich, *New American Militarism*, 235 n.20.

12. Elain Sciolino, "Don't Weaken Arafat, Saudi Warns Bush," *New York Times*, January 27, 2002 §1, 8.

13. Pape, *Dying to Win.*

14. U.S. Department of Defense, "DoD Responses to Transnational Threats, Vol. 2: DSB Force Protection Panel Report to DSB," Washington, DC, December 1997, 8, available at http://www.acq.osd.mil/dsb/reports/trans2.pdf.

15. Thom Shanker and Eric Schmitt, "A Nation at War: Strategic Shift: Pentagon Expects Long-Term Access to Key Iraq Bases," *New York Times*, April 20, 2003, 1.

16. Ed Blanche, "The Empire Digs In; Amid All Talk of Withdrawing Troops from Iraq, Bush Requests Funds to Build a Network of Super Bases Across the Country, Pointing to a Long-Term Deployment to Last Far Beyond the Insurgency," *Current Affairs*, May 1, 2006, 14.

17. Senator Joseph R. Biden, "Biden Amendment on Prohibiting Permanent Military Bases in Iraq Passes Senate," press release, June 22, 2006, available at http://biden.senate.gov/newsroom/details.cfm?id=257680.

18. Johnson, *Sorrows of Empire*, 242.

19. Bacevich, *New American Militarism*; Johnson, *Sorrows of Empire*, 183.

20. Johnson, *Sorrows of Empire*, 152 (quoting U.S. Senate Subcommittee on Security Agreements and Commitments Abroad, Committee on Foreign Relations, December 21, 1970).

21. Ibid., 288.

22. "The Terrorism Index."

23. Francis Fukuyama, *America at the Crossroads: Democracy, Power, and the Neoconservative Legacy* (New Haven, CT: Yale University Press, 2006), 188.

24. Stanley Hoffman, "Thoughts on Fear in Global Society," 71 *Social Research*, Winter 2004, 1033.

25. Miriam Pemberton and Lawrence Korb, *Report of the Task Force on a Unified Budget for the United States*, 2007, May 3, 2006, 2.

26. Bacevich, *New American Militarism*, 215.

27. "Ranking the Rich," *Foreign Policy*, May 2003, 60. In that study, the United States ranked twentieth out of twenty-one countries.

28. Scott Atran, "The Moral Logic and Growth of Suicide Terrorism," *Washington Quarterly*, Spring 2006, available at http://jurist.law.pitt.edu/forumy/2006/04/slippery-slopes-and-war-on-terror.php.

29. Pew Research Center, "U.S. Image Up Slightly, but Still Negative," Pew Global Attitudes Project, June 2, 2003, available at http://pewglobal.org/reports/display.php?ReportID=247; Pew Research Center, "Views of a Changing World," Pew Global Attitudes Project, June 23, 2005, available at http://pewglobal.org/reports/display.php?ReportID=185.

30. Daniel Benjamin and Steven Simon, *The Next Attack: The Failure of the War on Terror and a Strategy for Getting It Right* (New York: Times Books, 2005).

31. Ibid.

32. 9/11 Public Discourse Project, *Final Report on 9/11 Commission Recommendations,* 5, available at http://www.9-11pdp.org.

33. Richard A. Clarke et al., *Defeating the Jihadists: A Blueprint for Action* (New York: Century Foundation Press, 2004), 143.

11. MULTILATERAL SOLUTIONS TO A TRANSNATIONAL PROBLEM

1. For a compelling account of the Bush administration's hostility to international rules, before and after 9/11, see Philippe Sands, *Lawless World: American and the Making and Breaking of Global Rules from FDR's Atlantic Charter to George W. Bush's Illegal War* (New York: Viking, 2005).

2. "A More Secure World: Our Shared Responsibility," Report of the Secretary-General's High Level Panel on Threats, Challenges and Change (United Nations 2004), 39 (hereinafter "High Level Panel Report"). See also Statement of Stephen Rademaker, assistant secretary of state for arms control before the House International Relations Committee, Subcommittee on International Terrorism and Nonproliferation, April 28, 2005, cited in 99 *American Journal of International Law* 715, 716 (2005).

3. High Level Panel Report, 44.

4. James Traub, "The Netherworld of Nonproliferation," *New York Times Magazine,* June 13, 2004, 49.

5. James Traub, "Why Not Build a Bomb?" *New York Times Magazine,* January 29, 2006, 15, 16.

6. George Perkovich, Jessica Mathews, Joseph Ciriniciae, Rose Gottemoeller, and Jim Wolfsthal, *Universal Compliance: A Strategy for Nuclear Security,* Carnegie Endowment for International Peace, March 2005, 38.

7. Traub, "Netherworld of Nonproliferation."

8. Traub, "Why Not Build a Bomb?" 16.

9. High Level Panel Report, 35, par. 119. Program of Action Agreed to at the 2000 NPT Review Conference: "The Conference agrees on the follow-

ing practical steps: A diminishing role for nuclear weapons in security policies to minimize the risk that these weapons will ever be used and to facilitate the process of their total elimination." Nuclear Non-Proliferation Treaty Review Conference, *Programme of Action on Nuclear Disarmament*, available at http://disarm.igc.org/parag15.html. See also Nuclear Non-Proliferation Treaty Conference, *2000 Review Conference of the Parties to the Treaty on the Non-Proliferation of Nuclear Weapons Final Document*, available at http://disarmament.un.org:8080/wmd/npt/2000FD.pdf (accessed December 18, 2003).

10. Alyn Ware, "Rule of Force or Rule of Law? Legal Responses to Nuclear Threats from Terrorism, Proliferation and War," 2 *Seattle Journal for Social Justice* 243, 246 (2004).

11. SC Res. 984, UN SCOR 3514 Meeting, UN Doc. S/Res/984 (1995).

12. U.S. Department of Defense, *Nuclear Posture Review Report.*

13. Ware, "Rule of Force," 248.

14. High Level Panel Report, 42.

15. Carnegie Report, 35.

16. Ibid., 13.

17. Richard J. Goldstone, "The Future of International Criminal Justice," 57 *Maine Law Review* 553, 563 (2005).

18. The 2002 National Security Strategy stated: "We will take the actions necessary to ensure that our efforts to meet our global security commitments and protect Americans are not impaired by the potential for investigations, inquiry, or prosecution by the International Criminal Court (ICC), whose jurisdiction does not extend to Americans and which we do not accept." White House, *National Security Strategy of the United States* (September 2002), 31, available at http://www.whitehouse.gov/nsc/nss.pdf.

19. Cited in Diane F. Orentlicher, "Unilateral Multilateralism: United States Policy Toward the International Criminal Court," 36 *Cornell International Law Journal* 415, 422 (2004).

20. "Is a U.N. International Criminal Court in the U.S. National Interest? Hearings Before the Senate Subcommittee on Foreign Relations," 105th Cong. 724 (1998) (statement of John Bolton, senior vice president, American Enterprise Institute).

21. Pub. L. No. 107–206, 116 Stat. 820 tit. II (2002), *codified at* 22 U.S.C. secs. 7421–7433; Orentlicher, "Unilateral Multilateralism," 423.

22. Colum Lynch, "U.S. Confronts EU on War Crimes Court, Immunity Pact Issues Threatens Relations," *Washington Post*, June 10, 2003, A17.

23. Orentlicher, "Unilateral Multilateralism," 431.

24. Wesley K. Clarke, "Restoring America's Alliances," Remarks Before the Council on Foreign Relations, November 20, 2003; Anne K. Heindel, "International Human Rights and U.S. Foreign Policy: The Counterproductive Bush Administration Policy Toward the International Criminal Court," 2 *Seattle Journal for Social Justice* 345, 347 (2004).

25. Mark Mazetti, "U.S. Cuts in Africa Aid Hurt War on Terror and Increase China's Influence, Officials Say," *New York Times*, July 23, 2006, 12.

26. Ibid.

27. Richard Goldstone and Janine Simpson, "Evaluating the Role of the International Criminal Court as a Legal Response to Terrorism," 16 *Harvard Human Rights Journal* 13, 26 (2003).

28. Marc Grossman, Under Secretary of State for Political Affairs, "American Foreign Policy and the International Criminal Court," Remarks to the Center for Strategic and International Studies, Washington, DC, May 6, 2002, available at http://www.mtholyoke.edu/acad/intrel/bush/rome.htm.

29. Jackson stated that "if certain acts in violation of treaties are crimes, they are crimes whether the United States does them or whether Germany does them, and we are not prepared to lay down a rule of criminal conduct against others which we would not be willing to have invoked against us." Report of Robert H. Jackson, U.S. Representative to the International Conference on Military Trials, Int'l Org. & Conf. Ser. II, European & British Commonwealth 1, Dep't of State Pub. No. 3080, at 330 (London 1945).

30. President George W. Bush, "State of the Union Address," 2004, January 20, 2004, available at http://www.whitehouse.gov/news/releases/2004/01/20040120-7.html.

31. High Level Panel Report, 63.

32. Alan Dershowitz, *Preemption: A Knife That Cuts Both Ways* (New York: W.W. Norton, 2006), 208–9.

33. High Level Panel Report, 64.

34. Oscar Schachter, "Self-Defense and the Rule of Law," 83 *American Journal of International Law* 259, 264 n.24. (1989).

35. High Level Panel Report, 31.

36. Ibid., 31–32.

37. Ibid., 33.

38. Ibid.

39. UN GAOR, 5th Sess., Supp. No. 20 at 10 (UN Doc. A/1775 [1950]). The resolution states, "If the Security Council, because of lack of unanimity of the permanent members, fails to exercise its primary responsibility for the maintenance of international peace and security, [the General Assembly] may make appropriate recommendations for collective measures, including in the case of a breach of peace or act of aggression the use of armed forces when necessary, to maintain or restore international peace and security."

40. Security Council Res. 1368 pmbl. (September 12, 2001); 40 ILM 1277 (2001); Security Council Res. 1373, pmbl. (September 28, 2001); 40 ILM 1278 (2001).

41. Jose E. Alvarez, "Hegemonic International Law Revisited," 97 *American Journal of International Law* 873, 879 (2003); Steven R. Ratner, "Jus ad

Bellum and Jus in Bello After September 11," 96 *American Journal of International Law* 905, 909–10 (2002); Nico Schrijver, "September 11 and Challenges to International Law in Terrorism and the UN, Before and After September 11," in *Terrorism and the UN: Before and After September 11*, ed. Jane Boulden and Thomas L. Weiss (Bloomington: Indiana University Press, 2004), 55, 62.

42. Schrijver, "September 11," 58.

43. Karin von Hippel, *Improving the International Response to the Transnational Terrorist Threat—Terrorism in the UN*, 112.

44. Louis Henkin, "Notes from the President: The Missile Attack on Baghdad and Its Justifications," *ASIL News*, June 1993, 2.

45. The British Labour Party used this phrase to describe its 1998 initiative to make the European Convention on Human Rights directly enforceable in domestic British courts. The United Kingdom had for nearly fifty years been a party to the European Convention on Human Rights, but those rights could be vindicated only before the European Court of Human Rights. These rights are now enforceable both by British domestic courts, and by the European Court of Human Rights. By contrast, international human rights in the United States are generally not enforceable in either U.S. domestic courts or international tribunals.

46. For example, if international human rights protection of privacy or equality were interpreted to require the prohibition of speech that would be constitutionally protected in the United States, such as libel or hate speech, the Constitution would trump. But where international human rights simply offer greater protection to a given right than does our Constitution, there would be no constitutional barrier to our abiding by it. Thus, if international human rights prohibits the death penalty, there would be nothing unconstitutional about abiding by that standard, even though our Constitution has been interpreted not to bar the death penalty.

47. See World Trade Organization, "Dispute Settlement Understanding," 33 ILM 1125 (1994).

12. THE RULE OF LAW AS AN ASSET, NOT AN OBSTACLE

1. Geneva Convention (III) Relative to the Treatment of Prisoners of War, part 1, art. 3, August 12, 1949, 6 UST 3217, 75 UNTS 135

2. Joseph Blocher, "Combatant Status Review Tribunals: Flawed Answers to the Wrong Question," 116 *Yale Law Journal* 667 (2006) (arguing that the Combatant Status Review Tribunals do not meet the requirements set forth by the Geneva Conventions). As noted above, in the Military Commissions Act, Congress barred foreign nationals from raising Geneva Conventions violations in litigation against the United States or its officers, so it is possible that there will never be a judicial ruling on the issue.

3. While President Bush said that he would not treat the al-Qaeda detainees as protected by the Geneva Conventions, he did say that they would be treated humanely. White House Office of the Press Secretary, "Statement of the Press Secretary on the Geneva Convention," May 7, 2003, available at http://www.whitehouse.gov/news/releases/2003/05/20030507-18.html.

4. 50 U.S.C. §1811. "The Conferees intend that this [15-day] period will allow time for consideration of any amendment to this act that may be appropriate during a wartime emergency. . . . The conferees expect that such amendment would be reported with recommendations within 7 days and that each House would vote on the amendment within 7 days thereafter." HR Conf. Rep. No. 95-1720, at 34 (1978).

5. See generally David Cole, *Enemy Aliens: Double Standards and Constitutional Freedoms in the War on Terrorism,* rev. ed. (New York: The New Press, 2005), xx–xxi, 22–46.

6. *Hamdi v. Rumsfeld,* 542 U.S. 507, 509 (2004).

7. See Law Library of Congress, *Preventive Detention: Australia, France, Germany, India, Israel, and the United Kingdom* (July 2005). [TK]

8. See 117 *Congressional Record* H31551-2 (daily ed. September 13, 1971) (remarks of Congressman Railsback), cited in *Padilla v. Rumsfeld,* 352 F.3d 695, 721, 722 (2d Cir. 2003), *reversed and remanded,* 124 S. Ct. 2711 (2004).

9. 8 U.S.C. §1226a (a) (5).

10. "Statement of the Press Secretary on the Geneva Convention."

11. Lieutenant General John Kimmons, Defense Department New Briefing on Detainee Policies, September 6, 2006, available at http://www.washingtonpost.com/wp-dyn/content/article/2006/09/06/AR200609060 1442.html.

12. Alan Dershowitz, *Why Terrorism Works: Understanding the Threat, Responding to the Challenge* (New Haven, CT: Yale University Press, 2002).

13. Philip B. Heymann and Juliette Kayyem, *Protecting Liberty in an Age of Terror* (Cambridge, MA: MIT Press, 2005), 35–39.

14. The approach urged here is that taken by our early leaders. For example, Thomas Jefferson believed that executive officers might sometimes have to act unlawfully in an emergency, but must "act at his own peril, and throw himself on the justice of his country and the rectitude of his motives." Early military leaders, including future president Andrew Jackson, who acted unconstitutionally in response to wartime emergencies, were held accountable for their violations by federal courts and left to seek indemnification from Congress. See Lobel, "Emergency Power and the Decline of Liberalism," 98 *Yale Law Journal* 1385 (1989), 1392–97. Our proposal is in some ways similar to that taken by the Israeli Supreme Court when it outlawed the use of "moderate physical pressure" against Palestin-

ian terror suspects, but acknowledged that a necessity defense might lie under general Israeli law. *Public Committee Against Torture v. State of Israel*, HCJ No. 5100/94, July 15, 1999, 27, available at http://elyon1 .court.gov.il/files_eng/94/000/051/a09/94051 00.ao9.pdf. See also Oren Gross, "Are Torture Warrants Warranted? Pragmatic Absolution and Civil Disobedience," 88 *Minnesota Law Review* 1481 (2004). With respect to torture, we think it is preferable to limit exceptions to the general avenues of forgiveness that exist as a background matter for all criminal laws. Crafting a necessity exception, by contrast, would create a *legal* authorization, albeit after the fact, for conduct that international law prohibits under all circumstances.

15. Stephen Fidler, Mark Huband, and Friederike Tiesenhausen, "Bomb-making Material Discovered in London Warehouse Following 24 Dawn Raids by Five Forces and MI5 Officers," *Financial Times*, March 31, 2004, 1.

16. Don Van Natta Jr. and Stephen Grey, "Investigators Are Clear Who Carried Bombs, but Have Far to Go to Explain More," *New York Times*, July 18, 2005, A8.

17. Patrick E. Tyler, "Europe Trying to Act First Against Terrorist Networks," *New York Times*, April 7, 2004, A12.

18. Van Natta Jr. and Grey, "Investigators Are Clear."

19. Michael Isikoff, "Terror Watch: The Real Target?" *Newsweek*, November 17, 2004.

20. Adam Zagorin and Elaine Shannon, "London's Dirty-Bomb Plot," *Time*, October 11, 2004, 22.

21. Alan Cowell, "Britain Charges 11 in Plane Case; Bomb Gear Cited," *New York Times*, August 22, 2006, A1.

CONCLUSION

1. *Hamdi v. Rumsfeld*, 542 U.S. 507, 536 (2004)

INDEX